"Death does seem to have
all he can attend to"

"Death does seem to have all he can attend to"

The Civil War Diary of an Andersonville Survivor

GEORGE A. HITCHCOCK
Edited by Ronald G. Watson
Foreword by Edwin C. Bearss

McFarland & Company, Inc., Publishers
Jefferson, North Carolina

LIBRARY OF CONGRESS CATALOGUING-IN-PUBLICATION DATA

Hitchcock, George A., 1844–1915.
 "Death does seem to have all he can attend to" : the Civil War diary of an Andersonville survivor / George A. Hitchcock ; edited by Ronald G. Watson ; foreword by Edwin C. Bearss.
  p.   cm.
 Includes bibliographical references and index.

 ISBN 978-0-7864-7890-3 (softcover : alk. paper) ∞
 ISBN 978-1-4766-1400-7 (ebook)

 1. Hitchcock, George A., 1844–1915—Diaries. 2. United States. Army. Massachusetts Infantry Regiment, 21st (1861–1864) 3. Massachusetts—History—Civil War, 1861–1865—Personal narratives. 4. United States—History—Civil War, 1861–1865—Personal narratives. 5. United States—History—Civil War, 1861–1865—Prisoners and prisons. 6. United States—History—Civil War, 1861–1865—Campaigns. 7. Soldiers—Massachusetts—Ashby—Diaries. 8. Andersonville Prison—Biography. 9. Ashby (Mass.)—Biography. 10. Fitchburg (Mass.)—Biography. I. Watson, Ronald G., 1941– II. Title. III. Title: Civil War diary of an Andersonville survivor.
 E513.521st .H58 2014
 973.7'81092—dc23
 [B]   2014001054

BRITISH LIBRARY CATALOGUING DATA ARE AVAILABLE

© 2014 Ronald G. Watson. All rights reserved

No part of this book may be reproduced or transmitted in any form or by any means, electronic or mechanical, including photocopying or recording, or by any information storage and retrieval system, without permission in writing from the publisher.

On the cover: Twenty-year-old Private George A. Hitchcock, photographed June 12, 1863, at Mt. Sterling, Kentucky (courtesy Martha Hitchcock Price); *background* text from Hitchcock's diary

Manufactured in the United States of America

McFarland & Company, Inc., Publishers
 Box 611, Jefferson, North Carolina 28640
 www.mcfarlandpub.com

For
Martha Hitchcock Price,
George Alfred Hitchcock's great-great-granddaughter,
who wrote that she has come to appreciate her great-great-grandfather's
subtle sense of humor, his descriptive skills, his faith, and his ability to
endure incredible hardships. She hopes that all those who read his
original diary will find it most interesting and educational.
—R.G.W.

Contents

Acknowledgments	ix
Foreword by Edwin C. Bearss	1
Preface by Ronald G. Watson	5
Introduction by Ronald G. Watson	7
Introduction by George A. Hitchcock	11
1. Apprenticeship to Uncle Sam	13
2. The Maryland Campaign	22
3. The Fredericksburg Campaign	36
4. Winter at Falmouth	55
5. Removal to Newport News	65
6. Transfer to the Department of the Ohio	72
7. Spring and Summer in Eastern Kentucky	81
8. The East Tennessee Campaign	108
9. Winter in the Mountains	137
10. Hospital Life	148
11. Grant's Campaign	155
12. Captured at Cold Harbor	168
13. Prisoner of War	173
14. Andersonville, Georgia	178
15. Camp Lawton—Millen, Georgia	208
16. Florence, South Carolina	215
17. Release	218
18. Hitchcock's Commentary in 1890 on Union Prisoners of War	225
19. Hitchcock After the War	232
Bibliography	237
Index	241

Acknowledgments

I wish to express my sincere appreciation to Ruth Penka, former executive director of the Fitchburg Historical Society, for providing me with access to George A. Hitchcock's Civil War diary. Ruth and all her dedicated volunteers have always been extremely pleasant and helpful. Ruth's professional expertise and the Fitchburg Historical Society's excellent resource library provide Fitchburg, Massachusetts, with an ideal historical society for the Civil War historian. The collection of Massachusetts regimental histories is very comprehensive.

I was privileged to have access to two outstanding reference libraries which provided the major portion of the research material in this book: Davis Library at the University of North Carolina at Chapel Hill, the Perkins Library at Duke University and the Carol Grotnes Belk Library at Elon University. Many staff members extended valuable aid and great kindness.

The library and archives at the Andersonville National Historic Site in Georgia were very informative. I appreciated the help from Alan Marsh, Fred Sanchez, Mark Ragan and Bill Burnett. The Archives/Library Division of the Ohio Historical Society at Columbus was an outstanding resource. Steve Gutgesell, whom I met during a tornado drill, offered many good suggestions. The archives and library at the U.S. Army Military History Institute, Carlisle Barracks, at Carlisle, Pennsylvania, were very valuable resources. Archivist Richard Sommers was helpful identifying and researching material related to the conflict on June 2, 1864, near Bethesda Church. The Georgia Room at the University of Georgia in Athens was also a very valuable resource.

Martina Hines, data specialist, at the Kentucky State Nature Preserve Commission at Frankfort, Kentucky, was very knowledgeable about the Camp Nelson area and identified the Daniel Boone Cave in Jessamine County. Martha Sink, research librarian at the Central North Carolina Regional Library at Burlington, was helpful through the use of the "Library Stumpers" on the Internet.

Additional resources which provided important information included:

Acknowledgments

Fitchburg, Massachusetts, Public Library, especially the materials in the Henry A. Willis Room; Mercer University Main Library at Macon, Georgia, especially the excellent microfilm collection; Lexington-Fayette County Historic Commission in Lexington, Kentucky; and the invaluable General Reference Branch of the National Archives in Washington, D.C.

Many people were exceedingly generous with their time and expertise: Jane Matthews at the Thomas Public Library at Fort Valley, Georgia; Ruth Spiers at the Jenkins County Memorial Library at Millen, Georgia; Walter A. Gray, Jr., director of the Beaufort National Cemetery, at Beaufort, South Carolina; Janie Morris at the Special Collection Library, Duke University; Jeanine Bruce at the Lake Blackshear Regional Library at Americus, Georgia; Thomas Blake at the Florence National Cemetery, Florence, South Carolina; the research staff of the Florence Morning News, Florence, South Carolina; Nick Zeigler, a resident of Florence, South Carolina; Donald Norton, historian in Ashby, Massachusetts; Marja Leena LePoer at the Ashby Public Library; and Archivist Margot Karp at the Reference Library at Pratt Institute, Brooklyn, New York. Mark Anderson Moore—a writer, historian and mapmaker—provided the excellent maps to accompany Hitchcock's military journey.

I offer a special thanks to former National Park Service Chief Historian Edwin C. Bearss for reading the manuscript and for offering valuable suggestions. His evaluation and comments were very encouraging and supportive.

—R.G.W.

Foreword by Edwin C. Bearss

A happy combination of circumstances beginning in August 1993 led to the publication of *From Ashby to Andersonville: The Civil War Diary and Reminiscences, dated 1890, of George A. Hitchcock, Private, Company A, 21st Massachusetts Regiment, August 1862–January 1865,* by Savas Publishing Company in 1997. This book was welcomed by a broad constituency of Civil War enthusiasts—scholars, armchair buffs, and confirmed battlefield stompers.

The genesis of *From Ashby to Andersonville* dates to an August 1993 visit to the Fitchburg Historical Society by Ronald Grover Watson, a Fitchburg native long interested in genealogical research. By chance Watson examined "The Army Diary of George A. Hitchcock" that Hitchcock had rewritten, edited and enhanced in 1890 from his original 1865 diary. The diary had been donated to Fitchburg Historical Society more than 60 years before by Miss Anne Louise Hitchcock, the only daughter of George A. Hitchcock. Anne Hitchcock died on December 12, 1936.

Ron Watson, besides a deep interest in the Civil War, possessed excellent credentials for evaluating and carefully editing this Hitchcock journal. Born in Fitchburg, he graduated from the local high school in 1946, and Hartford's Trinity College in 1950 with a B.A. majoring in history. He taught high school for one year at Ashby High School in Ashby, Massachusetts, before being drafted during the Korean War.

After two years duty in the United States Army's Counter Intelligence Corps, Watson returned to college in 1953 and graduated from Springfield College with a M.Ed. in educational administration. Beginning in September 1954, Watson spent the next 30 years in public education, initially as a history teacher, and then as a high school principal. In 1992, President George H. Bush selected Watson as the 704th person in the "A Thousand Points of Light"—a national program recognizing community service.

Watson, in editing Hitchcock's 1890 diary, learned that he and George A. Hitchcock shared a number of experiences. He found that Hitchcock had been a member and deacon of Fitchburg's Calvinist Congregational Church and in 1901 authored the church's history. This was the church in which Watson was a member and taught Sunday school during his high school years. Hitchcock lived in Fitchburg, two houses from Watson's paternal grandfather's home. His father was ten years old when the old soldier died. George Preston Hitchcock, George's only son, taught chemistry and was principal of Fitchburg High School from 1893–1905—Watson's paternal grandmother graduated in 1894.

On Saturday, January 20, 1996, I met Ronald Grover Watson. I had traveled to the Raleigh-Durham area to speak to the Civil War Round Table of North Carolina. Knowing of my special interest in the Civil War, Andersonville, and the tragic prisoner-of-war story, Watson told me about his project and his desire to have the Hitchcock writings published. What I heard in our brief chat, reinforced by Watson's sincerity, satisfied me that the Hitchcock journals were not just another Civil War diary, and I told him I welcomed the opportunity of reading and evaluating his manuscript.

Within a week after my return to Northern Virginia, I received the edited and transcribed 1890 diary. Several weeks were spent with Hitchcock, and it struck a responsive chord. Few if any Civil War diarists with whom I was familiar had a better eye or talent for describing the countryside or the people.

Hitchcock's description of the great battles, such as Fredericksburg, in which he was a participant, are focused and evocative. In an afterword to what he wrote at the time, in 1890 he added pungent comments regarding the leadership of the generals who commanded the Army of the Potomac. Late December 1862 found the 21st Massachusetts on picket duty near Chatham, the home of Horace Lacy, a Fredericksburg landmark then, and now an historic property administered by the National Park Service.

The Ninth Corps, on February 4, 1863, was detached from the Army of the Potomac, and, after duty in Southside Virginia, was reassigned to the Department of the Ohio. What happened during these months, particularly when the 21st Massachusetts and the other units assigned to the corps' Second Division were on occupation duty in Central Kentucky, is not well known. Hitchcock's journal provides excellent insights into how the Yankees interacted with the civilians in a "loyal" state where slavery was legal.

In mid–September, the Ninth Corps began the long march that took Hitchcock and his comrades deep into East Tennessee. The marches, camps, battles and personalities that characterized Maj. Gen. Ambrose E. Burnside's successful campaigns in the region are described in an intelligent and insightful manner that enlightens and entertains.

On January 7, 1864, the regiment, having reenlisted, set out in a "blinding snow storm" back to Kentucky by way of Cumberland Gap. Some three months later, the peripatetic Ninth Corps was back in Virginia. After a stint in a Kentucky hospital and a furlough, Hitchcock rejoined his regiment on May 29 near Totopotomoy Creek. The regiment since May 5, when it crossed the Rapidan, had been an active participant in Lt. Gen. Ulysses S. Grant's bitter Overland Campaign. Hitchcock, as a casual, found the 24-day trip south from Boston to Richmond approaches vexing, irksome, and fraught with red tape.

Hitchcock was back with his unit less than a week before he was captured by the Confederates on June 2 after a bitter fight at Bethesda Church. The Rebels, always looking for an opportunity, took advantage of sloppy coordination between the Union Fifth and Ninth corps, dooming our diarist to spend the next six months as a prisoner-of-war.

Prisoner-of-war stories, with the theme of man's inhumanity to man, command public attention far beyond the Civil War community. More than 50 years ago, MacKinlay Kantor's *Andersonville* attracted a national audience of television viewers. I am no exception, finding Hitchcock's diary entries describing his experiences at Libby Prison, Camp Sumter (Andersonville), Camp Lawton (Millen) and Florence soul-searing.

In the years since President Richard M. Nixon signed into law on October 16, 1970, legislation establishing Andersonville National Historic Site, I have been professionally involved with the site of the nation's most infamous military prison. To facilitate plans for development and interpretation of the site by the National Park Service, I visited the area on several occasions in the early 1970s. In doing so, I became familiar with the history of the prison, its administration, and the prisoners. Out of my research came the *Historic Resource Study and Historical Base Map: Andersonville National Historic Site*. Then, in the mid–1990s, I was honored to be chosen to be one of the "talking heads" for A&E's *The Civil War Journal* with its focus on Civil War prisons. Prior to the showing of Ted Turner's *Andersonville*, I appeared on a program intended to provide an understanding that all Civil War prisons, whether Union or Confederate, were hell holes.

It was with this background that I evaluated Hitchcock's trials and tribulations, and came to understand its importance as a primary source. Hitchcock's diary, unlike most prisoners' accounts, is a day-to-day record instead of a reminiscence. As a World War II combat veteran, on returning to reunions, I have learned too often the hazards of reliance on old Marines' memories.

Employing the skills learned in college and honed in more than three decades in public education with a love and appreciation of history, Watson carefully transcribed and edited the Hitchcock journal. In doing so, he avoided the pitfall of too many editors—a heavy hand. Explanatory notes were informative but concise, not calculated to overwhelm the reader.

After reading and annotating the draft manuscript, I returned it to Watson on March 19, 1996. In encouraging its publication, I wrote:

> The diary ... is one of the best and most informative ... that I have been asked to read and comment upon. Particularly enlightening is Hitchcock's description of his service with the IX Corps during the period January 1863 to February 1864 and of the occupation and campaigns in Kentucky and East Tennessee, focusing on a theater of war that has not received the attention it warrants. Unlike the reminiscences of most Andersonville prisoners, Hitchcock's diary presents a balanced account of the more than four months he spent there. Not as well known are what the prisoners experienced at Camp Lawton and at Florence, how the exchanges were effected, and how the soldiers were processed upon reaching Camp Parole, Maryland. Now, thanks to Hitchcock's journal and your notes these can become common knowledge.

After the publication of *From Ashby to Andersonville,* Ron discovered Hitchcock's great-great-granddaughter, Martha Hitchcock Price, who lives in Fairport, New York. Martha, the Hitchcock family historian, sent Watson a copy of the 1865 Hitchcock diary, *The Army Experiences of George A. Hitchcock.* This diary had been originally in the possession of Hitchcock's only son, George Preston Hitchcock.

Now, Watson has revisited Hitchcock's diaries using Hitchcock's original 1865 diary with selective 1890 comments. The 1865 diary reveals new personal reflections that Hitchcock edited in 1890.

This new book is a major revision using Hitchcock's 1865 journal and will provide a treasure trove of information for Civil War historians and history buffs—a very rare and detailed account of a Civil War diary written daily and includes comments Hitchcock wrote twenty-five years later.

Edwin C. Bearss, historian emeritus of National Park Service and a United States Marine Corps wounded veteran of World War II, is a prominent military historian, an American Civil War expert and a guide of historic battlefields.

Preface by Ronald G. Watson

After the publication in 1997 of *From Ashby to Andersonville*—George A. Hitchcock's 1890 Civil War Diary that was edited and enhanced from his 1865 diary—I discovered Hitchcock's great-great-granddaughter, Martha Hitchcock Price, who lives in Fairport, New York a retired teacher and the Hitchcock family historian. I was thrilled when Martha sent me a copy of Hitchcock's 1865 diary that had been originally in the possession of Hitchcock's only son, George Preston Hitchcock. This 1865 diary is the record of Hitchcock's daily experiences exactly as he wrote them—occasionally during limited time under military pressure. The 1865 diary is the basis for this book. Within the diary pages of this book, Hitchcock's writings are in normal type while editor's comments and quotes from Hitchcock's 1890 commentaries are in italics. Research for this book was enhanced with the help of Martha Hitchcock Price and by the many excellent sources in the Bibliography.

By 1865 Hitchcock had written a vivid and well-organized journal that included accounts of: The Army of the Potomac's battles from South Mountain and Antietam through the disastrous Union advance toward Marye's Heights at Fredericksburg; a journey by rail through York, Pittsburgh, Columbus and Cincinnati to Paris, Kentucky; the protection of the Mount Sterling, Kentucky, area from guerrillas; an expedition from Camp Nelson in eastern Kentucky through the Cumberland Gap to eastern Tennessee; the skirmishes and battles in Burnside's Knoxville campaign; the arduous return-march to Camp Nelson during a severe winter with Confederate prisoners; the persistent effort to regain his health and return to his regiment; and an exceptionally compelling personal account of his capture at Cold Harbor and imprisonment at Andersonville, Camp Lawton and Florence Stockade and finally release.

From August 7, 1862, to January 1, 1865, Hitchcock composed this compelling and enthralling personal narrative, keeping a meticulous, detailed record of his daily activities in pocket diaries. Hitchcock has provided the reader with a fascinating chronicle of a soldier-traveler who spent many free moments exploring cities, attending church services and observing the environment.

His diaries were never published for many personal reasons. The 1890 revised diary was presented to the Fitchburg Historical Society by his daughter, Miss Annie Louise Hitchcock, on April 7, 1932, four years before her death. And there the diary remained, hidden away in a walk-in vault while the 1865 journal was held privately by his son's family.

Private Hitchcock in his 1865 diary expresses a very fresh point of view with a minimum of hostility. Such objectivity is seldom found in Civil War diaries. His personal commentaries written after the war, when he was struggling to regain his health and secure a pension while reevaluating his capture and imprisonment, are somewhat more partisan in tone—although by 1890 Hitchcock had ameliorated his comments on the Confederacy.

George Hitchcock was an intelligent, perceptive and religious Union soldier, and his detailed descriptions of his military experiences qualify as a quintessential Civil War diary. This may be the only daily narrative written by a soldier during the Civil War and then twenty five years later, reflecting on the past, provided new information and commentaries that have been included in this book.

Although Hitchcock's 1865 diary and his later comments vary to some extent, the changes in interpretations are limited after twenty-five years. The reader should note, however, the differences and fascinating patterns in Hitchcock's 1865 journal in the following areas compared to his 1890 commentaries and reminiscences: His emphasis on (and importance of) his deep religious proclivities that provided support for his survival at Andersonville; his comments on the hostile language toward the Confederacy; his specific acrimony directed at Henry Wirz and the grave conditions at Andersonville; his resentment created by prison of war suffering; and his reaction to Confederate prisoners. This book clearly shows how this articulate soldier's views changed after twenty-five years, especially concerning war, prisoners of war and the obstacles confronted by governmental bureaucracy.

Introduction
by Ronald G. Watson

George Alfred Hitchcock was a resident of Ashby, Massachusetts, a small town forty-two miles west of Boston in the northwestern extremity of Middlesex County bordering on New Hampshire. It was incorporated on September 4, 1767. The picturesque land offers a variety of hills and vales with rich pastures and farmland marked by meandering streams. In the 1860s, a majority of the people were engaged in agricultural pursuits—wheat, potatoes, corn, oats, barley, apples and dairy products. There were 1,091 residents in Ashby comprised of 532 males and 559 females, with no free colored. Ashby area residents were noted for their industry, frugality and hospitality. *The Ashby Evening Gazette*, dated December 22, 1869, editorialized that "the town early took measures to administer justice, or at least to correct violations of good order, especially on the Sabbath." This small town of farmers and merchants furnished 109 soldiers during the Civil War, including George Hitchcock—eighteen of his fellow townsmen never returned.

Hitchcock was born in Ashby on January 15, 1844, the third child of Eliza Sparhawk and George Loring Hitchcock. Three of the Hitchcocks' seven children died in their early youth. George inherited from his parents a strong "Yankee" conscience with an abiding sense of duty and responsibility. His uncompromising moral standards were rooted in Victorian values and enhanced by what he described as "strong parental love." In his diary he wrote that his father, a wheelwright, was his "congenial companion," an abolitionist and member of the free soil party, who believed in "free soil, free speech, free labor and free men."

In "Memoirs of Ashby in 1850," George Hitchcock wrote after the war that his home was located on the main road running north and south between southern New Hampshire and Fitchburg, Massachusetts. Adjoining his home was his father's carriage and wheelwright shop with its medley of old wheels and wagon parts. Throughout the village, each home had its connecting shop selling boots and shoes, harnesses, blacksmith, coffins, rope, carpet, and dresses. During the decade between 1840 and 1850, Ashby boasted of two unusual industries: Whitney's organ shop (one of the first in the country), and the Willard's shop, which sold time pieces that remain today cherished heirlooms. There were four stores in Ashby, including an apothecary. The southern part of town was called "Mill Village" with its dozen mills of various types including saw mills and producers of tubs, pails, carriages, and boots.

Farming was a cherished way of life in Ashby. According to Hitchcock, the farmer was the "captain of industry." Outside the village the entire township was dotted with large farms that had well-kept barns stocked with all kinds of domestic animals. The large families provided the necessary labor, and Hitchcock noted that "no unreliable hired help was then known." Before the railroads were built, Ashby was a relatively important stop on the great Boston and Burlington (Vermont) stagecoach road with its two enterprising hotels. A grand old tavern, Children of the Woods, furnished rest and refreshment for passengers and animals before the journey through the hills of Rindge, New Hampshire.

As his journal attests, the young Hitchcock was well educated. George recalled with fondness the small ungraded school located near the Ashby Commons crowded with 60 to 70 pupils. "The town was indebted for the high standard of excellence of such teachers as Mrs. Sara Wyman and Miss Susanne Augusta Wallis (afterward Mrs. Amasa Norcross)." Academic results were reflected in the high character of citizenship and domestic virtues of the scholars who were pupils of those teachers. "No more perfect discipline had ever since been attained and at the same time the development of individuality—an attainment well nigh impossible by the present graded methods. And with both of these teachers, the dominant trait which controlled was the law of love." Hitchcock attended the Ashby public school and continued an academic education at Appleton Academy in New Ipswich, New Hampshire, and Templeton (Massachusetts) High School, all with the intention of attending college.

If there was one distinctive trait of Ashby, differentiating this town from other old New England towns, Hitchcock believed that, while holding a high standard of intelligence, Ashby never harbored or claimed an aristocratic taint. Many towns of eastern New Hampshire and northeastern Massachusetts, whose settlements had been fostered by royalists, boasted of their highbred families. Neighboring towns pointed with pride to some dominant masterful family who bequeathed its spirit to later generations and gave it a character which Oliver Wendell Holmes depicted as the "true New England aristocracy." Hitchcock stressed that this was not so with Ashby, and no aristocracy or plutocracy could ever be anything but "an excrescence or offense in any true American community." Hitchcock felt that "the blossom and fruitage of Ashby in the 1850s was the sterling common sense which called no man master." The people looked to their ministers of God as their moral leaders, and their physicians were their leaders in educational thought—all men of superior intelligence and judgment. Yet Ashby was "never a utopia, simply a plain, common sense, healthy outgrowth of democratic ideas." Towns like Ashby "helped to make this nation the foremost in the world."

On August 7, 1862, the 18-year-old Hitchcock left Ashby to volunteer in the 21st Infantry Regiment of Massachusetts Volunteers—the same regiment that his older brother, Henry Sparhawk Hitchcock, had joined on August 23, 1861.

Introduction
by George A. Hitchcock

My first motive in preparing this diary was to preserve in compact form the narrative of events which would necessarily ever be of more value and interest to the writer than to anyone else. But the interest manifested by personal friends, to see the account of my army and prison life, led me to make a more extended and complete account than I at first intended. I am sensible to the fact that the "original" diary found, in the "field and dungeon" as well as the constant handling it has received since, has almost effaced the pencil-written pages and has therefore made this "copy" a matter of necessity. I have adhered to the literal of the original, generally, but as occasions of greater interest came up, I made more detailed accounts. The various quotations of scripture interspersed were found to be of such valuable comfort and encouragement at those dates, that they have found a place there.

Owing to the fact that my "proof-reader" is "out of town," I request all my friends to make all proper punctuations, additions and omissions to suit their individual tastes.

—G.A.H., 1865

1

Apprenticeship to Uncle Sam

"Orders came this afternoon for recruits to leave for the seat of war, which means me."
—Hitchcock, August 30, 1862

When George Hitchcock left Ashby, he looked forward to a reunion with his brother and membership in a proud regiment. His older brother, Henry Sparhawk Hitchcock, a resident of Templeton, Massachusetts, enlisted as a sergeant in Company A, 21st Massachusetts Regiment on July 19, 1861. The regiment was organized and trained during July and August at the Agricultural Fair Grounds in Worcester, Massachusetts. Henry received leave to marry Mary Miller Chamberlin on August 21. Prior to heading south, the soldiers were issued old smoothbore muskets, altered from flintlocks, to replace the makeshift, crooked-barrel guns which had been used for drilling.

On August 23, 1861, after being mustered into the United States service for three years, the regiment was presented with a silk regimental flag from the ladies of Worcester, and then they left for Norwich, Connecticut, by train, traveled from Norwich to Jersey City by boat and again boarded a train to Havre-de-Grace by way of Philadelphia. They were issued ball cartridges for the first time; the regiment expected a hostile reception in Baltimore. On August 25, the regiment arrived at Baltimore before noon, filed quietly from the train with fixed bayonets and loaded guns, and marched through the crowded streets to Patterson Park—with neither a welcome nor insults heaped in the unit's direction. Three days later the regiment arrived at Annapolis, Maryland, for temporary garrison duty. More reliable Enfield muskets from Massachusetts reached them just before their first Christmas of the war.

On January 6, 1862, the 21st Massachusetts Regiment boarded the steamer, Northerner, bound for Hatteras Inlet as part of Ambrose Burnside's Expedition to North Carolina. Brigadier General Ambrose Everett Burnside led a joint army-navy force to gain control of the Pamlico and Albermarle sounds. The 12,000-man land force (the Coast Division of the Army of the Potomac) was organized

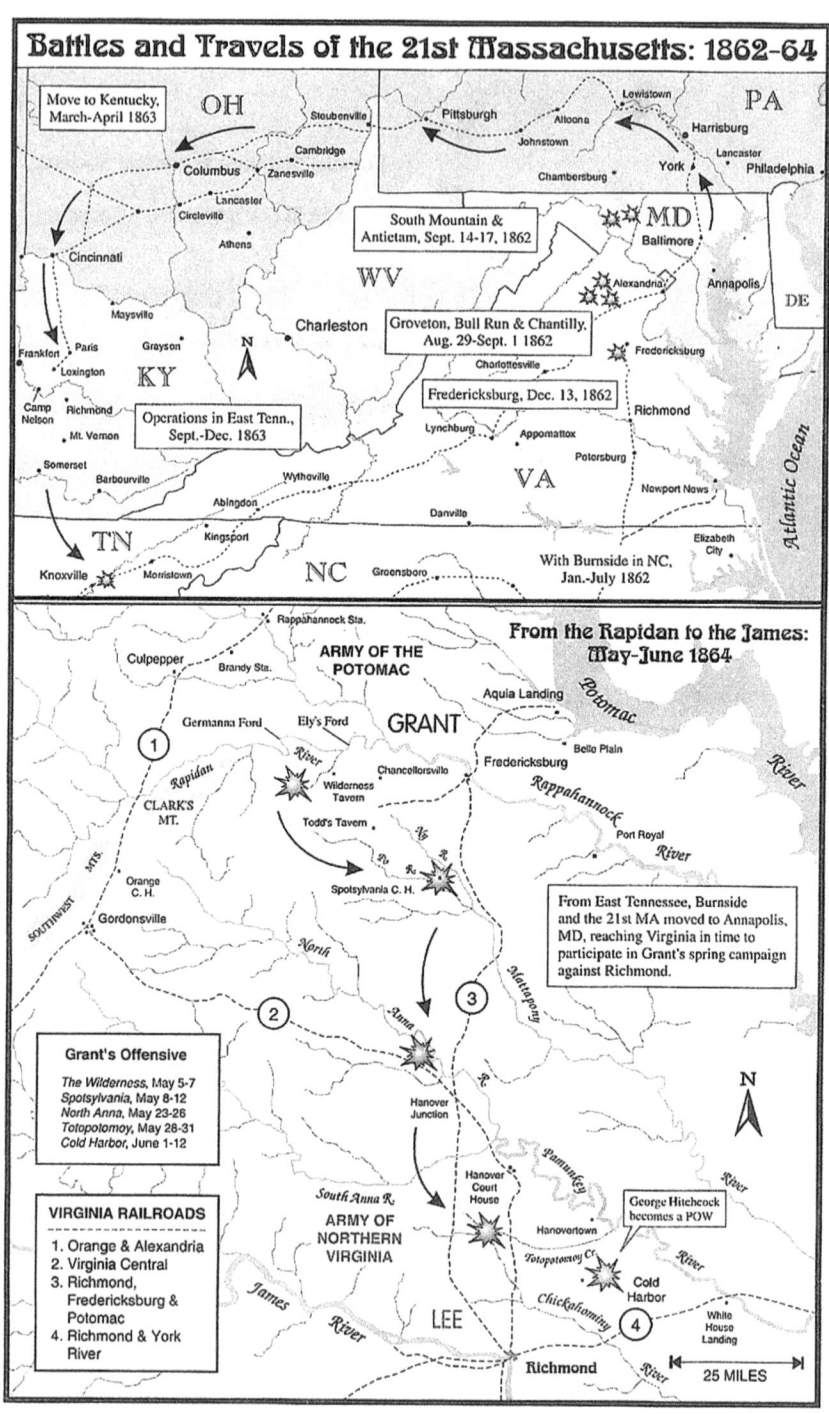

Engagements and travels of the 21st Massachusetts Regiment (© Mark A. Moore).

into three brigades, with the 21st Massachusetts Regiment part of Brig. Gen. Jesse L. Reno's Second Brigade. Three battles would turn the raw recruits into veterans. The strong Union force was victorious at the Battle of Roanoke Island on February 8, 1862 (700 soldiers from the 21st were engaged and 13 were killed or died of wounds and 44 others were wounded); at the Battle of New Bern on March 14, 1862 (675 soldiers from the 21st were engaged and 23 were killed or died of wounds and 35 others were wounded) and at the Battle of South Mills in Camden County on April 19, 1862 (500 soldiers from the 21st were engaged and four were killed or died of wounds, 11 others were wounded and one was taken prisoner).

On July 6, 1862, after the close of Burnside's campaign, the 21st Massachusetts Regiment left North Carolina and went into camp at Newport News. After spending the next month drilling and target shooting, the regiment became part of the newly organized IX Army Corps. The corps left Newport News on August 2, and arrived at Fredericksburg, Virginia, two days later.

* * * *

August 7, 1862—It was a fine, warm morning that dawned on the quiet little town of Ashby [*Massachusetts*] up among the hills of Middlesex [*County*] and the farmers made themselves busy in the hay-fields on either side of the road as Father and I rode to the depot. The familiar and peaceful scenes seemed to make my prospective future all the more intense and impressive, so that the repulses and difficulties met in the start did not dampen the ardor or overwhelm the patriotism. Lemuel Whitney and myself, armed with "Official Documents" from the Enlisting Officer Mr. B.W. Seamans of Ashby and countersigned by the Selectmen of the town, proceed to Boston to Adjutant General Schouler's office and after a short and very pleasant conversation, he gives us passes to the camp of rendezvous, Camp Cameron, which is situated in North Cambridge—six miles from the State House. Thither we proceed in the horse-cars. Reaching there before sun-down, we have but little time to look about us and hunt up the headquarters. Finding them we are disappointed in not seeing the commandant, Lieutenant Jordan, consequently cannot secure any quarters for the night. We therefore return to Cambridge and put up at the Market Hotel.

August 8—We are aroused early in the morning by the sounds of a heavy thunder shower. After breakfast we return to Camp Cameron and make several ineffectual attempts to secure recognition. We remain until afternoon and somewhat losing patience we leave camp, go into Boston, catch a train on the Boston and Maine Railroad and proceed to Lynnfield where we find the Ashby boys who left home a week earlier and are now joined to Company E, 33d Mass of which Colonel Maggi is commander. He was Lieutenant Colonel of the 21st and commanded that regiment in Roanoke and Newbern—a brave Italian officer who fought with Garibaldi for Italy's freedom.

Two regiments, the 33d and 35th, compose "Camp Staunton," a beautiful camping ground with a fine grove of trees in the rear and a large, clear sheet of water nearby. We find our boys all in fine spirits who urge us to go in with them, but we remain firm in our purpose to join the 21st. We witness the Dress Parade for the first time with great interest, after which the boys share with us their soldiers fare and we try a soldiers bed in a large "Sibley" or bell tent with the boys. Tired out, we sleep soundly as only healthy boys can.

August 9—The morning of the next day opens with showers while heavy sea-fogs come driving in, for we are very near the salt water. I camped down in a large Sibley tent with the boys and slept very well. Returned to Boston in the forenoon and dined at Campbell's, after which we made for Camp Cameron again. This time we (Lem and I) succeed in gaining a hearing and after waiting till half past four we were examined by a surgeon, accepted and quarters are assigned us in Barracks No. 6 with a piece of bread for supper. Weary and lame, we seek repose on the hard hemlock boards using our coats as pillows, and even thus finding refreshing rest.

August 10—We awake on our first Sabbath in camp to find a beautiful day and being so near the great city, swarms of Sabbath breakers overrun the camp all day bent on sightseeing. No religious exercises were held but during the morning the entire camp of recruits was ordered out and formed in a hollow square where the articles of war were read to us. These give instruction in the duties and laws governing each member of the army. The knowledge of them gives me new feeling of the important responsibility of even a private.

A great deal of drunkenness and many arrests during the day have made the sacred hours seem profaned to me since I have never before been away from the quiet and holy influences of a genuine New England Sabbath.

August 11—Slept about four hours last night, as the air was very chilly and I have not blankets yet. Found nothing especial to do, and the consequent lounging about seemed very tiresome. Nearly three hundred recruits left camp en route for Washington, but it does not change the appearance in camp as new ones are coming in so rapidly.

August 12—The morning is cloudy and threatening rain, but this clears away and the sun shines out very warm. Lem and I receive passes and go into Boston. We try to be sworn into service there, hoping in this way to be able to secure blankets, rations and other requisites for comfort. Being unable, we go into Tremont Temple Basement, which is used as an enlisting depot, and are tempted to reenlist into the Boston Quota, but giving that up; we return to camp somewhat out of temper, feeling that Government is using us rather shabbily, having been here nearly a week waiting and nothing accomplished as far as our "short vision peereth."

August 13—Today we are more successful. Lem's papers are made out and mine also, but red-tape has it that I, being a minor, must procure my father's written consent, which has to be countersigned on the enlistment papers. These I carried to Porter's Station and sent by express to Ashby. Tonight a large squad of recruits was sent away.

August 14—I went down to the Post Office at nine for my return papers; not finding them, I strolled over Cambridge to Charlestown, visited the top of the Bunker Hill Monument and the Navy Yard; from there into Boston, get dinner and go out to Porter's again, where I was happily surprised to meet father and Arthur who gave me the needed papers and then go on to Campello to visit Rev. Mr. Woods, while I trudge back to camp. [*Charles Wilkes Wood, George Hitchcock's minister during his youth, was the sixth pastor of the Orthodox Congregational Church in Ashby. He served from 1839 to 1858 and then moved to North Bridgewater, Massachusetts.*]

August 15—The morning was rainy, but that makes no difference to soldiers so we are ordered into line and have to march to headquarters to receive our bounty-money. On reaching there we were ordered back without it. Father returned from Campello in the afternoon, called out to camp and with some parting advice and a sad "Good Bye" he returned home. Recruits for the 2nd, 8th, and 22nd regiments left for the seat of war tonight.

August 16—The sergeant and corporal in charge of our barracks left today, so we are left in charge of green ones. Wrote to Henry. Went in the afternoon with a squad up to Spy Pond, West Cambridge, to bathe. Received tonight twenty-five dollars advance of Government Bounty.

August 17—Sunday: The Articles of War were again read to us this morning. An invitation from the Baptist Church, North Cambridge, was sent out to camp so a large number of us went down to afternoon service. [*In 1890 Hitchcock added: "I know not how soon I may have another opportunity to see the inside of a church so the occasion is an impressive one."*]

August 18 and 19—Had my first experience in guard duty on the camp guard. We form a living fence—each man having a "beat" of some three or four rods [*one rod equals five and one-half yards*] on which he tramps back and forth. Guard mounting begins at nine in the morning. First relief stands from nine to eleven; second from eleven to one; third from one to three and continuing through twenty-four hours. The occupation was not hard but very tedious and during the night the desire to drop to sleep was well nigh irresistible, but a healthful fear of the dread penalty kept me awake.

August 20—The monotony of camp life is broken by various peddlers who scent the soldiers bounty money and various articles, some useful, some useless, are exchanged for "shinplasters." I purchased a stencil with which I mark my various articles of wearing apparel:

G.A. HITCHCOCK Co. A, 21st Reg't M.V.

August 21—Received a box of goodies from home in which was a letter from Henry written from Culpeper Court House, where they have had fighting. Messrs. Foster, Seamans, Levi Burr and Ware of Ashby and Boyden of Boston visited us this afternoon.

August 22—News of the Evacuation of the Peninsula by the Army of the Potomac under McClellan. Eighty men for the 17th MVR [Massachusetts Volunteers Regiment] went away to the seat of war today.

August 26—Wrote home today. I was under drill today for first time. Battalion Drill under Major Hall of 1st MVR. Edwin Whitney and Henry Burr visited us bringing a box. Recruits for the 20th were sent off today. Attended a prayer meeting at No. 9 Barracks which was conducted by Rev. Goodhue of North Cambridge. Great interest was manifested.

August 30—No furloughs were allowed today. I received government clothing and equipments this morning. Packed my valise and knapsack, gave the valise in charge of the corporal of the barrack to be sent home. Orders came this afternoon for recruits for 2nd, 11th, 21st, 24th, and 27th to leave for the seat of war, which means me. Marched out of camp, rode in horse-cars to Boston, where several hundred of us formed and marched across the city, passing the Germania Band which was stationed on Washington St. discoursing excellent music and instilling patriotism into weak-kneed recruits. Packed into cars at the Old Colon R.R. depot at sundown and rode through the beautiful suburbs at beautiful sunset. Stopped at only Bridgewater till we reach Fall River at half past nine. Went on board the splendid Steamer "Empire State" and after finding a comfortable place in the main saloon where I leave my knapsack, I explore the vessel which is a little world of wonder.

August 31—Sunday morning finds us out on the Sound with lad on each side and vessels all about, which indicates the near approach of New York Harbor. The sky is clear and the atmosphere perfect as we sail up the harbor. We pass the shadow of the "Great Eastern," which lies at anchor not far from Hell Gate, [*section of East River, New York, a channel 200 feet wide at narrowest part*], her monstrous black hulk towering far above our decks. We arrived at the Pier foot of Courtland St. at 10 o'clock a.m. March up Broadway to the Soldiers "Rest" on Franklin St. Here we get rations and stop over night. Little does it seem like our New England Sabbath with scenes like these and so much noise about us. [*The* Great Eastern *had arrived in New York from England on August 31, 1862. This "greatest iron ship" was launched in London in 1858, and was five times the size of any ship afloat with a hull 693 feet long (18,915 gross tonnage). There were 800 cabins (some having their own bathtubs with hot and cold running water) and five gilded and mirrored saloons (grandest encompassing 3,000 square feet). The ship was designed to be propelled through the ocean at a mind-boggling 18 knots (never exceeded 14.5 knots) by twin 56-foot paddle wheels* *and a 24-foot screw propeller that were powered by coal in 10 boilers (carried 3,000 tons of coal). The ship, which also carried 6,500 square yards of canvas on six masts that were available only for auxiliary power, was put on the Atlantic run, but her 4,000 berths were never filled; she was beset by costly accidents and bankruptcies. The Great Eastern Company promoted by Cyrus Field bought the Great Eastern in 1864 and fitted the huge ship for the monumental task of carrying 2,000 miles of telegraphic cable to connect England and North America. The second attempt was successful: The* Great Eastern *left Valencia on the south coast of Ireland on July 13, 1866 and arrived at Heart's Content Bay, Newfoundland, on July 27, 1866.]*

September 1, 1862—We awake to find a stormy day. March to the Jersey Ferry and cross to Jersey City and wait three hours for transportation. Start for Philadelphia at noon and reach there at half past nine in the evening and find the rain pouring. Found excellent supper at the Soldier's Refreshment Saloon after which we march across the city to the Depot of the P.W. and Baltimore R.R. where we find two new regiments ahead of us awaiting transportation. So at about midnight we find quarters nearby in a Hall belonging to a Hose Company where we wait till morning.

September 2—Leaving Philadelphia at half past eight we pass out of the immense depot of the P.W. & B.R.R. I caught sight of Mr. Kenny and spoke with him; he is Master of Transportation here. The day is beautiful as we ride along through a beautiful fertile country and reach Havre de Grace at noon. The manner of crossing the broad Susquehanna is peculiar. Large ferry boats connect with the tracks and the entire train of cars is run on to the boat on three separate tracks and transferred to the Delaware side, into Wilmington, where I first see negro slaves and am made to understand that we have left the free land behind us. We arrive in Baltimore at half past two. Landing we pass through the famed localities of the "Mob" of last year, across the city to the Soldiers Relief Building where are eight hundred others awaiting transportation.

September 3—We find our quarters rather uncomfortable and are glad to embark on a very long train before noon. Before leaving B [*Baltimore*] a large train load of wounded came in from the battlefields of Bull Run and Chantilly, [*Casualties in Union forces, commanded by Major General John Pope, during the operations from August 16 to September 2, 1862, were: 1,747 killed; 8,452 wounded; and 4,263 missing.*] a sickening sight to raw recruits but we are in for it and may have an opportunity to see something more yet. From B to Washington our train moves very slowly and the warlike aspect increases as we approach the Capitol. Forts and fortifications on each side and soldiers all about. Reach Washington at noon and march down Pennsylvania Ave. to the lower end of the city and cross the Potomac in a steamboat to Alexandria.

"Death does seem to have all he can attend to"

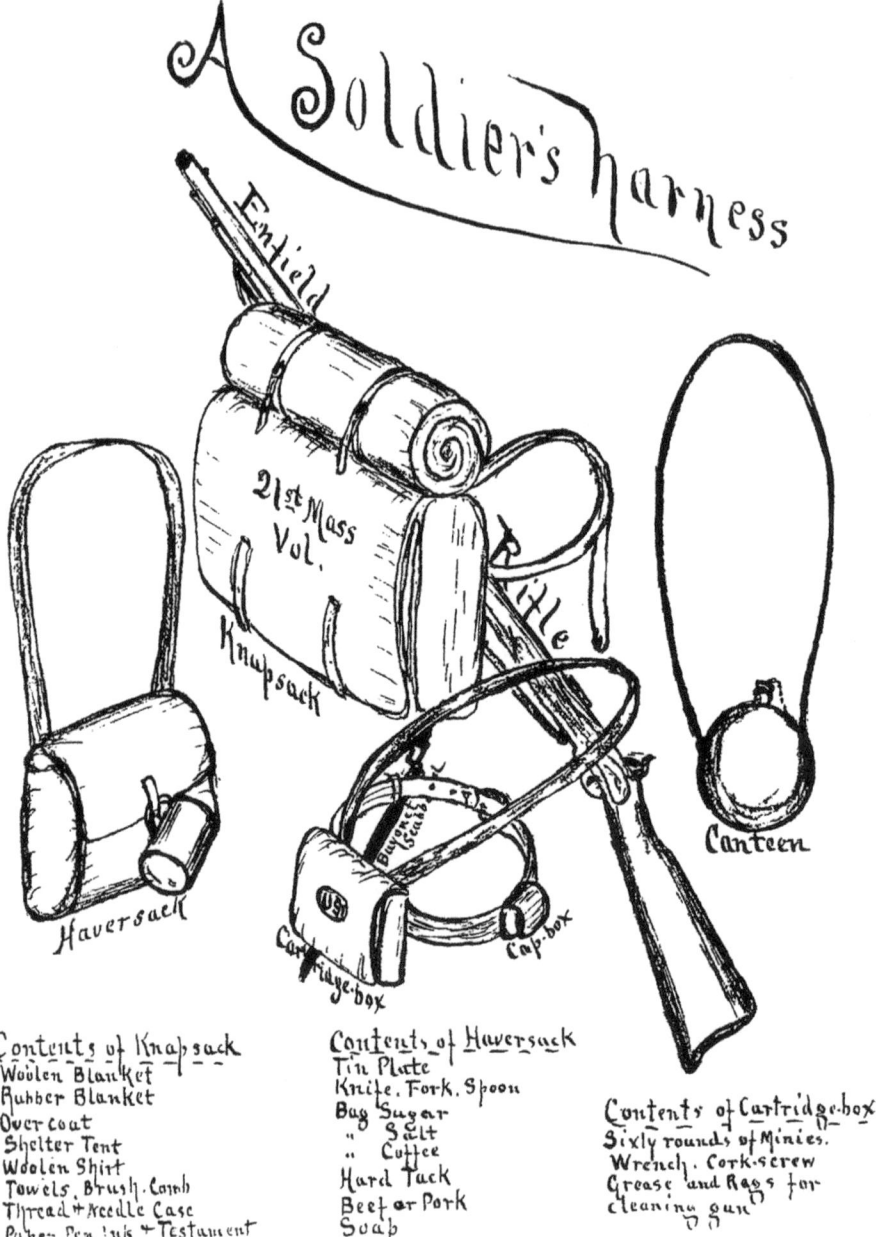

"A Soldier's Harness," drawn by George A. Hitchcock for his 1890 diary.

As we are crossing the stream we see several gun boats going up the river packed with troops and learn that the enemy is heading toward Maryland, having forced our army back to the Capitol defenses. Find supper in Alexandria, then march out two miles to Chestnut Hill which is a part of Arlington Heights near Fort Ellsworth. Here our commander orders a halt to camp down for the night, with the caution to "look out and not bump heads against the rafters when we get up in the morning." As darkness settled down over the surrounding country, what a thrilling impression is made as the innumerable camp fires of McClellan's army dot the valley thickly from Alexandria back for miles out on the Fairfax Road, which runs along the base of Chestnut Hill and myriad of drums and bugles sound the tattoo.

September 4—From our camping ground we can see Washington with its beautiful marble Capitol towering above, seven miles away, a long sweep of the broad Potomac ten miles down to Fort Washington and all the surrounding country. Have just heard from the 21st [*Massachusetts*] that Col. Clark and all his staff were lost in the late battles but have since been heard from. Lieut. Col. Rice was killed. Members of the 21st are engaged in the convalescent camp near here and report that the regiment has been badly cut up and in camp two miles out. Wrote home today. [*Colonel William S. Clark, from Amherst, Massachusetts, was not killed and remained with the 21st until his resignation on April 22, 1863. However, the regiment (400 soldiers engaged) suffered their heaviest casualties of the war at the Battle of Chantilly on September 1, 1862: 140 casualties—38 were killed or died from wounds, 76 wounded and 26 taken prisoner. Lieutenant Colonel Joseph Parker Rice was killed.*]

September 5—Started out to find the 21st but had not gone a mile before I learned that the regiment had gone to Chain Bridge, six miles up the river, so we expect to remain here until they are stationed somewhere. The entire army seems to be packing around Washington. I saw the celebrated "California Joe" of Berdan's Sharp Shooters. He is a rough looking pioneer. [*Truman "California Joe" Head served in Company C, 1st United States Sharpshooters commanded by Colonel Hiram Berdan. Head was born in Philadelphia and wandered across the country to California. A former gold prospector and bear hunter, he was one of many old gunners (52 years old) who became "Sharpshooters."*]

September 6—The sun beat down so hot that we rigged a shelter of our rubber blanket. It is rumored that the rebels are across the Potomac and endeavoring to surround Washington.

2

The Maryland Campaign

"He [President Lincoln] looks like the many pictures I have seen of him, good-natured, honest and homely."
—Hitchcock, October 3, 1862

On September 1, 1862, after the Union army retreated to Centreville, the Second Manassas, or Bull Run, Campaign came to a violent closure during a tremendous thunderstorm. Two Federal divisions fought a bloody but successful rear guard action at the Battle of Chantilly at Ox Hill, Virginia, against Thomas "Stonewall" Jackson's troops which were attempting to crush the retreating Union right flank. Two of the most promising commanders of the Union army were killed in the engagement: Maj. Gen. Philip Kearny, who commanded the First Division of III Corps, and Maj. Gen. Isaac Ingalls Stevens, who commanded the First Division of IX Corps. The 21st Massachusetts Regiment was engaged at Chantilly, where Hitchcock's regiment suffered the heaviest casualties it would experience during the war (3 officers and 19 enlisted men killed; 5 officers and 37 enlisted men wounded; and 3 officers and 37 enlisted men captured or missing).

President Lincoln removed Maj. Gen. John Pope as commander of the Union army the following day and replaced him with Maj. Gen. George Brinton McClellan. The soldiers were jubilant about the selection of McClellan and, notwithstanding their loss of morale from the debacle on the plains of Manassas, they were prepared to challenge the Confederate forces within a matter of days.

Meanwhile, on September 4, 1862, Gen. Robert E. Lee embarked on a bold raid north of the Potomac. His 55,000-man army moved north to Leesburg, Virginia, crossed the Potomac River at White's Ford into Maryland and its vanguard arrived in Frederick on September 6. When Lee's plan to resupply his army and to recruit soldiers failed, he evacuated the city on September 10 and marched toward the South Mountain gaps. The Federals, however, refused to abandon Harpers Ferry as Lee had anticipated. Lee divided his army, sending Jackson's troops to capture the 2,500 Union forces at Martinsburg and 10,400 at Harpers

Ferry. McClellan's advance arrived in Frederick on September 12, where the next day XII Corps soldiers on picket duty discovered Special Orders 191, which detailed the position and strength of the various segments of Lee's army. McClellan moved against Lee with more alacrity than usual, and on September 14, 1862, attacked three well-defended gaps in the South Mountain range: Crampton's, Fox's and Turner's.

The 21st Massachusetts Regiment was engaged at Fox's Gap where the fighting lasted until ten in the evening. Maj. Gen. Jessie Reno, commander of the IX Corps, was killed during the conflict and his loss devastated the men of the 21st. There was not a man in the 21st who did not love him. According to Augustus Woodbury, "he had a magnetic kind of enthusiasm and, when leading on his men, he seemed to inspire his followers and make them irresistible in action—a dauntless soldier, whose like we rarely see."

Late on the afternoon of September 15, McClellan halted the Army of the Potomac on the east bank of the Antietam Creek near the village of Sharpsburg. The Union right wing, composed of the I Corps and IX Corps, was commanded by Maj. Gen. Burnside; the center, composed of the II Corps and XII Corps, was commanded by Maj. Gen. Edwin V. Sumner; and the left wing, composed of the VI Corps and Darius Couch's division of the IV Corps, was commanded by Maj. Gen. William B. Franklin.

By the following evening. General Lee had most of the Army of Northern Virginia deployed on the heights crowning the west bank of the Antietam Creek. Lee's army, unofficially composed of Maj. Gen. James Longstreet's Corps and Maj. Gen. Thomas J. Jackson's Corps, was concentrated in front of Sharpsburg. Jackson's troops arrived on the field on September 16, one day after the surrender of Harpers Ferry. At sunrise the following morning the divisions of Maj. Gen. Lafayette McLaws and Maj. Gen. Robert Anderson arrived from Harpers Ferry. About 40,000 Confederate troops confronted 87,000 Federals.

The Battle of Antietam was fought on September 17, 1862. The fighting lasted from sunrise until after dark and resulted in the bloodiest single day battle of the Civil War. Union losses were 12,882 (2,157 killed, 9,716 wounded and 1,009 missing); Confederate losses were 11,530 (1,754 killed, 8,649 wounded and 1,127 missing).

The 21st Massachusetts Regiment was engaged in the afternoon phase of the battle at the lower bridge over Antietam Creek—popularly dubbed Burnside's Bridge. Five hundred Georgians (riflemen from the 2nd and 20th Georgia regiments) stalled the Union advance over the narrow span during the morning. When Burnside's troops finally crossed the creek in the early afternoon, the Georgians withdrew toward Sharpsburg. As Burnside's troops were driving across the fields and hills toward Sharpsburg, Maj. Gen. Ambrose P. Hill's Confederate division arrived from Harpers Ferry and drove the Union troops back to the heights near the bridge. Hill's tactical victory was the last significant fighting at Antietam. Lee, whose army had come within hair's breadth of being demolished, brazenly held his position the following day and began withdrawing his army across the Potomac River into Virginia.

Although the results of this very significant battle were not readily apparent (and are still hotly debated today), there were diplomatic, military, political and social implications. Robert E. Lee had failed in his bid to duplicate his successful string of battles north of the Potomac River. President Lincoln's political support hinged on military success since there had been discontentment growing in the Union. Lincoln had stated in 1861 that "we must settle this question now, whether in a free government the minority have the right to break up the government whenever they choose." Now, Lincoln had the opportunity to enlarge the purpose of the war beyond saving the Union. He expanded the purpose of the conflict to include slavery. On September 22, 1862, Lincoln issued the preliminary Emancipation Proclamation, which would take effect January 1, 1863. The document purported to free slaves held in those parts of the nation still in rebellion. The brilliant political document all but ended the threat of European intervention in the war and the movement overseas for diplomatic recognition of the Confederacy waned.

George Hitchcock finally joined with the 21st Massachusetts Regiment on September 9, 1862, in Maryland, a rather untimely association that cast him into one of the war's bloodiest contests. On September 14, 225 soldiers in the regiment (including Hitchcock) were lightly engaged at South Mountain and four were wounded. Three days later 150 soldiers of the regiment (including Hitchcock) marched with Ambrose Burnside across the creek and against the Sharpsburg heights. Almost 30 percent of these were killed or wounded—10 killed and 35 wounded.

* * * *

September 7, 1862—As I sat under our shelter reading this Sabbath morning, orders came for us to pack up and march. At noon we left Chestnut Hill and proceeded to Long Bridge. There we wait five hours and then cross what is said to be the longest bridge in the world, up Pennsylvania Ave to the "Soldiers' Rest" between the railroad station and the Capitol building where we lodge for the night. On our way through the streets we saw General Casey, a large gray haired man of about sixty, who is commander of the post. [*Long Bridge, crossing the Potomac River at the foot of Maryland Avenue, was the great outlet from Washington into Virginia for Union troops and supplies during the Civil War. The original Long Bridge over the Potomac River was built in 1809 at a cost of $100,000; however, the bridge was destroyed by a freshet in 1831. In 1835, a wooden bridge was erected at a cost of $113,000; the bridge was damaged in 1836 and again in 1840, but was reopened for travel in 1843. The bridge was 4,677 feet long and divided into three sections: The part over the channel was*

2,000 feet long with 13 fixed spans of 135 feet and one pivotal span of 182 feet. After being used since 1870 by the Baltimore and Potomac Railroad, the bridge was replaced in 1905.]

September 8—[*In 1890 Hitchcock added: "On arising from our rough quarters, I had my first introduction to the 'soldiers companion,' which sticketh closer than a brother, loveth darkness rather than light because his deeds are evil. He also loveth a warm corner and every cleanly soldier would gladly consign him to a very warm region (LICE)."*] Saw Herbert Lealand and other parolee prisoners of the 21st enroute for Annapolis. At one o'clock our squad leave Washington on the road to Annapolis Junction, march all the afternoon, halt in the evening till eleven when news comes that the regiment is only three miles ahead. Therefore we press along and find the three miles increased to four and afterward to five, passing Gen. Burnside's headquarters.

Sergeant Henry Sparhawk Hitchcock, Company A, 21st Massachusetts Regiment, was George's older brother (courtesy of Martha Hitchcock Price).

September 9—We soon find the 21st encamped by the side of the road at one o'clock in the morning. I soon found the sergeant's tent in darkness and called Henry's name. He answered me immediately and I was once more with my brother. My anxious inquiries were soon checked by him for he said I should need all the sleep I could get in the next three hours. In the morning I find Henry looking very thin and worn down with the terrible hardships of the past few weeks, but we are rejoiced to meet each other again. We are roused at half past four and at half past five Burnside's whole corps is on the road moving north westerly. I am loaded down with gun, cartridge box filled with cartridges, belt and cap box, two heavy blankets, overcoat, canteen and haversack. We halt in the afternoon, the brigade camping in a hollow about a mile and a half from Mechanicsville. This campaigning in real earnest comes hard with me and I am feeling well used up. We marched eight miles and camped near Brookville. Lem and I are in the first file of fours on the right of Company A—being two of the tallest [5'11"].

[*On April 19, 1862, the 21st Massachusetts and 51st Pennsylvania regiments landed at Elizabeth City, N.C. and started marching north. Each man carried rations for two days and sixty rounds of ammunition; they marched twenty miles in oppressively hot conditions and then successfully fought the Battle of Camden (South Mill, North Carolina). After a few hours of rest the regiments made the weary return march, encountering severe rain and very muddy roads (the entire expedition took place within twenty-four hours).]*

September 10—We did not move today, so laid about under a boiling sun. Troops have been passing by constantly all day, some on the Frederick road [*Frederick, Maryland*] and others more westerly. Am refreshed and better prepared for a march tomorrow.

September 11—Roused at half past four, on the move at half past six on the road to Frederick. We march all day, halting about every two miles for rest. We meet our cavalry pickets coming in with a rebel prisoner who reports the enemy six miles away. Marched fourteen miles and camp for the night in a nice level field. I try my luck at cooking meat for the first time.

September 12—Rained nearly all night so I am wet to the skin sleeping under water in the open air. We march fifteen miles and when seven miles from Frederick find the enemy only a short distance ahead. We hear cannonading as we approach the city. The road is full of troops hurrying forward to the scene of action. We arrive in sight of Frederick two miles before we reach the city where we go into camp for the night.

September 13—Our Division [*Second Division of the IX Corps commanded by General Samuel Davis Sturgis*] is under orders to march at a moment's notice and to be prepared for fighting, so I go to work and acquaint myself with my new friend, my gun, take it to pieces and clean it up, then load myself with knapsack, haversack, canteen and equipment, and lie on arms till four p.m. when the cannonading grows less continuous and we are ordered to move ahead. March through Frederick City with flying colors at sundown, out over a long level tract, then as darkness begins to settle down upon us we begin to climb the Blue Ridge. Up, up four long, weary miles till we reach the Gap which has been held all day by the rebels, and we now see marks of the struggle on each side of the road. We gain a small idea of the grand view which is before us though rapt in darkness, from the far distant signal lights and outline of mountains miles away beyond the Potomac, but we do not stop. Down we go at a rapid march and go into camp near Middletown ten miles from our last night's camp.

September 14—We have marched over seventy miles within the past week; a pretty good test for a raw recruit. We lie down on arms all the morning listening to the battle of artillery up the side of South Mountain and at half past one p.m. orders come for us to "Forward." As we go through the village of Middleton signs of conflict increase. The churches are filling up with wounded, and from their steeple-tops the signal flags are hard at work. The streets are packed with troops hurrying forward and as we begin to ascend, a steady stream of wounded come pouring down from the front. pouring down from the front. The sights fairly sicken me and John Wallace cautions me—tells me to look only straight ahead.

We rush up at double-quick to support a battery which is just planted in a more advanced place, when, just as we form into line-of-battle, [*Fox's Gap—Wise's field: Part of the struggle was for the wooded crest on the left of the field; Confederate soldiers were posted behind a stonewall near the Wise's house; on the left of Wise's house is the ridge road.*] a united volley from a rebel battery and musketry receive us crashing through the trees. Instantly the order comes "Lie down." Down we all go and remain flat for twenty minutes or less, when the force in our front seems to be trying to flank us and we are ordered over to the left of the road which is here called "Fox's Gap." As we cross the deep cut, we see the road literally packed with dead and dying rebels who struggled so tenaciously to force back our resistless tide of troops, and here the horrors of war were revealed as we saw the heavy ammunition wagons come tearing up right over the dead and dying, mangling many in their terrible course, while the shrieks were perfectly heart-rending. Soon we reach an open field between two pieces of timber and hardly had we formed in line again before we receive a volley from the enemy posted behind a stone wall a half dozen rods in front. We lie down till the first volley is over and then charge up nearly to the wall but find the New York 51st just in front halting for orders. None of our field officers can be found, so Capt. Richardson orders us to fall back to the timber in our rear, and from thence back a few rods to a cornfield, where we reform, having found Col. Clark. Here we learn that Gen. Reno has just been shot nearby. By this time darkness had settled over the conflict and the battle lulled, so we remain in our position all night, constantly expecting an attack but receiving none. The rebel loss is very heavy. [*In 1890 Hitchcock added: "What were my feelings when first under fire? I was fearfully that the rebels would hit somebody and I wished they would not hit me. How did I feel? My brain was constantly telegraphing to my legs to take me down the hill. Yes, strange as it may seem, I did not want to be shot and I thought I might be if I remained. I was not brave and I did not want to be a coward so I watch the others and did just as they did, carrying on a conflict on my own private account in my heart and with the help of God I won a victory."*]

September 15—After a very uncomfortable and sleepless night we arose at five to find the enemy gone. Looking about us on the other side of the wall we find the ground covered with rebel dead. While one man lies hanging over the wall, shot in the act of climbing over, we are startled by two or three shots in the woods in front and ordered ahead at double-quick, but find that our pickets fired upon some rebels who came into our lines by mistake thinking the place occupied by their own troops. Finding out their mistake, they tried to escape but were captured. We lay on arms all the morning. Many of the troops venture away from the line and bring in trophies from the field of action taken from the rebel dead. At noon Gen. Burnside rode by and passed down the road amid the cheers of his men. He is followed by division after division and after a while our turn comes and South Mountain is left behind. Marched till night through a beautiful, fertile country, camping near Boonsboro. Reports that the main rebel army is cornered between us and Harper's Ferry where Gen. Wool is engaging them. Also that they are much demoralized and skedaddling in all directions, and Stone Wall Jackson killed. [*Rumors abounded but were frequently false. Thomas Jonathan "Stonewall" Jackson was mortally wounded by his own men at Chancellorsville on May 2, 1863.*]

September 16—The morning is foggy but the artillery is hard at work and continue so. Constantly the different batteries are moving from one position to another. Quite often the rebel range becomes uncomfortable for us and the shells and "railroad iron" come screaming through the air burying in our midst. Gen. Burnside came along and spoke to the troops encouraging us. He says the artillery has driven the enemy back a mile. Gen. McClellan with a long train of staff and body guard passed us in the afternoon. At four we move forward a mile and rest on arms supporting a battery for the night. Our stock of food which had been consumed is replenished in the evening as the trains succeeded in reaching us.

September 17—We had a good night's rest and are sent to support a battery at the foot of a hill on our right. Here we remain all the morning while the roar of artillery is constant and incessant. While here we receive a large mail in which Col. Clark learned from home that extensive preparations had been made for the funeral, his friends supposing he was dead. At about one o'clock p.m. the terrible order came to our brigade, "Move forward to the left and charge down the hill." As we go over the brow of the hill, heavy volleys of musketry greet us and the batteries opposite us just beyond Antietam Creek pour their destructive fire into our ranks, which is well answered by the battery we have just left, whose shells go screaming over our heads and tear up the earth along where the line of fire is seen, which is making havoc in our ranks. We halt a few moments in a cornfield, close up ranks, then file out onto a side hill sloping down to the creek, some twenty rods from the rebel line, and open fire. I saw two or three sharp shooters drop from the trees skirting the opposite side of the creek. Our position is so exposed here that our loss is very heavy. Bullets spatter like hailstones and scores of our boys are killed and wounded, but my time is too fully occupied to notice the poor fellows around me. But a glance away to the right along the elevated lands give a faint idea of the general struggle which is fairly opened. After half an hour we charge down to the creek and have the satisfaction of seeing the gray backs running up over the hill. After a few moments more of brisk firing we charge across the bridge, the 51st N.Y. Regt. taking the lead. As soon as the 2nd Brigade is fairly across the rest of the Division follows. Gen. Burnside comes galloping down and across the creek, hastily scans the outlook and orders the Division line of battle to move forward up over the brow of the hill, when the enemy falls back to the edge of a cornfield a short distance from us and checks our advance, so we lie down behind a rail fence and give them more cartridges. Here we find we have pushed our part of the main line far ahead of the rest so that 35th Mass. Regt. receives a raking flank fire which doubles back that part of our line. By this time ammunition begins to give out and the regt. is ordered to crawl back a few rods where our position is not so exposed. Whitney and I who have not learned to be so expeditious have several rounds left and we are so intent on our work that when we have used up our ammunition look about us and find only dead and wounded all about. So we crawl back and find the boys. It is now dusk and we fall back to the foot of the hill by the edge of the creek where we rest on arms. At about ten o'clock the rebels set fire to the village of Sharpsburg, and after a few minutes the blackness of night is lighted all about us, adding a gloom to the battlefield which with the groaning and screaming make the night truly terrible. Our loss has been very heavy.

September 18—This is my first experience on the skirmish line. Our regiment was sent to the left out by the edge of the field where the rebels held last night. The day is dark and cloudy and there is not an attack during the day. Both sides have suffered so severely there seems to be a hesitancy about making any move though rumors at night are that the enemy is drawing away from our front. Where I lay I can see rebel officers ride out and take observations though too far away for bullets to reach.

We are relieved at night by fresh troops and return across the creek where we camp for the night in an apple orchard. Here we first learn that Daniel Daily was killed. He was shot in the leg and bled to death.

September 19—We wrote and sent letters home this morning. Our regiment numbers seventy-five fighting men with two Captains and one Colonel. It is supposed that the enemy has retreated into Virginia. Our regiment was sent forward as advance guard for the Division. We deployed about a rod apart and advance to reconnoiter after marching about four miles when we came in sight of the Potomac and the enemy on the opposite bank. After remaining here awhile we ascertain that the rebels are securely planted. At night we are relieved and go back out of range of the rebel batteries, and support Capt. Benjamin's Battery.

September 20—We did not move today and Col. Clark has told us that

Gen. Burnside promises a fortnight's rest. Fighting has been reported a few miles up the river where it is said that two or three rebel regiments have been captured in trying to cross into Virginia. Stragglers have been coming into camp all day and we can now muster nearly two hundred men. All hands have been writing home.

September 21—Today has been washing day. I have strolled about some, though I dare not venture far from the regiment. The routine of camp has been established and Dress Parade was held for the first time since I joined. Services were held by Chaplain Ball. Reading the scripture and prayers, he spoke very touchingly of Lieut. Col. Rice who was a Christian and beloved by all the regiment. Col. Clark read and order from Gen. Burnside tendering his thanks to the 21st for their bravery in the late battle.

September 22—I have been washing clothes and cooking. Think I shall soon be an experienced housekeeper. Several regiments passed by to Harper's Ferry today and we expect to go soon. The 36th Mass have just arrived out and have been put into our Corps, camping near us. There is a company of Templeton boys in it so we have been visiting.

[*Templeton is a small town southwest of Ashby. George Hitchcock graduated from Templeton High School.*]

September 23—Our bugle sounded before light for us to pack up and prepare to march. After waiting in the boiling sun till noon we again spread our blankets and in the afternoon the orders are countermanded. Dr. Hitchcock, Porter Kimball, Norman Stone, Ben Prentice and Alvah Crocker visited the regiment in the afternoon. They were sent out by the town of Fitchburg to look after the wounded.

[*Fitchburg was an industrial town of 8,000 in 1860—south of the Village of Ashby. Six members of the Fitchburg Soldiers' Relief Committee visited the Antietam battlefield with supplies for the sick and wounded. Every disabled Fitchburg soldier in the 15th and 21st Massachusetts regiments received a gift of five dollars. The committee included: Alfred Hitchcock (no relation to George), a surgeon; Alva Crocker, paper manufacturer; Alpheus Porter Kimball, deputy sheriff and jailor; Norman Stone, coal dealer; Benjamin Prentiss, blacksmith; and Alonzo P. Davis, former lieutenant in the 21st Massachusetts Regiment (resigned on January 16, 1862).*]

September 24—We had a smart shower in the forenoon but I kept dry under our rubber shelter. I received letters from home and wrote. There seems to be much excitement at the North over the nine months enlisted. I first read President Lincoln's Proclamation Emancipating all slaves after the first of next January which I believe is "just right."

September 25—The morning is cold with heavy dew. We are drummed up before light and prepare to march. At noon orders come for us to march at one o'clock, when we move out of camp some twenty rods and rest in line till half past four. Again the order is countermanded and we return to camp for the night. The New York Herald containing the account of the late battles has been brought into camp and received with great interest.

September 26—Orders come again today for us to move and at eleven o'clock we leave camp, move down across Antietam Creek where it empties into the Potomac. Here we are joined by the rest of the Brigade and proceed into camp two miles from the former camp, near Gen. Burnside's headquarters. We are in a large level field with the whole 2nd Division. We expect to remain here several days so the boys are busy erecting tents and shelters of boughs. We have to go about a half mile for all our water at a large spring which furnishes water for thousands of troops.

September 27—Camp duties have been established, roll call twice a day, camp guard detailed, guard mounting in the morning and dress parade at night at six when the time for different duties is established. Orders were read lamenting the death of Gen. Reno. The novelty of camp life long since over, the spare time hangs heavily, now something to read would be acceptable.

September 28—Roll call at five. Breakfast at six. Inspection of arms and equipment at eight. After this our duties are done till five p.m. when comes dress parade. Wrote home. Several new recruits from Camp Day Cambridge arrived. Saw Henry Colby of the 36th. We have just heard of the deaths of Captains Frazer and Kelton of the 21st who were wounded at Chantilly. The 9th N.H. Band discoursed some very fine music at sunset.

September 29—The 21st received orders to pack up and proceed down to Antietam Bridge below the hill where we are kept as reserve picket during the day. At night we return to camp. "All is quiet along the Potomac."

September 30—Company drill this morning, recruits drilled separately. As part of the regiment was on picket, Battalion drill was omitted. Burnside visited camp to see the condition of his boys. We were ordered to pack up in the afternoon, which was countermanded as soon as we were ready. This lolling about under the hot sun is not very pleasant for us. Lem Whitney is sick with headache and diarrhea and was excused from duty today.

October 1, 1862—Received a heavy thundershower in the afternoon but managed to keep pretty dry under the rubber blankets. In the evening, our long expected mail arrived. Henry and I receive letters and papers from home which are most welcome.

October 2—Sent letters home. I drilled with the company at eight and battalion at half past three. It was rumored that President Lincoln would visit us today but he did not put in an appearance. Have been reading an account of the Battle of South Mountain, in the Congregationalist, which was a hard fought battle.

October 3—We are called up at seven and ordered to make ourselves as neat and uniform as possible. The 2nd Division join the rest of the Corps which is composed of several Divisions of Infantry, Cavalry and Batteries, drawn up in line. At half past ten, President Lincoln appeared on horseback, with a long train of escort, among which were many notables, Generals and officers of all ranks and members of his cabinet. As he passed up and down in front of each line I had a fine opportunity to see him. He looks like the many pictures I have seen of him, good-natured, honest and homely. Salutes were fired and bands played "Hail to the Chieftain" as he passed off the field up the road in the direction of the Potomac where the rest of the Army lies.

October 4—I was on guard today at the gun which was the first time since I came out. Saw the big "Army Balloon" up and away in the north. Read a good letter from Rev. Mr. Bell to Henry. Our company drilled in skirmish drill today. Heard cannonading in the direction of Harper's Ferry and soon after saw a heavy column of black smoke rising in the same direction, but do not hear the particulars of it yet. Heavy shower came up in the afternoon which continued till dark with but little rain and much wind which threatened to overthrow our frail shelter.

October 5—The shower cooled the atmosphere so that we have a nice cool breeze today. A mail came in today but no letter for me so I return good for evil by writing. A supply of clothing and shelter tents arrived today. Lem and I received pieces of shelter which we put up, and it proves to be decided improvement of the blanket. Chaplain Ball made some excellent remarks at Dress Parade, with reading scriptures and prayers, and the regiment sang Old Hundred [*Psalm 100*].

October 6—The night was so cold I could not sleep so I sat by the cook's fire and kept warm. Battalion drill was omitted today and we are under marching orders with one day's rations. Lemuel and I have closed ourselves into our tent so that we can be more comfortable tonight.

October 7—Arose at three in the morning, got breakfast, and packed up before light. At eight the 2nd Division left camp and marched away toward Harper's Ferry. Our route was over a narrow rugged road and we progress very slowly most of the way climbing up until at half past one p.m. we reach Maryland Heights, from which we have an extensive prospect of the surrounding country of the long range of the Blue Ridge stretching away far back into Pennsylvania and across the Potomac down into Virginia, while opposite us some two or three miles to the south east is another range running parallel with this, inclosing a beautiful picturesque valley, dotted with farm houses and cultivated fields. As the eye follows the valley along toward the Potomac, it meets the bold rugged cliffs of Bolivar Heights rising perpendicularly back of Harper's Ferry, and then beyond lies the far-famed Shenandoah Valley. After feasting the eye on these beautiful pictures both sublime and lovely, we descend into Pleasant Valley and go into camp in a very pleasant place, a large field sloping to the south about three miles from Harper's Ferry. The camp is laid out with regularity. The different regiments of the Brigade arranged in sides to a hollow square, the parade ground in the center.

October 8—Camp duties have been instituted and camp-guard put around camp. The sun shines very hot. The sound of the Iron Horse can be plainly heard two miles away on the Baltimore & Ohio R.R. As it is more than a month since we have been with this sound of R.R., it seems pleasant and reminds us of peaceful times. A mail brought me a letter from Maria C. who is at Framingham Normal School.

October 9—I was placed on guard today; my post was in front of the Quarter Master's and Commissary Tents. Duties are to keep off intruders and thieves, which was not arduous except at noon when the sun shone down so very hot. Henry was officer of the guard today. Lem Whitney was guard at Gen Sturgis' Headquarters to protect an apple orchard.

October 10—The day has been cloudy and mild. Was off guard at eight this morning and had no duties till Battalion Drill at three p.m. the 11th New Hampshire Regt. joined the Brigade, a new regiment just from the "Granite Hills" command by Col. Harriman. Several of our boys were arrested by the guard for stealing apples.

October 11—During the night the storm set in with high wind. Was awakened by the sound just in time to save our tent from destruction, but many others were torn down. During the day we have but little rain though so very chilly we have to bundle ourselves in overcoats and shut us up in tents with blankets. Major Foster joined the regiment from Mass. He is quite lame yet from the wound received at Roanoke Island. Orders were read at Dress Parade for us to prepare for inspection tomorrow morning at eight. A mail came in during the evening with letters from home, for self and Henry.

October 12—The morning opens very chilly and cloudy. I was on guard and got a soaking as it rained hard all night. Gen. Ferrero inspected the 2nd Division this morning and excused Companies C and F from all duties today as a premium for their neatness and order. A continuous cannonading was heard through the day down the Potomac. I wrote home sending for a box. Today is the Sabbath but religious services were omitted as Chaplain Ball has gone to Washington.

October 13—A cold north-east storm with but little rain today. As I am not feeling well today and the weather will not allow us enough warmth for comfort, the blues have me. Henry is trying for a furlough. We hear today that Stewart's [Stuart's] Cavalry made a dash into Pennsylvania and returning, cross the Potomac at Point of Rocks where they met with resistance. This explains the cannonading yesterday. The Yankee will be the Yankee where ever he is. A large cornfield has been discovered not far away and general harvesting by our boys has resulted in our having a grand old "Hasty-Pudding" for dinner. Each man is his own grist mill grinding up the corn on the cartridge box which is conformed into a grate by punching it full of holes with the bayonet.

[*James Ewell Brown "Jeb" Stuart, Confederate major general who commanded the cavalry of the Army of Northern Virginia, made his second ride around McClellan's Army of the Potomac (October 10–12, 1862), raiding as far north as Chambersburg, Pennsylvania, and on October 12 recrossed the Potomac River north of Poolesville, Maryland, at White's Ferry. Although there was a brief skirmish near the mouth of the Monocacy River, Stuart avoided Union troops waiting near Point Rocks and Poolesville. White's Ferry is two miles below the junction of the Monocacy and Potomac rivers and ten miles below Point of Rocks.*]

October 14—The weather has cleared up somewhat though still cloudy and chilly. Today we feasted on hasty-pudding and molasses for breakfast, stewed beans for dinner and pudding and sugar considered a fine change from the everlasting indestructible, indomitable standard hard-tack. Major Foster took command at Battalion Drill. He shows himself an energetic skillful officer. He found some difficulty in keeping on his high-spirited horse owing to his game leg. My candle ration fell short so I spend the evening with Lemuel in darkness.

October 15—I am on guard today at the Quartermaster tents. Am nearly sick. A mail came in tonight with a good letter for me. Father says he has gathered twelve barrels of apples. The Ashby Quota of nine months have gone into camp at Groton; they are in the 53rd Regt. Also received intelligence of Mr. Silas Rice's death. Henry rec'd letter from Capt. Hawkes who is at Camp Parole not yet exchanged. [*In 1890 Hitchcock added: "He was captured at Chantilly."*]

October 16—Clouds and Sunbeams are the order of the days weather. At seven this morning cannonading opened above Harper's Ferry continuing all day. The First Brigade have received marching orders and ours are expected tomorrow. A Brigade Guard was mounted and no one allowed outside the lines without passes. Announcement was made at Dress Parade that we are to receive full supplies of clothing at once.

October 17—Heavy Thundershowers continued through the night. Our Army or a portion of it under McClellan crossed the Potomac at Charlestown, Va. where it met with resistance and had a hard skirmish. J.E. Clapp received his discharge papers tonight. Gen. Burnside came through camp to see his boys before Dress Parade.

October 18—A beautiful day but cold. I have been writing letters. Gen.

Ferrero commanded us at Brigade Dress Parade. Regimental Drill was omitted this afternoon in order to prepare for Sunday morning inspection tomorrow. A mail came in tonight with a bundle of letters and papers for me.

October 19—Rained at intervals during the night and day. Inspection at eight. Dress Parade and Religious Exercises were omitted on account of the rain. I spent quite a portion of the day in reading my home papers.

October 20—I was on guard today. As there is a very cold searching wind I am obliged to have a fire at my post which is in the valley. In this manner I keep quite comfortable. Brigade Drill this afternoon. A straw-stack has been discovered somewhere in the region which has been transferred into camp much to the comfort of the "sojer boys."

October 21—Endured a cold night and found the ground covered with a heavy white frost in the morning. Company drill at ten. Regimental drill at two and Dress parade at four fill up the hours till almost dark as the days are grown so short. The weather has changed so decidedly that we find ourselves unprepared for the wintry air.

October 22—Fred Sanderson was Captain of the Guard today so Henry took command of the company at Drills and Dress Parade. I rec'd letters from home and wrote to Jus. Hayward. Lem was on guard. Enlistments from the volunteer to the regular army are going on and several have left the regiment to join the regular cavalry.

October 23—At Dress Parade, a circular was read that no more clothing will be drawn, in view of the "impending movement" so we surmise that we are to leave here soon. Henry stopped overnight with me.

October 24—There was another heavy frost this morning. I have been on guard today at the headquarters of the 35th Mass. Regt. A regimental inspection of arms and equipments was held this afternoon. I have been reading in Massachusetts papers of a draft in Boston and other places. The home-patriots begin to see that this is a very determined war and not boys'-play. Enlistments into the regular army are producing quite a havoc in our regiment as a large number have already left us.

October 25—Preparations for marching soon have begun, all the extra clothing and baggage of the regiment has been packed and forwarded to Washington. This afternoon the Brigade received orders to march with two days cooked rations tomorrow morning but at half-past eight in the evening the order was countermanded. Albert Davis of New Ipswich of the 6th N.H. Regt. has been over to see me. His Brigade (the First) is under marching orders.

October 26—Storm began at nine this morning; at ten we again received orders to march which were again countermanded on account of the pouring rain. Continued rain all day. Kept under tent all day as all exercises were omitted. Sent a line home.

3

The Fredericksburg Campaign

> "All over the field in front is strewn the dead and wounded of the ranks that had preceded us. But we do not stop an instant to consider the spectacle."
> —Hitchcock, December 13, 1862

On November 5, 1862, President Lincoln relieved General McClellan from command of the Army of the Potomac; General Burnside assumed command two days later. McClellan had continuously failed to exploit the Union's military advantage by being extremely cautious and delaying any aggressive maneuvers. He had also become a prominent opponent of the Lincoln administration and its policies. His steadfast refusal to undertake offensive action resulted in his removal.

Burnside reorganized the army into three "grand divisions," with each wing composed of two corps of three divisions plus artillery and a cavalry brigade. Major General William Franklin commanded the Left Grand Division (47,000 men including the I and VI Corps with 100 pieces of artillery), Major General Joseph Hooker commanded the Center Grand Division (40,000 men including the III and V Corps with 100 pieces of artillery) and Major General Edwin Sumner

Major General Ambrose Burnside, George A. Hitchcock's favorite commander (National Archives).

commanded the Right Grand Division (30,000 men including the II and IX Corps with 60 pieces of artillery). The XI and XII Corps, with the mission of covering Washington, constituted the army's reserve, numbering about 27,000. Burnside moved the mammoth 122,000-man army to Falmouth, across the Rappahannock River from Fredericksburg, a city of 5,000 inhabitants and one of the country's most historic cities. His plan was to cross the river quickly and drive his army to Richmond with his supply line secured by the Union naval control of the tidal rivers. Union generals were obsessed with the emphasis of "on to Richmond," while Lincoln repeatedly stressed that the objective of the army was the defeat of the Confederate army.

General Sumner's Right Grand Division reached Falmouth by November 17 and by November 22 the entire army had arrived before Lee could shift Confederate troops to block a river crossing. The 21st Massachusetts Regiment was assigned to Sumner's Grand Division as part of Brig. Gen. Edward Ferrero's brigade, Brig. Gen. Samuel D. Sturgis' division, Brig. Gen. Orlando B. Willcox's IX Corps. The Massachusetts men moved slowly through a drizzling rain and entered Falmouth at noon on November 19. They eventually went into camp near the river opposite Fredericksburg. Sumner was anxious to cross the river at one of the fords and to occupy Fredericksburg and the adjoining heights. Hooker suggested that his troops could cross at a ford below Fredericksburg. Since the pontoons needed to bridge the river had not arrived, Burnside rejected the recommendations because the army, he believed, was not sufficiently supplied for such an undertaking. He also feared heavy rains could cause the river to flood, isolating the troops that had crossed. Although the bridges across the Rappahannock River had been burned, the stone piers were in good condition. Federal engineers could have built temporary structures across these piers within hours if Fredericksburg was secured. Two days later, James Longstreet's troops arrived in Fredericksburg, and the river rose rapidly because of heavy rains. Lafayette McLaws' division arrived on November 25 and William Barksdale's Mississippi brigade of 1,600 men occupied Fredericksburg. Meanwhile, on November 26, realizing the serious threat that confronted him, General Lee requested support from Jackson's divisions that were operating in the lower Shenandoah Valley. Jackson's men arrived on December 1 after marching 150 miles.

On November 22, while waiting for the pontoon trains to arrive, Burnside wrote to Brig. Gen. George W. Cullen, Chief of Staff in Washington:

> It is very clear that my object was to make the move to Fredericksburg very rapidly, and to throw a heavy force across the river before the enemy could concentrate a force to oppose the crossing and supposed the pontoon train would arrive at this place nearly simultaneously with the head of the column. Had that been the case, the whole of General Sumner's column—33,000 strong—would have crossed into Fredericksburg at once over a pontoon bridge in front of the city. Had the pontoon bridge

arrived even on the 19th or 20th, the army could have crossed with trifling opposition. But now the opposite side of the river is occupied by a large rebel force under General Longstreet. The pontoon train has not yet arrived, and the river is too high for troops to cross at any of the fords. The President said that the movement, in order to be successful, must be made quickly, and I thought the same.

By the time the pontoons arrived, however, Longstreet's corps was entrenched on the slope of the heights above the city holding a position of great natural strength. Burnside was cognizant of serious dissension among his subordinates. A majority of the corps and division commanders, who had been designated to assault Marye's Heights, disapproved of attacking the Confederate army through Fredericksburg. Lee had established a permanent position and could remain all winter if he chose; the pressure on Burnside from the Lincoln administration and the northern public was intense—*offensive action was expected.*

In the predawn darkness of a cold and foggy morning on December 11, Union engineers began laying three pontoon bridges in front of Fredericksburg, while two additional pontoon bridges were being constructed two miles below the city. The operation opposite Fredericksburg had an immediate problem: Barksdale's Mississippi and Florida sharpshooters firing from buildings and rifle-pits picked off the engineers. A heavy artillery bombardment failed to deter the Mississippians and Floridians. Finally, four Union regiments (7th Michigan, 19th and 20th Massachusetts and 89th New York) crossed the river in boats and successfully dislodged the Confederates in house-to-house fighting. The two bridges at Franklin's crossing below Fredericksburg had been completed by eleven in the morning with little opposition from the Confederates, but Burnside prevented Franklin from crossing until all the bridges were completed. That evening a third bridge was constructed at Franklin's crossing. On December 12, after the Union army had entered Fredericksburg, soldiers looted the town, destroying much of what they found in the houses abandoned by the city's 5,000 inhabitants.

While Burnside remained at his headquarters, Lee visited his corps and division commanders, inspecting his 275 guns and correcting faulty battery positions. Longstreet's corps of 40,000 men were entrenched in a frontage of five miles, while Jackson's corps of 39,000 men were positioned in depth along a two mile front southeast of the city.

On December 13, Franklin's troops attack Jackson's corps at Prospect Hill. Major General George G. Meade, commander of the Third Division, led the assault and achieved temporary success before being driven back to his original position. Franklin, who utilized less than a quarter of his men during the attack, failed to send additional troops after General Meade and Brig. Gen. John Gibbon's troops had penetrated the Confederate defense. Later, Franklin refused to renew the attack even after receiving orders from Burnside to do so.

The second attack focused against the heart of Lee's defenses on Marye's

3. The Fredericksburg Campaign

Heights directly beyond Fredericksburg. Union soldiers attacking the heights were savaged by fire from enfilading artillery on Lee's Hill and by artillery on Marye's hills and by four ranks of Confederate infantrymen standing in a sunken road, with a four-foot-high stone wall which continued for over 500 yards. From late morning till dusk, 14 brigade-size attacks were thrown against the Confederates—assaults as courageous and hopeless as anything during the war. Wave after wave of Union soldiers charged toward Marye's Heights, crossing open ground which was broken only by small ravines and a canal. Approximately 6,000 Confederate soldiers and twenty guns had withstood the continuous attack of seven divisions, resulting in more than 7,500 Union casualties in front of the stone wall. When the day ended, Lee had won his most one-sided victory of the war. The Army of the Potomac lost 12,653 men, while the Army of Northern Virginia suffered 5,377 casualties. The 21st Massachusetts Regiment suffered heavy losses— 200 soldiers engaged and suffered 66 casualties (13 killed, 52 wounded and one captured)—a loss of one-third of its battle strength. Private George Hitchcock was very fortunate to survive this disastrous battle.

A distraught Burnside was dissuaded by his commanders from leading a final charge with his old IX Corps on December 14. Lee expected Burnside to renew the attack by attempting a turning movement; however, during the rainy and windy evening of December 15, following a truce to allow for the burial of the dead and recovery of the wounded, the Union forces withdrew across the river. The greater superiority of Confederate generalship was reinforced. The strongest and bitterest criticism leveled at Burnside dealt with his continuous attacks on the stone wall and his failure to coordinate Franklin's attack on Lee's flank. Burnside had labored under extreme physical and mental exhaustion, and although he had remained at his headquarters and was unable to witness the battle, he failed to communicate with his commanders and to sufficiently delegate duties. On two previous occasions, Burnside had been offered command of the Army of the Potomac, but he had refused because he did not consider himself qualified for the position.

* * * *

October 27, 1862—The weather changed during the night which brought on a high wind demolishing several tents. Orders for marching came at ten and at eleven broke camp and marched out of Pleasant Valley leaving the monotony of camp life behind for new scenes and untried experiences before us. After a two mile tramp we come in sight of the Potomac at Sandy Hook, a small village on its banks. Here we pass by some of the grand scenery of America, under lofty rocky precipices, hundreds of feet in height where looking up in a perpendicular line we see trees and shrubs growing out of the rocks far above us. On the opposite side of us runs the B and O R.R. and the canal. These, with the turnpike on which we are moving, are crowded into the narrowest possible space between the banks of the Potomac and the lofty wall. Before turning our faces southward down the river we catch a distant view of Harper's Ferry and the heights back of the town and the ruined bridge across the river. We can also see where the broad Shenandoah meets the Potomac and beyond and back of this the far-famed Shenandoah Valley running away into distant blue.

We plod through the sticky mud, cross the railroad, pass through Knoxville and follow along the tow-path of the canal some three miles to Berlin; here we cross the Potomac on a pontoon bridge near the solid abutment of the burnt bridge at Berlin. We march up through a piece of woods, pass by a new Yankee regiment which is composed of stalwart Down-Easters who bitterly complain of the rough usage which has no allowed them any soft-bread for three days or any straw on which to sleep for a longer time. Of course they find the tender-hearted sympathy of our veterans. We reach camp at sundown near Lovettsville [*Virginia*].

October 28—We experience a very cold night, heavy white frost covering everything. Daylight opens to us a grand and beautiful picture. The lofty Blue Ridge running away to the southwest is lost in the hazy blue and before us is stretched many miles of the notably rich and beautiful country of the "Old Dominion." We are camped near the great broad pike leading to Leesburg and to Winchester. I was on guard today. Lieut. Saunderson made out the descriptive lists for Lemuel and myself so that we can be paid off with the regiment.

October 29—Orders came at noon for us to start and at two we were on the pike marching towards Leesburg. Pass through Lovettsville which presented more of the appearance of a military headquarters than anything else. The country all along the route is very beautiful and appears highly cultivated. We go into camp about eight miles from our last nights camp. Before breaking ranks, Major Foster cautions us to be on the alert as the enemy are right in front. Henry has been appointed Acting Adjutant in place of Lieut. Howe who has been promoted to Quartermaster of the regiment.

October 30—We were drummed up at three in the morning. At sunrise we are on the march toward Leesburg through the same beautiful country. We halt before noon near Wheatland, about seven miles from Leesburg. A large number of troops passed by our camp during the afternoon. Several boxes from home arrived for different members of the regiment but mine did not come. Henry formed the regiment at Dress Parade. The regimental payrolls have been made out.

October 31—Slept very poorly last night on account of the cold and rough ground. I was detailed as guard as supernumerary consequently my duties were very light, my two hours watch in the night were spent by a large camp-fire in a grove near Headquarters. The Brigade was mustered in for pay which we expect we may get next week.

3. The Fredericksburg Campaign

November 1, 1862—Our Brigade was drilled at ten this morning. Orders were read at Dress Parade for us to pack up and be ready to march in the morning. Our company was detailed as picket guard at the cross-roads three quarters of a mile from camp. Had a good nights rest and stood guard only two hours during the night, which was made far from being lonesome by continual chuckle of coons in the neighboring corn fields, dogs baying far and near at the farm houses, and owls and whippoorwills joining in the chorus.

November 2—Returned to camp at sunrise and packed up. At ten o'clock the whole Division were on the road to Leesburg. Quite early in the day cannonading opens a few miles in front of us which was kept up all day showing that our advance was being disputed. After marching a short distance we struck off from the Leesburg road leaving it on our right. Very soon we met three ambulances filled with wounded showing that the noise ahead meant something serious. Although our route was very circuitous we kept the cannonade directly in our front and toward night we halt and camp about two miles from the scene of the days action after a twelve mile march. Get supper and go to bed.

November 3—I slept well though a very chilly wind rose during the night. A rebel prisoner belonging to Stuart's Cavalry was found in a house nearby and was brought into camp in the morning. He reports that Lee's Army is moving down the valley on our right. Marched at half past two in the afternoon, move five miles and camped on the same ground of the rebel troops of yesterday in the village of Bloomfield. Several commissions reached us today among which was one making Henry 2nd Lieut.

November 4—Started on the march at half past nine. Hooker's Corps which came up with us during the night is also on the road and when we come to any long stretch of road we see that the road is full of troops for miles in both directions while other lines are keeping pace with us on different roads. I saw Gen. Couch and staff whom we passed while on the march. We camp near Ashby's Gap outside Upperville where we pitch tents. Here we receive supplies of bread, meat, coffee and sugar. The heavy booming of ammo reverberates up through the mountains occasionally through the day. We discover a large persimmon tree near camp loaded with ripe fruit and as we experience some difficulty in securing it the tree is felled and had a feast of luscious fruit.

November 5—Another cold frosty night. The enemy keep ahead of us from six to ten miles all the time. Left camp at half past seven, marched through the rebel village of Upperville to the tunes of Yankee Doodle and "Down with the Traitors." Kept in a southerly direction, crossed the Manassas Gap R.R. at Paris and halted after a brisk tramp of seven miles. We passed several fine looking residences showing the wealth of the planters in this beautiful fertile valley. We rested in the afternoon and get a mail in the evening.

November 6—A dark chill windy November day, we left camp at ten but on reaching the road have to halt for the 2nd and 12th Corps to pass along. We content ourselves in the mean while with singing which becomes a grand chorus as the entire Brigade enter into the spirit of song which "Psalm singing Company A" has the honor of commencing. At half past one we march out leaving over a mile of burning fence behind us to warm the hands and cool the hearts of the well-to-do neighborhood. March briskly till six and after a most wearisome tramp of twelve miles go into camp near Salem.

November 7—I tried to sleep but made a failure and spend the latter portion of the night, first warming my feet and freezing my back, then "vice versa." At nine in the morning a Snow Storm began which kept up till four when we again move. After a most dismal discouraging tramp of about three miles through the snow, darkness settles down upon us fast as we reach the ford of Rappahannock which proves to be too deep for us and fortunately too, as it afterward proves, for the enemy were hoping to trap us. After standing about an hour or more it is ascertained that we were under the guidance of a very drunken Gen. Sturgis, and then about-face march back two miles then on another road and finally worn completely out, discouraged, mad and cross, we turn into some woods and settle down at ten o'clock into the mud. I managed to get considerable rest, between two fires for three hours.

November 8—At nine o'clock we start on the turnpike to Warrenton, march three miles and stack arms near the edge of woods for coffee. After an hour we crossed the Rappahannock on a temporary bridge and made a hurried march for six miles. Pass through the village of Glen Mills and Jefferson camping just outside of J., a deserted village containing only three families and a slave-pen.

November 9—Snowed during the night. I was on guard. The sun came out and started off the snow before noon. We are advanced beyond the main army and are not more than two miles from the enemy in the direction of Culpepper. Religious services were held in the church by the Chaplain of the 21st Mass. and the 11th N.H. An order was issued for prayers at Dress Parade giving thanks for Gen. Burnside's victories.

November 10—The day was bright and mild. General Ferrero with a company of cavalry made a reconnaissance this morning and found the enemy pickets two miles from camp. They were fired upon and one frightened cavalryman came dashing into camp arousing camp. The long-roll was beat and we were all turned out to resist an attack. After a few shots from our battery we returned to quarters. Severe cannonading was heard in the Gap up in the mountains and away toward Culpepper where the enemy are in great force.

November 11—Another pleasant day and another reconnaissance was made which resulted in having our cavalry driven in, after which our battery went out and returned fire re-establishing our pickets. Provisions are getting short in the Brigade and it is reported that a train of seventy-five wagons have been captured, among which were our supplies.

November 12—I woke at one a.m. and found the regiment quietly preparing to march. At four, we quietly left camp and taking a northeasterly direction toward Warrenton marched swiftly and silently through the darkness about five miles and at daylight reached and encamped near the famous Sulphur Springs which was one of the great summer resorts of Southern aristocrats and F.F.V.'s before the war. Nearly all the large buildings, hotels and c. are now in ruins, one of the results of the war which Southern chivalry consider the outcroppings of northern vandalism. We encamp by the side of the broad pike leading to Warrenton seven miles distant. We are very short of supplies and teams have been forwarded to W. but we shall not receive them before tomorrow. The First Brigade came in and encamped opposite us tonight. We learn that we narrowly escaped being entrapped by the enemy who were in very strong force on two sides of us and were about ready to swoop out small force.

November 13—We are having our Indian summer. Hardtack & Salt Pork arrived in the morning and we have a dinner of Pork & Beans so we are all right again. The rebels came out in sight of us on hills about half a mile distant and sent a few cannon shots at us to inform us that they had reoccupied our yesterday's line of march. Two shots from our battery planted square in their midst send them back out of sight. Albert Davis came over to see us.

November 14—Fair and mild. The Division is being supplied with provisions. This afternoon, clouds of black have been passing over to the south, directly over our heads we can plainly see that they are composed of myriads of crows passing over in immense flocks to winter quarters. The hum of their innumerable "caws" and the strange appearance of the sky is a sight and sound that I never before witnessed.

November 15—High wind. We are roused at five and march eastward. After moving about a mile out the enemy discover our movement and fire on our wagon train which they keep up quite brisk till all our artillery composed of several batteries are planted and open on them. A general artillery engagement continues for over four hours till the enemy guns are silenced. Our regiment in the beginning of the fight was sent to support a battery when we receive the fire from two or three of the enemy's guns. Quite a number were killed or wounded mostly battery-men and we were obliged to lie and see the rebel shells burst all about us. At eleven we continue our march five miles and encamp near Fayetteville in the afternoon.

November 16—Started at nine this morning and marched toward Warrenton Junction. We pass a great many troops encamped along the road which is quite level and most of the way through the woods. A brisk march of seven miles and we encamp by the side of the Alexandria & Orange R.R. two miles from Warrenton Junction. Our forces hold the R.R. as far as the Rappahannock Station fifteen miles below.

November 17—The night was stormy but today only clouds. Began our march at half past twelve in a south easterly direction striking off in the open fields one division of each side of the road and one in the road with wagon trains and batteries. We ascertain the Burnside is in command of the army and he is changing base, that we are now bound for Fredericksburg with the intention of flanking the enemy. After a ten mile march we camp on the side hill, a very rough piece of ground in sight of thousands of troops.

November 18—We had more rain last night; were roused up at four and at daybreak were on the march. Our route lay through a very dreary and uninteresting country. Burnside passed us with his escort. Halted at one in the afternoon after thirteen miles march and go into camp seven miles from Fredericksburg. I was on guard from eight till ten in the evening at the Quartermasters tent.

November 19—Move at seven this morning our Division taking the road while other Divisions are on either side but the roads are blocked with number of troops and trains so we make very slow progress through the Virginia mud. At half past twelve we reach Falmouth one mile above Fredericksburg on the north side of the Rappahannock. We passed Gen Couch's Corps in which is the 15th Mass. where we find acquaintances. Our Division goes into camp opposite Fredericksburg at two p.m. The day is one of the genuine dark chilly November days which makes us all think of comfortable homes. The 21st is detailed to support a battery which is planted on the heights over-looking the city of Fredericksburg within stones throw of the river. Before making our camp many of the boys take a general survey of the situation. We find the advance of the rebel army have outrun us and are already in possession of the city. We see the grayback cavalry pickets all along the river bank and after considerable bantering talk on both sides we are convinced that the enemy force is not very great in the city yet.

November 20—Rained hard all night. Rebel troops and trains can be distinguished moving about the streets and as a large train was discovered moving away from a flour mill near the river bank and our battery opened on it with several shell. The heights of Falmouth which extend quite a distance along the river, give us favorable positions for placing batteries to command the city and the day has been spent in moving and placing our artillery along the Heights.

November 21—Stormed hard all night and day. The rain beating through our thin shelter tents has nearly soaked us and I have a severe clough on my lungs, in consequence of which the surgeon excused me from duty, giving me medicine. Our regiment has been taken out in squads during the day to discharge pieces and then clean up putting them in fighting order. Tonight the reflection on the clouds back of the city indicates that the rebel army is fast arriving and massing in strong force, which will probably dispute our further advance.

November 22—Today the weather has cleared up somewhat but it is still cloudy. A beautiful mail arrived tonight but I was unfortunate in not receiving a single letter. Commissions in the 21st are published in Mass. paper, Capt. Hawkes to Major, Foster to Lieut. Col. A few shells were fired into a departing train over in the city but without apparent effect. We are now situated where we are in ignorance of the movements of our army at large.

November 23—Clear today but cold and chilly, which brings on the "Shakes" and I am made painfully aware of that interesting disorder. Sunday morning inspection at ten o'clock. Lieut. Saunderson has been promoted to the Captaincy so that our company now has its complement of commissioned officers. For a change we draw rations of "Salt Horse," considered a luxury after a month of fresh meat. Nearly everybody is using the leisure time in writing letters.

November 24—Cold and frosty morning. The battery which we have been supporting left us and another took its place. I was again excused from duty and continue to take medicine for my cough. A rebel house a few rods from us has fallen prey to us northern vandals and everything in shape of furniture, books and papers have been transferred to camp for the satisfaction & amusement of the boys. I have at last received my long looked for home letter just a month old which notifies me of a box which was forwarded at the same time which does not come to hand.

November 25—Another sharp frosty morning. Answered my home letter and another mail arrived with letters from home, and bringing the commission for the new officers, Henry's with the rest, dated Sept. 25. The Second Brigade moved today and is now two miles from here. Several members from hospitals joined the regiment.

November 26—Another hard rainy night but cleared away cold again today. A regimental inspection took place at ten this morning. Our Division Wagon Master tells us that twelve days rations have been drawn (of regular camp rations) at headquarters which indicates a stop. I therefore send home for needed articles. Lieut.'s Clark and Hill joined the regiment from hospitals.

November 27—Thanksgiving day in Mass. as well as in several other states. The chaplain read Gov. Andrew's (*Mass.*) Proclamation at Dress Parade accompanied with excellent remarks and prayer. The Adjutant read an order from Gen. Wilcox, 9th Corps, praising the troops for their patient endurance during the march and expressing the hope and conviction that this campaign might end the war. Capt. Davis has joined the reg't just from home. I am on guard tonight and am feeling miserably having taken more cold.

November 28—Was again excused from duty on account of sickness. The morning is cold and frost and I feel about played out. Col. Clark came down from Acquia Creek this morning in the first train that has run over the road since our forces held the road last summer. The enemy run all the rolling-stock across to Fredericksburg and destroyed the bridge so that our government has sent down new locomotives and cars for the use of the army. Capt. Goss and Parker returned with him, back from Camp Parole. Clark is looking finely. Brother Henry made me a present of his dress coat which comes very opportunely and is highly appreciated. Orders arrived this evening for us to join the Brigade tomorrow at sunrise.

November 29—Roused up before light, ate breakfast of hasty pudding. Struck tents at daylight and at sunrise being relieved by the 2nd Michigan march back and join the Brigade. On our way we pass large camps laid out with great regularity. Our Brigade is encamped on a broad upland plain entirely devoid of trees, and in the form of a hollow square. The 21st composing one side, 35th Mass. another, 11th N.H. and 51th N.Y. another and 51st Penn. another. The ground enclosed between the regiments is called the Parade Ground where Dress Parade and Guard Mounting is formed. Gen. Ferrero Headquarters are back of the 21st, just outside camp. The entire camp lies on an exposed place where we get all the bleak winds. Wood and water can only be had by going nearly half a mile; these compose our principal inconveniences. The usual camp duties are instituted. Brigade services were held at eleven conducted by the chaplains of the different Regt's on the Parade Ground. Rations of beans, rice, molasses, salt pork, vinegar, hardtack, sugar and coffee have been drawn by the companies. Henry goes into Co. I of Pittsfield boys, and Geo. C. Parker and Lawrence into Co. A.

December 1, 1862—Cloudy weather and changeable. Company drill at ten. Brigade guard mounting at nine. Battalion drill in the p.m. was omitted as the paymaster is in camp. I signed the payrolls for forty dollars and sixteen cents and in the evening Company A marched up to headquarters and rec'd pay, so the boys go to bed in high glee.

December 2—Fair and cold. I went off to a neighboring camp (the 18th N.Y.) and found the sutlers tent. I fell in line with several hundred others who were waiting turns single file to exchange greenbacks for butter crackers, cheese and pigs feet. Battalion drill at two p.m., Col. Clark commanding. We were drilled mostly in the fighting manual and we know not how soon we may have to put it in practice. I sent thirty dollars home by the chaplain who goes on to Massachusetts to carry money for the regiment. Today's "Baltimore Clipper" contains President Lincoln's Message.

3. The Fredericksburg Campaign

[*President Lincoln's Annual Message to Congress on December 1, 1862:*

"Fellow-citizens, we cannot escape history. We of this Congress and this administration, will be remembered in spite of ourselves. No personal significance, or insignificance, can spare one or another of us. The fiery trial through which we pass, will light us down, in honor or dishonor, to the latest generation. We say we are for the Union. The world will not forget that we say this. We know how to save the Union. The world knows we do know how to save it. We—even we here—hold the power, and bear the responsibility. In giving freedom to the slave, we assure freedom to the free—honorable alike in what we give, and what we preserve. We shall nobly save, or meanly lose, the last best, hope of earth. Other means may succeed, this could not fail. The way is plain, peaceful, generous, just—a way which, if followed, the world will forever applaud, and God must forever bless."]

December 3—Cloudy and a cold wind. Company Drill was omitted. I have been helping build a fireplace for Capt. Saunderson of pine logs and mud. There was quite a row caused by a large number of the 21st boys charging on an apple cart belonging to the 11th N.H. Brick-Bats flew lively and Major Mitchell the officer of the day drew his revolver on the crowd but being threatened did not dare to fire. Three companies of the 11th N.H. were called out under arms when the crowd dispersed, the only damage being the loss of apples to the owners.

December 4—Today was beautiful. Passes for three privates, two non-com. and one commissioned officer are granted daily from each company and as I received one today I have been on a fruitless search for sutler's tent. There was a grand review of the 5th Army Corps about a mile south-east of camp.

December 5—Snow and rain and a very disagreeable day generally. I was detailed on guard as supernumerary, and being the third relief, my posts was at the guard quarters fire, a very satisfactory post for a comfort-loving chap like me. [*In 1890 Hitchcock added: "A supernumerary's duties are to be ready to respond to any call—similar to a policeman's in a civil life."*]

December 6—During the night the weather cleared up very cold and as I was on guard when the moon came out from behind the clouds, I saw the total eclipse of the moon which lasted about four hours. While on my beat I suffered severely from the cold, but a teamsters tent near my beat had a magnetic power over me as well as the sentinel next my beat, so we took turns in keeping guard over the tent, one to keep off intruders and the other to take care of the fire inside. All drills were omitted today on account of the cold.

December 7—Very cold and real zero weather. There is considerable suffering among the troops for want of clothing and better shelter. A large share of the regiment was excused from duty on account of poor shoes. Company A reported ten men for duty.

December 8—Very cold, freezing hard last night. Gen. Ferrero has ordered all drills for today and tomorrow to be omitted that the men may fit up their quarters more comfortably, and three teams have been detailed for each regiment for the purpose of bringing logs and boughs, so we are enlarging our tent, building a miniature log house three feet high, roofing it with our shelters, banking our tents outside with boughs and dirt. I secured a pass and went down to Falmouth. [*In 1890 Hitchcock added: "I went down to Falmouth, a dingy looking village, seemingly entirely occupied by our army officers for headquarters."*]

December 9—Weather has moderated and is again quite mild. I am on guard again. The boys build chimney of pine sticks and mud. Mail comes in regularly each evening. The 2nd Brigade have orders to keep on hand three days' cooked rations, preparatory for marching at any hour. One hundred from the 21st have been detailed for fatigue duty probably to lay pontoon bridges.

December 10—Mild and thawing. Charles Wyman [*owned Charles Wyman Hotel near the Commons in Ashby*] was in camp this morning. He left Ashby three weeks ago and is employed in the Quarter Masters department. Brigade inspection was held at one o'clock. Orders have been received to have everything packed ready to start eight tomorrow morning.

December 11—We were drummed up at four o'clock and in the dark chill morning prepared ourselves for the eventful, thrilling times in store for us. At half past four, the still night air was broken by a most terrific roar from all the Union batteries of over a hundred guns all along the heights this side of the river which open simultaneously, reverberating far up and down the banks of the Rappahannock. This terrific opening from our guns was supposed to be the signal of throwing the pontoon across directly in front of the city together with a large force before light. Such a deadly raking of the city, it was expected, would give us an opportunity to carry out this plan, but almost as soon as we had accustomed ourselves to the roar of artillery the rattle of musketry from sharpshooters told us that our brave advance were finding hot work. The roar of artillery was kept up without cessation till nearly noon carrying destruction to one of the aristocratic centers of the Old Dominion. At light we could see large columns of smoke rising up beyond the Falmouth Heights which hid the city from our sight. At half past eight we left camp and marched out toward the sound of conflict, when about half way we were halted. Here we remained all day witnessing the massing of the immense Army of the Potomac all about us near the defiles and approaches to the river's edge. Little idea could we gain of the horrid butchery which was to lay so many of these thousands cold in death just beyond that fated and fatal city, but our apprehensions were very great, knowing from our own observation what advantages and what complete preparations the enemy had. Soon after noon it became clear that a general crossing could not be effected until dark, so after much

3. The Fredericksburg Campaign

palavering and indecision and tramping we were allowed to return to our old camp ground and were not disturbed till morning. During the night our forces succeeded in throwing three pontoon bridges across with as many Corps.

December 12—At daylight our turn comes and we hurriedly march down and across the river amid an ominous silence from both sides. We halt under the banks in the upper part of the city, the enemy having retreated to the farther side of the city. All about us are packed thousands of troops waiting for the terrible order to "forward." The enemy is strongly entrenched in some high hills half a mile back of the city, and our forces have crowded their skirmishes back under cover of their guns which are constantly firing on our troops as they file down to the river and cross. Although the city could be completely raked by the enemy's and great havoc made with our troops (which are massing in its streets), they avoid doing so, probably hoping to save the city in case we retreat. The Union soldiers have spent the day in plundering stores, banks and houses, taking away valuables of all descriptions. As we are not allowed to leave our posts I do not participate in the general plunder but see a great deal of stuff that is brought down to the river banks. While lying about in the mud during the day, we witness some startling scenes. A few rods from our rendezvous lies a "Gray Back" [*Barksdale's Mississippian sharpshooter*] whose entire head down to his chin has been taken off by a shell, who was sharp-shooting from behind a shed against which he lies in a half upright position. During the afternoon a regiment came marching over one of the heights by one of our batteries instead of more prudently passing around through the defile which most of the troops had used. Being in plain sight of the rebel batteries and in good range a shell came over and planted itself, bursting right in the midst of their ranks. Without the least formality, ceremony of red tape maneuvering they skedaddled pell-mell to the foot of the hill leaving two or three wounded to take care of themselves.

Still later in the day a mounted band rode down to the bank of the river and thinking they were out of sight and range of rebel guns began playing "Bully for you" much to the amusement of us who were packed in thousands on the opposite side watching them. Suddenly a solid shot came screaming over striking in the edge of the water throwing spray into their very faces. Stopping their tune right in the midst of its melodies, away they galloped, some uphill, some down into the water, some up the river and some down. Amid the perfect storm of yells and cheers from our side, and in less time than it takes to say it not one solitary horse man could be seen.

December 13—Spending a comfortless night in the mud lying on arms. I rise very early in the morning and take a quiet stroll through some of the principal streets of the city. I see the strange and awful spectacle of desolated, ruined and plundered city. The streets and sidewalks are packed with troops, burning ruins of solid blocks on every side and streets and yards strewn with furniture and articles of all descriptions. I gather a few books & c as mementos, an account book from the steps of the ruined "Bank of Virginia," a small piece of an immense mirror nearly three quarters of an inch in thickness and several books from a large book store on Caroline St. At about nine we were ordered up and through the city, halt in a small back street on the side nearest the rebels, and here we deposit knapsacks, shelters and extra baggage in a house. In meanwhile the increasing din of artillery from the rebel works, shells crashing through the streets and into buildings about us, prepare our minds for the worst, which is about to open on us. Some of our boys while waiting for the terrible orders improve the time in eating their rations, but most are looking with earnest faces into each others in silence and many can be seen whose thoughts are far away. How many of those faces were cold in death before the sun went down.

Soon our troops come pouring out of the city, forming in line of battle just a few rods away, begin their onslaught on the works about St. Mary's Heights, and now the battle is fairly begun in all its terrible realities. One continuous crash and rattle of musketry and roar of heavy artillery form in our home-loving minds a grim outline of the horrors yet in store for us. For my part, I do not believe a soldier gifted with reason and given time for reflection can ever prepare himself for battle as our army did in this, without the thought crowding itself uppermost on the mind "Prepare to meet thy God." Many and fast were the silent prayers for strength and deliverance sent up as the order came to us at one p.m. to "Fall in." We (the 2nd Brigade) file out at double quick into a large field unobstructed by fence, tree or building. Prepared most perfectly for our reception by the rebels. Forming in line of battle we stand face to face with the long line of rebel earthworks crested with a sheet of flame from the well protected troops behind them.

All over the field in front is strewn the dead and wounded of the ranks that had preceded us. But we do not stop an instant to consider the spectacle. With the charge and Union cheer the veteran 2nd Brigade rush over the field without breaking only as the terrific fire thins out our ranks. Closing up as we go we are ordered to halt when within a few rods from the rebel works, falling flat we are partially protected by the rising ground just in our front and begin firing rapidly. Our color-sergeant John Collins of my own company is killed here when one of the supporting corporals seizes the colors, hardly had he raised them when he is killed. Sergeant Plunkett then grasps them and a shell takes off one arm, forcing the staff into the ground with the other arm he again raises them, when soon comes another shot which takes off the remaining arm and sends him reeling headlong down the slope. After brisk firing with apparently no success our ammunition is exhausted. Being beyond the reach of our ammunition supplies and impolitic for any of our troops to be seen retiring we lie in our places with the leaden hail spattering all about us. We see Brigade after Brigade come out from the city and receive the fiery ordeal we had already passed through. Some lines of new troops would break and skedaddle, but most did nobly coming up to where we lay would keep the rattle of musketry unabated. At sundown the Famous Irish Brigade came up over the plain in such a perfect unbroken line although receiving the concentrated fire from batteries which had before been engaged in other directions. With the reckless Irish bravery, they came yelling up and past us but were soon forced back to the same slight shelter the rest of us had. During the afternoon our heavy guns on Falmouth Heights could not be used without endangering us and one battery was sent out onto the fatal field, thinking to help us. Hardly had they shown themselves on the field before two or three horses were shot when they prudently retreated. All the daylong our balloon could be seen high in the air over the Falmouth Heights and repeated attempts were made by the long-range guns of the enemy to bring it down, but without success. Thus through all that fearful day we lay in this exposed situation and before the setting sun draws the curtain of darkness over the scene, our little Company A finds only ten of its twenty five members left on the field, the remainder have been killed or wounded. The entire Brigade seems to have suffered in the same proportion. Under cover of the darkness we steal off the field, receiving a parting volley from the enemy and the battle lulls. Stumbling over the dead all along the exposed field we enter the city, pass through it down to our old position by the river's bank, drop down thoroughly exhausted, sleep putting all remembrance of the terrible defeat out of mind for the while.

December 14—Sunday opens, a bright mild day and although no general engagement took place; there was an incessant rattle and roar of skirmish and artillery firing through the day. Household furniture strews the streets and John Wallace, Whitney and I secure a feather mattress which we appropriate to use (preferring it to the muddy bed of last night) camping down at half past seven we anticipate a comfortable night. Hardly had we begun to sleep when we hear the familiar voice and order of Gen. Ferrero. "Fall in! 2nd Brigade." Up through the city again we go out on the field and relieve the pickets holding the line we left yesterday. We lie in position all night, cold, sore, weary and comfortless, unable to sleep at all. About midnight we receive a volley from the rebel pickets a few rods away who were frightened by the approach of a pig from our lines but no damage was done to us.

December 15—Taking advantage of the darkness we throw up a slight ridge about a foot in height with the aid of a bayonet, cups and plates which although no protection from the enemy's fire gave us a sort of screen and as daylight begins to approach instructions and cautions are sent from mouth to mouth along the line. We all understand that we are to lie flat in almost one position all day. Raising a head or getting up on hands and knees will be done at the peril of ones life where a whole rebel army are acting as sharpshooters. The sun comes up bright and we can look back over the field and take in a new view of its horrors. Although all the wounded had already been taken off the field, it was thickly strewn with all kind of equipment and arms, fragments of human bodies and horses, artillery wagons & c & c, and without moving the head I could count over seventy-five dead bodies in that part of the field nearest where we lay. How many hearts were apt to bleed which in their far off homes had not yet heard of these fallen heroes. One sad sight was to see a poor horse which lay just as it had been shot, in the harness somewhere about the hind quarters, occasionally raise itself up on its forefeet looking so imploring toward us for help, and groan so like a human being as to be perfectly heartrending and then fall back in exhaustion, dying by inches by pain, starvation and thirst.

A few careless heads were picked off during the day which would come up above the earthwork high enough to invite a rebel bullet. Just before sundown, the enemy succeeded in planting a new siege gun in a manner to rake our line, and sent one shell squarely through our ranks killing and wounding several, but before they could bring it to bear with the same effect again, darkness came to our relief and a relief it was too, for it seemed as if we could hardly wait for perfect darkness to settle down so weary had we become of this one position. As night draws on we begin to look for a new relief but hour after hour passes and none come, so Col. Clark goes down to the city to find Ferrero and at midnight orders come for us to leave the field one by one. As we crawl off silently, rendezvousing in a railroad cut we begin to understand that we are to be the last skirmish line on that field and that a general retreat is in progress. After an hours waiting the entire brigade is drawn off and we march back to the city.

December 16—We pass through the streets crowded with ambulance trains filled with our wounded all headed toward the river. When we reach the pontoon bridges, we find them thickly covered with sawdust to deaden all sound to aid us in making a safe retreat. On our way back to our old camp ground we pass the great bivouac of wounded where preparations are rapidly going on to pitch tents for their shelter. We reach our "home" at three in the morning tired and everybody cross. After sleeping a couple of hours we wake and find it raining. Pitch our tents again and as all duties are of course suspended we write home. Well after all it is a relief, but such a discouraging relief as we think of the overwhelming defeat to our army. Sergeant Davis comes around at evening to our tent and details Lemuel who with twenty others from the regiment are sent back across the river under flag of truce to bury the dead. Troops have been passing by all day back to their old camping grounds.

3. The Fredericksburg Campaign

Hitchcock's Comments in 1890—General Burnside assumed the responsibility for the defeat in these chivalric words in his report to the President: "For the failure of the attack, I am responsible, as the extreme gallantry, courage and endurance, shown by our troops was never exceeded and would have carried the points had it been possible. To the families and friends of the dead I can only offer my heartfelt sympathies, but for the wounded I can offer my earnest prayers for their comfort and final recovery."

Looking backward twenty seven years, we have found that the responsibility must be shared by the treacherous subordinates who failed to give him the willing help which they ought in the flank movement on the left. It must also be shared by the authorities in Washington which failed to have the pontoons ready on his arrival but forced him to make the advance at an inopportune time.

It is futile to suggest what might have been the result if the cooperation had been hearty. Yet, granting all this the country still claims that his judgment was in error in attempting to throw his brave troops against an impossible barrier, forgetting that General Grant found equally impossible barriers two years later at Spotsylvania and Petersburg with as equally terrible slaughter.

All the previous and later triumphs of General Burnside failed to place him in the first rank by an indiscriminate public. A callow youth may be forgiven the effusive homage paid to his commander for those qualities which deservedly render him popular; namely, a dashing, magnificent presence combined with a cheerful, gracious temperament; a watchful interest in the welfare of his men and a pride and confidence in their prowess (as evinced in his determination to send the veterans of the 9th Corps to accomplished what the whole army had failed to perform); but he is not to be judged by such a tribunal. Neither is he to be judged by the critics who passed judgment adversely on every one of the leaders of the Army of the Potomac excepting General Grant.

Perhaps not one of them suffered this unrighteous judgment more than General Pope, who accepted the unwelcome position with soldierly obedience with full knowledge that he was to be the victim of the damnable spirit of revenge on the part of the satellites of General McClellan. From this standpoint of history we claim for General McClellan the credit of organizing the grandest army of modern times out of an unwieldy mob of self-asserting Yankees. This mission ended with the Peninsula campaign, but the nation's gratitude should be cheerfully rendered for what he did.

General Pope's soldierly qualities and ability should in no sense be dimmed for the failure which a discriminate people rests upon the heads of General Fitz-John Porter and others whose names are not worthy. And this also in face of the defense pleaded by them, because their loyalty (in spirit) was withheld from their rightful commander.

General Hooker's failure may be said to have the least excuse, for with whatever talents he may have possessed must ever be associated the criminal folly of drunkenness at a critical hour. As a "chain is only as strong as its weakest link," so he was weakest of all. No finer generalship was displayed with grander results than that of General Meade in the culmination of the war, in the Gettysburg campaign and its credit is solely due to him, but in its stead, he received the cruel letter from General Halleck which he justly resented.

But how the country has almost forgotten him in eulogizing General Grant. We would take no laurels from General Grant which belong to him; but many have been bestowed which belong to others. General McClellan as an organizer; General Pope by his example of obedience; General Burnside by his bravery and sturdy patriotism in the midst of the darkest hours of the rebellion and a disloyal army; General Meade by skillful tactics overwhelming the invincible General Lee; all had a share in turning over to General Grant an army perfected by discipline, and an administration willing at last to bestow autocratic power upon him.

The Supreme Arbiter of events gave each his appropriate work, but myriad causes united to end the war and General Grant was only one instrument in its accomplishment. The error of judgment then rests with the critics of General Burnside, and we therefore claim for him as high attainments as any commander of the Army of the Potomac.

4

Winter at Falmouth

"Some of the time it [rain] came down in torrents threatening to inundate the army."
—Hitchcock, January 21, 1863

Morale of the Army of the Potomac plummeted after the Fredericksburg disaster. As days passed, Union soldiers became discontented and demoralized. Large numbers fell out for sick call and daily desertions increased to 100 or more. Several unscrupulous and self-serving high level commanders disseminated negative information about General Burnside both within and outside the army that further damaged Burnside's already tarnished reputation. By contrast, General Lee's prestige regained some of its luster that was lost in the Maryland Campaign.

General Burnside still believed that the Confederates' position could be flanked. General Lee, not cognizant of Burnside's future intentions, sent Maj. Gen. J.E.B. Stuart and 1,800 cavalry on a raid deep behind the Union lines. Stuart returned on New Year's Day without news of Union plans. Lee continued to strengthen his defenses fronting Fredericksburg with his left anchored on Taylor's Hill and his right on Hamilton's Crossing. The Confederate army spent a bleak Christmas in shelters on the heights and in the woods near Fredericksburg. Union pickets, accepting an invitation by the Confederates, crossed the river at the rocky ford above Falmouth and celebrated Christmas at huge campfires with Confederate pickets. When fifty Confederate soldiers returned the visit a few days later, they were seized while smoking and joking around the fires with Union pickets. Shortly thereafter, the Confederate soldiers were returned to their side of the river and stringent orders against fraternization were issued and enforced by Union commanders.

With weather favorable, Burnside made preparations for a cavalry raid bypassing the Confederate lines with the mission of interrupting communications and creating alarm in Richmond. On December 30, the day the raid was scheduled to begin, Burnside received a dispatch from Lincoln that stated: "I have good reason for saying you must not make a general movement of the army without letting me know." Two dissident officers, who had been granted leave for personal business prior to a military action, went to Washington to convince officials that Burnside was incompetent and his campaign must be halted. President Lincoln met with the two malcontents: Brig. Gen. John Newton, commander of the Third Division of the VI Corps, and Brig. Gen. John Cochrane, commander of the First Brigade in Newton's division. Burnside met with the president and offered his resignation. On January 8, Lincoln wrote to Burnside: "I do not yet see how I could profit by changing the command of the Army of the Potomac, and if I did, I should not wish to do it by accepting the resignation of your commission." Fortified by this support, Burnside prepared a new plan to cross the fords above Fredericksburg and turn Lee's left flank.

On a cold and sunny January 20 following an unusually dry month, Franklin's and Hooker's troops headed for Banks' Ford, five miles above Fredericksburg, while Sumner's troops delayed a day before their planned crossing in front of Fredericksburg. Confederate troops were placed on the alert. Then, a fierce, three-day winter storm struck; the rain fell in torrents and the roads were reduced to ribbons of mud. Columns of miserable troops dragged to a virtual halt and pontoons and artillery pieces failed to move. On the morning of January 22, Burnside ordered the army back to their camps. The march was extremely difficult— for the next twenty-four hours, muddy and tired soldiers slowly plodded back to their quarters. Franklin had demoralized his command and his troops were discouraged by the dissident generals. After the "Mud March," Hooker openly denunciated the commanding general. When Burnside heard the despair and negative rhetoric, he traveled to Washington and submitted General Orders, No. 8, for Lincoln's consideration. The order dismissed from the service Generals Joseph Hooker, W. T. H. Brooks, John Newton and John Cochrane, and relieved from their positions Generals W. B. Franklin, W. F. Smith, Samuel Sturgis, and Edward Ferrero and Lt. Col. J. H. Taylor. On January 25, 1863, instead of a wholesale dismissal, Lincoln relieved General Burnside from command of the Army of the Potomac and named General Hooker to command the army. General Franklin was relieved, and at his own request, Lincoln relieved General Sumner.

General Hooker, a popular choice with the rank and file, reorganized the cavalry into separate corps using the Confederate model, curtailed corrupted quartermasters, improved rations, cleaned up the winter quarters and granted more leaves. Although there was an immediate improvement in morale, the efficiency of the command had been seriously impaired by the internal dissensions and by a lack of cooperation from subordinate officers. Discordant elements persisted in the Army of the Potomac until Maj. Gen. George G. Meade assumed command on June 28, 1863. Morale was high in the Army of Northern Virginia, but there was a consciousness in the ranks that a persistent and determined Union army had an unlimited supply of men and materials to replace their loses.

* * * *

December 17, 1862—John L. Hildreth of New Ipswich was in camp today. He tells us that Albert Davis was shot dead on the field. Our forces have evacuated all the south side of the river, and the enemy have reoccupied the city. Several exchanged prisoners joined the regiment from Annapolis today.

December 18—A very cold windy day, ground froze hard. Major Hawkes arrived last evening and I spoke with him at regimental drill for the first time since we left Mass. He brought bundles of shirts and stockings from home with excellent letters. I took dinner with Henry, had soup and ginger snaps from Templeton.

December 19—Maj. Hawkes brought down to my tent today a new pair of thick mittens, a present

Captain George P. Hawkes was taken prisoner at the Battle of Chantilly on September 1, 1862, and was exchanged a few months later. He was promoted to major in September and to lieutenant colonel in December 1862.

from Aunt Lee, and a real god-send to me for the cold weather and guard duty will render them valuable indeed. I drew a pair of pants from government and have been rigging up anew. Col. Maggi of the 33rd and formerly of our regiment called on us today. I with two others from our regiment was detailed to support Dr. Butler at the Division Surgeon's hospital about a mile from camp tonight.

December 20—It was cold but pleasant. We were quartered in a large hospital tent for the night, and today we have been at work fixing up around the tents of the wounded, putting them in more comfortable shape. Joined the regiment at night.

December 21—Very cold. Sunday morning inspection at half past ten. The 35th Mass., 21 Mass. and part of the 11 N.H. have been detailed to go out on picket tomorrow morning at light. At Dress Parade orders were read from Gen. Ferrero thanking the 21st for their bravery in the late battle. I have been up to Sanderson's tent singing with Maj. Hawkes, Henry and others.

December 22—Milder today. I was excused from duty on account of poor shoes and did not go with the regiment but spent most of the day in my tent reading and writing. The Army Balloon was up at three this p.m.

December 23—A load of Express boxes via Harper's Ferry arrived with one for Henry and myself from home. There was a grand review of the Ninth Corps by Gen. Sumner near camp today. Our regiment came in from picket in time to join in it. Col. Maggi brought over his band to play to us tonight.

December 24—Pleasant and thawing. The regiment went out on picket again and I was again excused by the surgeon. John Mayo and Eliab Churchill of the 33rd were here to see me today. The army balloon was up this afternoon. Before night, the reckless Irish Company B showed signs of demoralization. They had secured a lot of whiskey from Falmouth and prepared for Christmas eve by getting fighting drunk. Numerous knock-downs occurred and my tent was stove in before the row was quieted.

December 25—Mild. The regiment came in from picket and at half past twelve went as escort for train load of wounded to the depot, who were enroute to Washington. Henry and I send home a box of books. Rations of whiskey were served out to the regiment today with which to celebrate Christmas. As I celebrate without the use of whiskey, I refuse my ration.

December 26—Letters from home tell me that Massachusetts is seeing a very cold winter with hardly any snow. Brigade Drill this afternoon by Gen. Ferrero. At Dress Parade commissions were announced for Whitney, 2nd Lieut. and Sampson, 1st Lieut.; resignation from Col. Foster and Lieut. Clark. I have been drawing clothing, pants and shoes.

December 27—I was on guard at the Brigade Commissary Headquarters.

December 28—Very mild. E. Churchill of the 33rd came over to see me today. Rev. Mr. Paine of Holden [*Massachusetts*] addressed the regiment at Dress Parade. He was the first chaplain appointed, but resigned on account of ill health.

December 29—Had two hours squad drill in skirmishing and an hour and a half Battalion drill. I received a bundle of papers from Mr. Seamans.

December 30—We were roused up before light and at eight went down to the river two miles away on picket. I was on the first relief. My post being near the edge of the river and my nearest companion, a rebel picket opposite me just a stones throw across the river. Maj. Hawkes detailed me to assist him after my first beat and for the remainder of the time that I was on picket I quartered with the officers in the parlors of the "Lacey House," a handsome residence of some wealthy aristocrat, which stands on a commanding elevation overlooking the entire city of Fredericksburg and beyond. the main parlors which are connected by large folding doors, show signs of an elegance and taste which correspond with the rest of the place. Numerous outbuildings,

4. *Winter at Falmouth* 59

During the war the mansion was referred to as the Lacy House, after its wartime owner, J. Horace Lacey. During the Battle of Fredericksburg, the mansion served as the command post for General Sumner, Union Right Grand Division commander. Two pontoon bridges spanned the Rappahannock River immediately below the mansion. Hitchcock served there in December 1862 (National Archives).

slave quarters and barns all are deserted or given up by the owners and the remaining furniture shows the rough usage from Union soldiery. A fine looking piano with the organ combination stands in one of the parlors, receiving severe treatment from unmusical hands.

[*This large Georgian mansion known as Chatham had stood on Stafford Heights near Fredericksburg for ninety years before the Civil War. In the eighteenth century, it was the home of William Fitzhugh, a wealthy landowner. During the war the mansion was referred to as the Lacy House, after its wartime owner, J. Horace Lacey. During the Battle of Fredericksburg, the mansion served as the command post for General Sumner, Right Grand Division Commander. Two pontoon bridges spanned the Rappahannock River immediately below the mansion.*]

December 31—Rained during the night and this morning has cleared away very cold. Before leaving our picket quarters the mischievous portion of the regiment, each and individually took some part of the organ away with them, and at eleven a.m. we create a sensation on entering camp, by the innumerable discordant sounds arising from the confiscated pipes of the organ. Henry found a valise full of goodies from home consisting of apples, cake, jelly, brown bread, pies, butter and coffee, a most acceptable New Years Present. Mustered in for pay this p.m. Major Hawkes took charge at Dress parade. The 11th N. H. Band serenaded the Field and Staff of the different regiments of the Brigade in the night. The hospitality with which it was received became very marked after each succeeding treat so that when the last Headquarters had been "done" each member was playing on his own hook regardless of time and harmony.

January 1, 1863—It being a public holiday, all drills were omitted. Henry and I had a Feast on the contents of the home box. Capt. Saunderson received a box from Harper's Ferry.

January 2—Company Drill in the morning and Brigade Drill in the afternoon. Part of the 9th Army Corps was reviewed near us today. Henry's box via Newbern arrived today having been en route for six months. The contents excepting the shirts and the like were valueless.

January 3—Lieut. Col. Foster came to the regiment last night and today Lieut. Parker of Co. A.

January 4—Sunday. Fair and mild. John Mayo came to see me.

January 5—Fair and warmer. A grand review of Hooker's Corps by General Burnside took place on our drill grounds today.

January 6—Gen. Burnside reviewed the entire 9th Corps near Gen. Sumner's headquarters, "Phillips House."

[*The Phillips House was General Burnside's headquarters during the Battle of Fredericksburg. Located east of the Lacy House, it was owned by Alexander K. Phillips and called "Mulberry Hill." General Sumner had occupied the Phillips House but moved to the Lacy House on December 12, 1862. Phillips House burned in February 1863.*]

January 7—The 21st and 35th Mass. went out to picket the river, my post, third relief from eight to ten, gave me opportunity to see large numbers of rebel soldiers on the opposite side. Spent most of the night on the dirty and old brick floor of the negro quarters connected with the Lacy House.

January 8—My poor accommodations of last night have given me a sore throat.

January 9—Drilled in skirmish in the morning and in the afternoon, Division Drill, Gen. Nagle of the 1st Brigade commanding. It included a great deal of heavy standing around.

January 10—Rained all day without intermission, passed the time in our leaky tent, reading, singing and eating.

January 11—Cold and clear, Sunday morning inspection.

January 12—According to orders, tents have been cleaned out and aired, ditches dug, and streets cleaned. Received letter from Rev. Mr. Wood of Campello. Heard that Charles Wyman has been sent to Washington sick with fever.

4. Winter at Falmouth

January 13—Threatening rain, I am on guard at the Brigade Commissary tent. Capt. John Proctor and Mr. Ruggles of Fitchburg visited the regiment.

January 14—Regiment went down on picket again. Sidney Hayward rejoined the regiment.

January 15—Cloudy, high wind and warm. Saw a pontoon train moving up toward Falmouth, and it is rumored that another attempt is to be made to cross the river above Falmouth.

January 16—Very raw cold wind. Lemuel and I securing passes went off on a tramp, found our way down to Falmouth and over to camp of the 33rd Mass. where we saw old acquaintances. Our Division has received marching orders and rations have been dealt accordingly.

January 17—Cleared off cold. Skirmish drill this morning. Three days rations are to be kept constantly on hand.

January 18—Very cold. Read news of the capture of all our Signal Books at Murfreesboro, Tenn. Lieut. Asahel Wheeler has been promoted Captain of Co. G.

January 19—Company and Battalion Drills. Lemuel is on guard at Gen. Ferrero's Headquarters.

January 20—About ten o'clock this morning, batteries began moving through our camp toward Falmouth and continued till noon. Then troops composing Franklin's and Hooker's Corps commenced moving up in the same direction and continued all the afternoon. We have received orders to be ready to march early tomorrow morning.

January 21—Began to rain last evening and has continued hard all day. Some of the time it came down in torrents threatening to inundate the army. As no general movement seemed advisable this morning, the 21st were ordered to relieve picket at the Lacy House. Maj. Hawkes being commander of the picket he detailed me to wait on him so I was favored and did not have to stand on guard at all. There was much talk among the officers about projected move and unusual commotion could be seen across the river, horsemen riding hurriedly out from Fredericksburg to the northward. Lie down to sleep in very fine comfortable quarters in the Lacy House thinking of the thousands of poor fellows up the river lying on arms, shelterless, and in this horrid Virginia mud. [*In 1890 Hitchcock added: "I feel almost ashamed of this 'parlor soldiering.'"*]

January 22—Storm continues with heavy fog. Mud, Mud everywhere and streams very high. The Rappahannock in many places has overflowed its banks. Received papers from home and saw yesterday's edition of the Richmond Examiner brought over in the Flag of Truce boat with dispatches for Gen. Burnside. The Rebs have stuck up an image on their picket line with a large placard attached bearing the words "Burnside stuck in the mud."

[*The* Richmond Examiner, *January 21, 1863—John M. Daniel, editor,* *reacting to peace movements in the Confederacy and in the North, wrote: "... It is not for us to give advice to any party at the North, but in this case the maxim is certainly true, which holds that it may be wise for them to learn from an enemy. The lesson which we would teach the Northern conservatives is simply this, that <u>honesty is the best policy</u>. Let them not go before their people with a delusive and false programme. Let them not deceive their people into the belief that the South will unite in the convention which they propose. The Union is broken, and broken forever. Like the beautiful bubble blown from a pipe, once broken, it can never be restored. The blood which has been shed can never be washed out. The grievous wrongs which have been inflicted upon us can never be repaired, forgotten, or forgiven. The South, even if she could consent to dishonor herself, could never consent to defame her dead, or turn a deaf ear to the voices appealing from fifty thousand graves against the enemy of their country and their race. She cannot consent to reconstruction; and the Northern conservatives, if they have hearts and feelings, know it. Their hands, no less than those of the Abolitionists, are stained with Southern blood; their consciences are equally loaded with the guilt of this wholesale and wanton bloodshed; and we will not, we cannot grasp them in friendship. It is a fraud and false hood to teach the Northern people that we will unite with them in convention."]*

January 23—Cleared off pleasant at night. The troops returned to their camps today and this move was a failure. Toward nine in the evening muttered words and mysterious movements among the unruly members of our regiment indicated some unusual commotion which broke out in a riot near the Brigade Sutler's tent in which large numbers from different regiments engaged. They made a grand charge on the tent but were checked for a few moments by the two occupants who showed resistance, but soon surrounding them, the roughs tore down the tent, carried off all the merchandise and two of their number who were shot in the melee.

January 24—Maj. Hawkes has been promoted to be Lieut. Col. and Capt. Richardson to Major.

January 25—Sunday morning inspection. I have been reading the "Life of Adjutant Stearns" of the 21st who was killed at Roanoke. He was the son of President Stearns of Amherst College.

January 26—I have found my time fully occupied today washing clothes; Company drill in the morning, Battalion drill in the afternoon and Dress Parade at night, where the Brigade received and welcomed Gen. Ferrero, who has just returned from a furlough, with cheers and music.

January 27—I was detailed with forty others to build a corduroy bridge no far from Quartermaster Thompson's Headquarters over a swollen stream which has heretofore been forded. Orders were read at Dress Parade changing command of the Army of the Potomac from Gen. Burnside to Gen. Hooker and the 9th Corps from Gen. Sumner to Gen. Couch. [*Hitchcock's reaction in 1890 to Burnside's dismissal: "So our old commander leaves us much to our regret."*]

January 28—Severe storm began last night and snowed all day. Went out on picket by the river and stood two hours during the day on a post about half way between Falmouth and Fredericksburg on a knoll, exposed to the piercing winds which swept the river the air being filled with driving sleet and snow. There was nothing within reach with which to make fuel and so, binding my overcoat cape tightly over my head, my woolen blanket about my shoulders and my rubber blanket over the whole, I trotted swiftly back and forth on my beat until completely exhausted I would sink down in the snow and rest for a few moments, then up and go it again. The only human being to be seen was rebel picket just across the river who sat during the whole time crouching over his faint and struggling fire. I think I never suffered so much from the cold and never again came so nearly perishing, and when I espied the solitary man come plunging through the snow which was to relieve me, I felt as if I could not have held out much longer. The ordinary rules for relieving picket were ignored, the sergeant of the picket guard instead of marching his entire guard around with him, simply sent out his men one by one to their respective posts. I return to the rendezvous of the guard which is a cave in the banks of the Rappahannock adjoining the grounds of the Lacy House. We were relieved and returned to camp at night. Found a letter from Mrs. Ide who notified me that she had sent me a box of goodies.

January 29—Wallace, Whitney and I crawled under our blankets snuggling closely together to keep out the cold and early in the evening went to sleep. Did not wake until broad day-light when we found the sun shining brightly and the snow piled in a small drift over our blankets adding to the warmth of our nest. Drills and Dress Parade were omitted on account of the snow. Henry was in to see me.

January 30—A court martial is being held in our hospital tents trying the men engaged in the riot at the sutler's tent. Wallace and I have been fixing up our quarters.

January 31—Tonight the mail brought a Congregationalist [*paper*] from home. Orders announcing the assuming of command by General Hooker were read.

February 1, 1863—Sunday morning inspection in charge of Col. Hawkes. Furloughs are being granted to officers and privates of our Brigade.

February 2—I was detailed to go out on picket with detachments from the different regiments of the Brigade. got along more comfortable than I did the last time.

February 3—My post was on a terrace below the Lacy House, overlooking the river and Fredericksburg, with orders to give notice to the officers at the House if anything unusual occurred in our front. As the duties were unnecessary during the daytime, I stood guard only at night. The weather grew very cold during the night, the air very clear and nipping. The moon came out from the clouds full and bright, giving me, from my elevated post, a beautiful picture, in one direction the handsome Lacey House with its fine surroundings (or those that had been spared by our troops), shade trees, shrubbery and pretty summer houses; in another direction, the fated city with all its spires and towers reflected in dark relief against the sky; and beyond and above, the dark forests which seem more gloomy as I think of the thousands of thousands who are hidden behind their shelter ready to meet us in deadly conflict. Then in the foreground, down at my feet flows the swollen Rappahannock with its sullen roar as if to chide the sinful humanity which it separates, for their Satan-born propensities to fight. Yes, it gives the soldier on picket in the silent night ample time for reflection, and it is not strange the thought arises: Is not this restless mighty God's mouthpiece to soothe the turbulent spirits which cry out from one side "I shall have my slave," and from the other, "You shall not." [*In 1890 Hitchcock added: "Standing thus, hour after hour in this silent night, it is hardly strange that the soldier on picket finds time for moralizing."*]

February 4—The morning is the coldest of the year but the weather moderated before night and looked like snow. A Brigade Bake House is being built in the rear of our regiment.

February 5—A cold stormy day, snow and rain. No duties today. Sigel's Corps is said to be moving today. Brooks of the 2nd Mass. Regiment, a Templeton boy, was here to see us today.

February 6—The 9th Corps received marching orders today, but we do not have any idea what it means.

February 7—Henry has been detailed Aide-de-camp for Col. Hartranft commanding the Brigade. Orders have been received to march at an hours notice having knapsacks packed.

February 8—Inspection this morning at ten o'clock.

February 9—At 4 o'clock our bugles and drums sounded out the order "Prepare to march" and after a hasty breakfast, the Brigade packed up and left camp at day-light.

5

Removal to Newport News

"The Monitor with several other gunboats are cruising about the mouth of the James River but a short distance away."
—Hitchcock, February 15, 1863

On February 6, 1863, George Getty's division of the IX Corps left winter quarters on the Rappahannock River, near Falmouth, proceeded by train to Aquia Creek, was transported to Fort Monroe, and then proceeded to Newport News, Virginia. Edward Ferrero's division left on February 9 and Orlando Willcox's division followed the next day. On February 10, 1863, the IX Corps, commanded by Maj. Gen. William F. "Baldy" Smith, was separated from the Army of the Potomac, and remained inactive for the next six weeks.

On January 30, 1863, 1,800 Confederate troops in Brig. Gen. Roger A. Pryor's Brigade, defending the lines of the Blackwater River, engaged Brig. Gen. Michael Corcoran's 4,800 Union troops at Deserted House (Kelly's Store), Virginia, nine miles west of Suffolk. The Confederate troops were forced to retire because of the overwhelming Union force and a shortage of ammunition. Both sides, however, claimed victory. There were 39 Confederate casualties (8 killed and 31 wounded), while the Union forces suffered 143 casualties (23 killed, 108 wounded and 12 missing).

In March, Brig. Gen. Getty's division was sent to Suffolk, about twenty miles southwest of Norfolk, where Confederate troops threatened Union works. Getty's division never rejoined the IX Corps, being reassigned on March 2, 1863, to the Department of Virginia. On March 19, Maj. Gen. John Grubb Parke assumed command of the corps.

* * * *

February 9, 1863 (continued)—Embarked on the cars for Aquia Creek. As the day was bright and the air mild, we enjoyed the ride very much. Along the route for the most of the way laid the camps of different Divisions and Brigades of the Old army of the Potomac. Arrived near Aquia Creek early in the afternoon, left the cars and march about a mile through a very lively scene. This being the base of supplies for the two hundred thousand soldiers of the Army of the Potomac, it had the appearance of an active city: hundreds of moving army wagons, immense store houses, and large camps of Quarter Masters' tents. We reach one of the wharves and after some delay are marched onto the decks of the large steamer "Louisiana" at four in the afternoon with the 35th Mass. and 51st Penn. After a great deal of hustling about, the men secure and appropriate different portions of the vessel for individual use, Company A finding a place in the fore part of the lower deck. The vessel swings out into the center of the Potomac and cast anchor.

February 10—Early in the night two schooners loaded with the remainder of the Brigade are taken in tow by our steamer, weighed anchor and move slowly and grandly down the broad Potomac. During the fore noon we enter the Chesapeake Bay and the steamers "Georgia" and "North America" pass us loaded with the first Brigade. The day is glorious and the men are drinking in the enjoyment of the holiday excursion, lying about on the sunny side of the decks reading, writing, playing cards and singing. The officers appropriate to their use the staterooms of the vessel, so Henry finds fine quarters with the staff officers of the Brigade.

February 11—The weather changed during the night and morning dawns cloudy with a chill nor-easter blowing in from the Atlantic on which we are now resting. Having reached off Fortress Monroe, at midnight we cast anchor until daylight, when we again weighed anchor and sailed into Hampton Roads, stopped a few minutes at Fort Monroe and then sailed up past the Rip-Raps [*a manmade island across the navigational channel from Old Point Comfort in the middle of the mouth of Hampton Roads*] and landed at the wharves at Newport News, near the spot where the terrific combat between the Monitor and the Merrimac took place. The half submerged hulk of the "Cumberland" [*30 gun frigate*] lies a short distance off and nearer still, the masts of the buried "Congress" [*50 gun frigate*]. Pitched camp a quarter of a mile from shore. I was detailed to help unload baggage from the schooners. [*In 1890 Hitchcock added: "It is unnecessary to say that the War Department did not give us information in regard to its plans or the reasons for the removal of so large a body of disciplined troops from the front of Lee's Army on the eve of Hooker's advance. In the absence of definite information, the rank and file are not fully united in their views. One theory was that Burnside was to return to North Carolina with his 9th Corps and resume offensive operations. Another was that a strong force at this point would so threaten Richmond from the same lines of McClellan's old campaign that Hooker would have less opposition."*]

February 12—Foggy and heavy sea-breeze. The camps are being laid out with great precision and regularity. The tall straight pines in the rear of the camp split up so nicely that we are making fine stockades for our tents. Soft bread was issued today and the regular camp duties instituted.

February 13—Company & Battalion drills on the broad grounds overlooking the James River and Hampton Roads. I was detailed to unload express boxes from a schooner at the wharf.

February 14—I have found work in the woods gathering fuel and stockade stuff and down at the wharves again unloading boxes.

February 15—The Monitor with several other gunboats are cruising about the mouth of the James River but a short distance away. Doing picket duty.

[*The* Monitor *and* Merrimack *duel at Hampton Roads, Virginia, on March 9, 1862, was the first battle between ironclad ships. The* Merrimack *was destroyed on March 9, 1862, to prevent capture. The* Monitor, *not very seaworthy, sank off Cape Hatteras on December 31, 1862, in heavy seas while being towed to the Carolina coast. Her escort,* Rhode Island, *rescued forty-seven men—sixteen men were lost. Hitchcock must have seen an ironclad similar to the* Monitor.]

February 16—Capt. Hill of Company D drilled us in squad drill. I was detailed to shovel around headquarters and was therefore excused from Battalion drill. At night assisted to unload hospital tents from a steamer. Gen. Ferrero resumed command of the Brigade and Henry has returned to the regiment.

February 17—Col. Clark has just returned from Mass. where he has been on furlough for ten days. A steady deluging rain which began in the night has almost entirely overflowed our level camp ground and I was obliged to fill in with mud to keep myself and trappings out of water.

February 18—Storm continued unremitting all night and day. All my blankets, clothing and knapsack are soaked and having no duties, I sit most of the day under my shelter unable to find any occupation in such a storm.

February 19—Wind shifted and weather cleared up. The Brigade are receiving the A tents and therefore Cole, who is now tenting with me, has been assisting in putting our quarters in better weather-proof shape. Lemuel Whitney received a box of goodies from home which contained valuables for me in shape of dried apple, sausage, cakes and pies.

February 20—Went out on picket. The line extends along the edge of a tall pine forest and our part of the line being about a mile back of camp. Duties very simple and light.

February 21—Cleaned up gun and equipments for tomorrow's review, We pitched our A tent and moved in. Received letter from Walter Lamb, Newbern, N.C.

February 22—Snowed very hard all night and turned to rain at daylight, which continued till afternoon. Our tent barely escaped overthrow from the high winds and we kept busy bailing water from our flooded tent.

February 23—I exchanged tents and tent mates with Osgood and am now with Wilbur Potter in a shanty made of slabs with a roof composed of several pieces of shelters. The 51st New York had presentation of colors at Dress Parade.

February 24—I was on guard on the Parade Ground. Brigade Drill in charge of Col. Hartranft.

February 25—Stood on beat from one till five in the night and having no fire was very cold. At about nine in the morning, batteries and regiments began to center in our front and by ten, our Brigade was marched out in line. After a short time, the whole 9th Corps could be seen spread out on the long parade ground over a mile in length. Soon the guns of the man-of-war Frigate "Minnesota" fired a salute as General Dix landed and rode onto the field with his Staff. He then, accompanied by Gen. Smith commander of the Corps, rode up and down the lines amid the cheers of the troops and music from the numerous bands. The whole Corps of thirty thousand then passed in review before him and I had an excellent opportunity to see the old soldier, gray haired man of sixty. Crowds of Army and Navy officers came up from Fortress Monroe to witness the review with their ladies.

February 26—Built a chimney and fire-place of split sticks and mud for our tent, making it much for our comfort.

February 27—Rec'd letter from home containing pictures of the family.

February 28—The regiment was mustered in for pay. Inspection by Col. Clark and Hawkes. I was detailed on guard posted at Gen. Ferrero's Headquarters. Rec'd papers from home.

March 1, 1863—Regiment inspection by an army officer.

March 2—Regiment drilled in squad drill as a regiment. Brigade drill in the afternoon.

March 3—On guard in front of camp; stood four hours consecutively in the night. Gen. Ferrero drilled the Brigade. Lieut. John F. Lewis, formerly of Company A, resigned on account of fever and ague [*a malarial fever marked by successive cold, hot and sweating fits*] and received an honorable discharge.

March 4—Company drill in the afternoon. Capt. Saunderson and Aldrich received furloughs and went home. Jack Reynolds returned to Company A from the hospital. Rec'd letter from home.

March 5—I went down to the wharves with a hundred others on detail this morning and unload a schooner containing bales of hay. Brigade drill this afternoon.

March 6—Last night was very cold. Drilled in squads in the facings. A sad and impressive sight was witnessed today; a young man of the 35th Mass.

was buried with military honors. The band playing Pleyel's Hymn [*Ignaz J. Pleyel—melody written in 1791*] as the regiment marched with reversed arms down past our camp to the burial place.

March 7—Drilled without arms this morning. Col. Hawkes and Henry went down to the Fortress Monroe in the afternoon on the mail boat which runs up from the Fort twice a day. I received a package of papers from home tonight.

March 8—Sunday. Very warm and mild. Cleaned up gun and equipments for Brigade inspection which took place at one o'clock. Several of our boys have received furloughs and gone home.

March 9—Company and Battalion drills in facings under command of Capt. Walcott who is Acting Adjutant.

March 10—Burnside was said to be here today.

March 11—I was on guard at Col. Harriman's tent, 11th N.H.

March 12—Company drill in the afternoon.

March 13—The Third Division left Newport News for Suffolk where Corcoran is reported to have retreated. Company drills morning and afternoon.

March 14—Brigade guard was changed to regimental as the 51st N.Y. and 51st Penn. have just vacated. Duties & Drill were omitted today in honor of the Battle of Newbern anniversary.

[*Battle of New Bern: On March 14, 1862, New Bern, North Carolina, was captured by the Coast Division of the Army of the Potomac led by General Burnside (thirteen regiments of infantry). The official record indicated that the "21st Massachusetts, from its exposed position and the daring of its officers and men, suffered the greatest loss"—58 casualties.*]

March 15—I went out on picket today. My post was the farthest one on the line, on the beach below the promontory. An interesting sight was spread out before me. Seven miles away over the water, the trim and massive gray walls of the Fortress Monroe rose from the blue sea, the low sandy beach connected with the main land further to my left where lay the village of Hampton, prominent in which arose the shiny dome of its seminary. Back of this and running almost up to the beach in the intervening distance was a low level of unbroken pine forest. Off to the right of Fortress Monroe in the middle of the "Roads" arose the black ragged rocky Rip-Raps solitary from the water, and away to the south partially exposed to view was Norfolk. A large fleet of vessels can be seen anchored around the Fort. As the weather was mild and duties light I had a very easy picket.

[*When construction was completed in 1834, Fort Monroe was referred to as the "Gibraltar of Chesapeake Bay"—the most powerful fort in the Union. The Fortress at Old Point Comfort was a bastion of the Union in Tidewater, Virginia.*

It was at Fort Monroe in May 1861, two years before Abraham Lincoln issued the Emancipation Proclamation, a Union commander, Major General Benjamin Butler, declared that three fugitive slaves there were contraband, war spoils, effectively freeing them. This act sent a flood of slaves to the "Freedom Fort." Confederate president, Jefferson Davis, was locked up in a casemate in the wall of the fort from May 22, 1865, to May 13, 1867.]

March 16—Received and read a Congregationalist [*church bulletin*] from home.

March 17—Lieut. Lawrence drilled us today. I drew clothing and pants today. In the afternoon the regiment broke camp, moved down about a mile below near the beach and pitch a new camp where we find better water and a more convenient place generally.

March 18—Fixed up quarters and went down to the wharves and Sutlers Shops about the beach. The officers of the 2nd Brigade were invited to a Grand Ball which was held on board a splendid steamer at the wharves this evening.

March 19—I was placed on guard over some old barracks to prevent them from being torn down by the men who are anxious to secure the boards for tent flooring. The 1st Division embarked for Baltimore en route for Dept. of Ohio and there are surmises that we shall have to follow them soon. A battery left us this morning for Hampton. Commenced snowing tonight.

March 20—Storm continued, snowing all day and very cold. Wilbur Potter and I laid abed most of the day, this being the only way we could keep comfortable. The old barracks near us are filled with the 27th New Jersey who are waiting for transportation.

March 21—Storm continues. I received papers from F.W. Seamans. Several returned from furloughs today and more troops went away.

March 22—Clear and warm. Snow going rapidly. Col. Hawkes started for a ten days furlough to Massachusetts. Inspection at ten o'clock. Several Frigates and ironclads are anchored off the beach in our front. The Minnesota and Keokuk are among the number.

March 23—Our regiment is doing Provost duty at the wharves and storehouses. The 36th Mass. embarked for Baltimore this morning. Gen. Burnside has taken command of the 9th Corps and is transferring it to the West, to Department of the Ohio. Fixed up our tent.

March 24—I was on guard as Provost. From my post near the beach in the night, I could hear the watches on the Minnesota as they cried out the hour of the night and "All's well." Found good quarters when offbeat among the numerous bales of hay.

March 25—The First Brigade left for Baltimore and our orders were read at Dress Parade for us to march tomorrow afternoon. Five days rations are being cooked for the journey.

March 26—At eight o'clock we are packed and down to the wharves. Went on board the steam-transport "Kennebec" at noon. I was detailed to assist in loading officers baggage which lasted till three when we move off amid the cheers of those we leave behind. Sail down the Roads through a fleet of vessels carrying the ensigns of various foreign nations, just stop at Fortress Monroe for mails and then put out to sea.

6

Transfer to the Department of the Ohio

> "Nine tenths of the regiment were more or less under the influence of liquor and a majority of the remaining tenth had all they could do to help the drunken pack to the cars."
> —Hitchcock, March 29, 1863

On August 19, 1862, the Union Department and Army of the Ohio was reorganized by the War Department. The new department included the states of Ohio, Michigan, Indiana, Illinois, Wisconsin and that part of Kentucky east of the Tennessee River, including the Cumberland Gap. On August 23, Maj. Gen. Horatio G. Wright assumed command of the department with headquarters at Cincinnati. This reorganization was made in response to a resurgence in Confederate fortunes that began in mid-June. Southern armies had boldly seized the initiative along a 1000-mile front, extending from Virginia's tidewater to the Indian Territory.

President Lincoln intuitively understood the importance of keeping Kentucky in the Union and was aware of the long-heard pleas of East Tennessee Unionists to free them from the "heavy hand" of Confederate despotism. These circumstances provided President Lincoln with the means to rescue General Burnside from oblivion and give him a meaningful mission. After his dismissal as commander of the Army of the Potomac, Burnside was directed on March 16, 1863, to resume command of his beloved IX Corps and relieve General Wright as commander of the Department of the Ohio. He was also to take the IX Corps to Ohio with him. Burnside arrived at Cincinnati on March 23 and assumed command on March 25.

Confederate raids coincided with Burnside's arrival. On March 22, the 8th Kentucky Cavalry (a detachment of Brig. Gen. John Hunt Morgan's cavalry), commanded by Col. R. S. Cluke, raided Mount Sterling, Kentucky, taking 300 prisoners and seizing horses and supplies. Cluke reported that his "command is elegantly mounted and clothed—in better condition than they ever have been." On the following day Brig. Gen. John Pegram led a 1,500-man cavalry expedition to obtain beef cattle for the Confederate army. He attacked Danville, 40 miles southwest of Lexington and forced five Union regiments to retreat.

These raids caused alarm and anxiety among the inhabitants of Kentucky and Ohio. Burnside recognized the need for a larger military force in the area. Such a force would serve to restore the peace in Kentucky, impress the "Peace Democrats," "Copperheads" and other antiwar activists in Ohio, Indiana and Illinois with the presence of military authority and accomplish the deliverance of East Tennessee.

On March 26, soldiers of the IX Corps, including the 21st Massachusetts Regiment, boarded the steamer Kennebec at Newport News, arrived at Baltimore on March 27 and headed west the next day on the Northern Central Railroad. The troops had an unfortunate clash with local militia at Columbus, Ohio, on March 30, which was never officially reported by the military. The IX Corps was welcomed by Burnside at Cincinnati on March 31, and then transported to Paris, Kentucky, some 70 miles south. The soldiers were surprised that the inhabitants showed no open hostility and seemed to be glad to see them.

* * * *

[**Hitchcock's comments in 1890**—*"It was definitely announced at last that the 9th Corps was to be transferred to the Department of the Ohio. General Burnside having been assigned to its command, he desired that his old soldiers should go with him. The 9th Corps was formed out of the original "Burnside expedition" and its peculiar mission rendered it, if not somewhat clannish, at least exclusive in its interests and purposes from the Army of the Potomac; certainly it acquired none of its jealousies and rivalries.*

"General Burnside widely discerned that such a body of men loyal to each other and to their commander would be a very effective force in the independent line of action laid out for and by him. Subsequent results proved his wisdom of choice and gave success to the plans of the East Tennessee campaign. Although withdrawn from participation in the glorious Gettysburg campaign, a portion of the Corps took part in the equally glorious Vicksburg campaign, but the grand strategic value of its work was the East Tennessee campaign.

"Although Sherman's march to the sea received the wider admiration, one object attempted and accomplished was the same with each army, namely: severing the Confederacy and thereby forcing each part of fight without the assistance of the other. By the whole sale transfer of so large a body of veteran fighters into the heart of the Confederacy, our government was also able to open up a large section of the South notable for its Union sentiment.

"The summer of 1863 found bodies of "Yankee" soldiers scattered through

Kentucky engaged in the missionary work of converting its citizens to the knowledge that the Union had the power and would eventually conquer the rebellion. It was this experience that made Kentucky the first state to swing solidly back into the Union.

"When the reunited 9th Corps reached the valley of the Holston (river in East Tennessee), it was planted squarely in the pathway between Lee and Johnston. At the nearest northern base of communication and supplies was two hundred miles away, separated from it by natures great barriers of lofty mountain ranges and broad rivers."]

March 26, 1863 (continued)—The air is mild and the sea calm and before dark we are out of sight of land—for me the first time. I stay on deck till long after dark enjoying the new and strange scene. Ongoing below the scene changes. Whiskey has been procured and all the reckless potion of the regiment are fight-drunk. From the hurricane deck to the lowest hold all is boisterous confusion.

March 27—Many are so crazy that safety of life is fairly in danger. Those officers who are sober worked long and late trying to keep their men from doing others harm, but as it was, there was a multitude of knock-downs, and bruised faces. Co. A's quarters were in the gangway and in the coal bin opposite the engine room where there was a continual passing. I find a retired spot in the coal bin and retire to my "downy couch" of coarse coal not being able to find even a board with which to soften the rough points and corners. In this strange bed I shut my eyes at midnight from all the worldly trials and vanities and wake at broad daylight after a truly refreshing sleep. We are allowed to boil our coffee, by the good-natured fireman, in the furnaces where but a moment was needed of its intense heat for each cup to boil. going on deck we find ourselves sailing up the broad Chesapeake with the low sandy reefs of Eastern Maryland on our right. We constantly meet and pass vessels of all descriptions among which, a massive screw-propeller which went dashing past us with wonderful rapidity. Before noon we passed in sight of Annapolis though several miles away from it. At about two in the afternoon we drew near to the granite walls of Fort Carroll which guards the entrance to the Patapsco River. Passing this we approach the enlivening scenes of a large city which, to a weary soldier, long time away from all scenes of civilization except of war, it is exceedingly refreshing. we plow up to the wharves of Baltimore right under the guns and parapet of Federal Hill and Fort McHenry which look down in a most threatening manner at us. Before we had fairly touched land, scores of enterprising ragamuffins swarm about us in boats bringing pies, cake and fruit to sell, and they find ready purchasers. Owing to the intoxicated state of most of the regiment we are not allowed to land. the authorities wisely thinking we are safer where we are than waiting transportation about the city.

At nine o'clock in the evening we are landed and march across the city through several of the principal streets, two miles to the Depot of the Northern Central R.R. Here we are again detained several hours awaiting the making up of trains. The soldiers catch the few undisturbed moments, some to secure a nap and many others to find whiskey in the neighboring saloons. I find a comfortable nook in the bulkhead of a block of dwelling houses where I sleep till I'm roused by the sound of tramping footsteps and discover the Brigade moving off. I barely escape being left behind but succeed in finding the car where the Co. A boys are and at two in the morning we move out of Baltimore. We are huddled into old freight cars without room enough for all to lie down at once, so take turns about, and in this manner I secure some sleep before daylight, which finds us entering Free-Pennsylvania!

March 28—The train was delayed some time in morning at York and later at Glen Rock. Early in the afternoon we came in sight of the Susquehanna [*River*] which we followed to Bridgeport. Stopping here a few minutes we have a fine view of Harrisburg across the river with its towering dome of the capitol building. After leaving here we approach and enter a very mountainous country. Nearly every mile shows us the activity of the mining region, little wooden railways run from some distant hole in the mountains to the main railway. Sometimes they are only a few rods long however, running up a steep inclined plain in some overhanging cliff and on these are numerous trucks laden with coal trundling down to be transported to every part of the Union. The day has been cold and stormy and our old rickety car leaks badly, so the sights which would otherwise interest us exceedingly are often forgotten in our efforts to keep dry. toward night we enter the enterprising town of Mifflin up in the mountains. We remain here till dark and then begin to ascent the Allegheny Mts. As darkness shuts out all sights of interest and our weary bones are aching from the continued jostle of our cars we try the mathematical puzzle of having different bodies occupy the same space at the same time. In this process, human natures (which are the same everywhere) rebel and discordant music from unruly tongues lull me to sleep.

March 29—After a night of broken rest daylight opens to us the approaching scenes of Pittsburgh. At nine o'clock we leave the cars and march into the City Hall where we are feasted by the bounteous hospitality of patriotic gentlemen and ladies. Toasts were given and responded to by Gen. Ferrero, Col. Clark and Dr. McCook. After "three time three and a hearty tiger," we march back to the depot where, in spite of the guards, the regiments were thinned out with surprising rapidity, each man taking himself out of the way and before night as they began to scatter back, each one appeared to have found and taken himself a raging devil. I never saw a large body of men who were so completely intoxicated as was our regiment when they marched or rather staggered through the streets to the depot of the Columbus R.R. I presume that as many as nine tenths of the regiment were more or less under the influence of liquor and a majority of the remaining tenth had all they could do to help the drunken pack to the cars. The disgraceful scene did not end here. [*In 1890 Hitchcock included officers in the drunken pack.*]

March 30—Our train with its drunken freight went speeding out of the mountainous region of Pennsylvania into the broad prairies of Ohio, riding all night. The daylight found us near Coshocton. The weather had cleared off finely, and many of us changed our close-quarters to the tops of the cars where the clear air and swiftly moving panorama made a desirable change. My time was occupied during the forenoon in keeping a drunken fool of Co. C from rolling off the car. After leaving the town of Newark someone unshackled two or three rear cars while the forward part went on and left them. As soon as it was discovered at the engine, we were backed until the connection was made, when it was found that it was part of a plan by which a number of reckless intoxicated ones, who had broken into and robber a liquor store of a barrel of whiskey, had succeeded in concealing it on board the disconnected cars. When we reached Columbus in the afternoon we were met by generous friends who brought us lunch of sandwiches and boiled eggs. In return for the attention, the raging, drunken fellows made a fuss with the Provost Guard whose orders were "not to allow our men to leave the depot and train." the difficulty became serious when a large crowd of our men attacked the Guard with clubs and brick-bats knocking down and severely wounding one or two. The whole Company of Provost were then turned out who were ordered to load and fire a round of blank cartridges into the crowd, hoping in this way to avoid bloodshed. This served only to madden the rioters the more, when a round of ball was put into the crowd which killed one and wounded several. Large numbers then rushed to the cars to secure their arms. In the car where I was there was fighting and struggling by men endeavoring to keep them in the car. In the midst of all this disgraceful scene Col. Clark jumped on board the engine and ordered the engineer to move along. So away we went leaving a large number of our boys who, we afterwards learned were <u>properly</u> cared for.

We stop at dusk for a few minutes at London and another night shuts us in. A majority of the men are already sleeping off their potations and the inventive mind of those who have not succeeded in finding room to lie down brings into use the sailor's hammock, which we construct out of our shelters, tying up each end and fasten them swinging to the top of the cars. By ten o'clock our car is filled with them, and the ludicrous scenes which ensue—"First one, then another" of the insecure fastenings give way and the occupants unceremoniously go down, some head-first, others feet-first astride an unlucky sleeper beneath.

* * * *

Newspaper Reports on the Incident at the Railroad Depot on March 30, 1863 in Columbus, Ohio:

1. Daily Ohio State Journal, *Columbus, Ohio, March 31, 1863—"An Unfortunate Affair: Riotous Proceedings, Soldiers Attack the Provost Guard. They are fired upon with serious and fatal results. We regret to be called upon to announce the occurrence of a serious affray in our streets yesterday that led to fatal results to some of the parties concerned. During the afternoon, three immense trains of cars, having on board a large portion of a brigade of troops appertaining to Gen. Burnside's command, en route for Kentucky, arrived at our depot. In view of preventing straggling, a small force of the Provost Guard was stationed near the depot. After the trains had stopped, a considerable number of soldiers left the cars and were making their way up into the city. As they emerged from the depot they were halted by the guard; to which the soldiers (being somewhat heated with drink) offered some slight resistance and much abuse. They were, however, turned back by the guard and quietly forced to return to the depot. There the soldiers heaped upon the guard the most vile abuse. The soldiers being reinforced by a large number of their comrades from the cars began to make demonstrations of violence, hurling stones, sticks, and mud at the guard. The soldiers were without arms; but being so greatly superior in numbers, and had become so violent in their demonstrations that Captain Skyles, commander of the guard, sent a reinforcement of some 25 men to their support, and also ordered a much larger detachment to move within supporting distance. Excited by drink and irritated by the firmness of the guard, the soldiers made a rush upon them, striking, beating, and maltreating the guard in a brutal manner. Lieut. Sullivan, of the guard, who had twice thrown up the pistol of one of the guard who threatened to fire, was struck and seized by several of the soldiers, who threw him, and were beating him when one of the guard struck the men upon the Lieutenant with the butt of his musket. This released the Lieutenant, and the soldiers thereupon made a rush for the alley east of High Street, with the view of flanking the guard. But they found a force of the guard posted there also. But now grown desperate, and being still further reinforced by several hundreds of their comrades, they made a rush upon the guard, who, thus overwhelmed by numbers, were forced back before the pressure. At this juncture the order was given to "fire." The guard at this opened fire, but firing almost entirely over the heads of the mob, for such now the soldiers had become. Sergeant Clough, however, cooler than the others, drew his revolver, and ordered the soldiers to fall back. They paid no heed to the order, but were rushing upon him, when he fired three successive shots, and every shot brought its man. Others of the guard now began to apply the bayonet and one of the soldiers received a severe bayonet thrust. Intimidated by the firmness of Sergeant Clough, who stood there like a hero, with determination stamped on every line of his countenance, the soldiers halted in their mad career.*

"At this moment orders came from Captain Skyles, commander of the guard, to cease firing. At the same time officers began to arrive from the depot and ordered the soldiers to the cars, which were then, at the suggestion of Captain Skyles, about to start from the depot. The soldiers, seeing that matters were becoming decidedly serious for them, soon after returned to the cars and were immediately carried off by the moving trains. One of the soldiers was taken up as dead. Two others remain, severely wounded. They were sent to the hospital and everything was done for them that possibly could be. Two of them are mortally wounded; the third will probably recover.

"The whole matter was a sudden and impulsive outbreak, incited by bad liquor with which the soldiers had been supplied from some source unknown to their officers, who did all that was possible to quell the disturbance; which occurred so suddenly that no means could have been taken to prevent it.

"Too much praise cannot be awarded to Capt. Skyles, the commander of the guard, for his prompt and consistent course in the premises. While the order to fire was not inopportune, the order to cease firing, given by Capt. Skyles, was most discreet and timely; for had it been continued, it would doubtless have brought out the whole force of the solders, with their arms, and the results must have been most serious and lamentable.

"The whole conduct of the guard was highly commendable. They calmly encountered the abuse and insult, and even observed order when assailed by missiles from the hands of the soldiers; and only fired when ordered, at the last extremity, to do so. One of the guard was severely hurt by a stone thrown at him, and several were struck by blows from the fists of their assailants. Sergeant Clough's coolness and intrepidity in the face of the mob were admirable.

"The whole affair was a most unfortunate one. The soldiers were spoken of by their officers as excellent men, orderly and well disposed. The mischief lay in the fact that liquor had been smuggled into the cars and the soldiers had unduly partaken of the mischief working spirit of rum. We are glad to learn the Captain Skyles has closed the rum shops of the city for the present, in order that no more mischief of like kind may be manufactured within."

2. Daily Ohio Statesman, *Columbus, Ohio, March 31, 1863*—"*Unfortunate Military Conflict; Three Men Shot.* An unfortunate affair occurred at the depot yesterday afternoon. Freight cars, conveying some twelve or fifteen hundred Massachusetts and Pennsylvania infantry and a battery, part of Gen. Burnside's old army corps, arrived from the East and stopped for a short time at the depot. As some of these soldiers manifested a disposition to straggle off into the city, a small detachment of the Provost Guard stationed here was posted across High Street, near the depot, to prevent this.

"A small party of the soldiers excited by liquor and partly perhaps from some other cause, attempted to break through the guard and make their way into the city. Finding themselves opposed, they attacked the guard with clubs and stones, and drove them back. The mob soon swelled to a hundred and fifty unarmed soldiers, who made use of such missiles as they could pick up in the street. The guard was reinforced by detachments sent up from Captain Skye's headquarters on West Broad Street.

"A most determined attempt to break through the guard was made in the alley east of High Street. Missiles were thrown, which struck and slightly wounded several of the Provost guard. The latter fired several shots at their assailants, wounding three of them, one of whom was said to be mortally wounded, but at the last accounts we heard of him, he was still living.

"The soldiers, with the exception of the wounded and a very few stragglers, were soon placed on board the cars, which started off on their way to Cincinnati."

3. Columbus Gazette *(published weekly), Columbus, Ohio, April 3, 1863*—"'Riot.' On Monday afternoon, while a portion of the troops of the Ninth Army Corps, en route from the East to the West, were halting at the Depot, receiving the edibles provided by the citizens of Columbus, some of their number who had managed somehow to get some whisky, attempted to pass or break through the guard place at the different streets, and finding that they could not do it, commenced using insulting and obscene language, and finally threw stones, billets of wood, etc., at them, whereupon the guard, having borne the insults with patience thus far, and patience ceasing to be a virtue, fired blank cartridges at them, which failed to produce any good results, and the storm of boulders and wood growing thicker and thicker, the guard fired but not with blank cartridges, for one of the insurgents fell mortally, while others were severely wounded. This settled the matter, the crowd dispersed, and the soldiers returned to the train which immediately moved off. The Colonel of the regiment justified the proceeding, and remained to attend to the wants of the wounded. We hear it rumored that one of the soldiers has since died, and that another is in a precarious condition.

"Whisky was the cause of the difficulty, but how it was obtained is a mystery, as it could not be had at the saloons near the depot. Just so long as our soldiers are allowed the use of liquor, or others are allowed to sell it to them, just so long will the community be afflicted with such discreditable affairs as that of Monday last. And it is not confined merely to the private or common soldiers. Night after night, soldiers who wear straps on their shoulders, embellished with the different insignias of their positions, have been seen in our saloons, making night hideous with their demoniac yells; but in the daytime they are brushed and primped up, looking for all the world as if they had just emanated from a bandbox. And our people welcome them into society. Bah! Is the officer better than the Private? We can't see it."

4. "The Crisis, *published in Columbus Ohio on April 1, 1863*—As several regiments of Eastern soldiers, mostly from Pennsylvania and Massachusetts, were

stopping at the depot in this city, on Monday, on their way West; a number of the soldiers, as they had plenty of time, concluded to visit the city, without orders. Our Provost Guard forbid their leaving the railroad station and a fight ensued and several of the soldiers were badly wounded. Unfortunately and deeply to be regretted as this affair is, no blame can be attached to the Provost Guard, as they only performed the duty required of them. Where were the officers of these regiments? They are to blame, for not being present. The Provost Guard deserves great credit for their forbearance under the trying circumstances."

[Charles F. Walcott, who was a captain in the 21st Massachusetts Regiment and present at Columbus, stated in his book, History of the Twenty-First Regiment of Massachusetts Volunteers, *in 1882 that the incident at Columbus was "a murderous attack upon our men, and this inhuman outrage might have provoked a fearful revenge, if the officers of the brigade had not exerted themselves to the utmost to calm the excitement of the men, and keeping them from their guns forced them on board the cars and hurried them out of town."*]

* * * *

March 31—Daylight cloudy. At three, entered the city of Cincinnati. Marched up to Fifth St. Market House and found breakfast ready for us, after which march down toward the river, halt a few moments in front of Burnett House where General Burnside comes out on the balcony and addresses the troops with a few fitting words of welcome and praise. We then cross the river on ferry-boats, march through Covington to the depot of Kentucky Central R.R. At night we go on and again bring our hammocks into use. During the night we reach Paris where our experience on these cars is finished for the present.

7

Spring and Summer in Eastern Kentucky

> "They are a very rough and ragged looking set but nearly all look wide awake, daring and determined."
> —Hitchcock, June 18, 1863

General Burnside assigned the troops of the IX Corps to various locations in Kentucky, including Lexington, Paris, Mount Sterling, Big Hill, Hustonville, Somerset, Liberty, Glasgow, Louisa, Tompkinsville, Lebanon, Hickman's Bridge, Monticello, Winchester, Middleburg, Lancaster, and Frankfort. The Daily Ohio State Journal, *published in Columbus reported on March 31, 1863, that the IX Army Corps had been "quietly transported by regiments, without attracting particular attention, by different lines, to their destination." The newspaper also reported that "with these troops in Kentucky all apprehensions of an invasion of that State may be set at rest." The 14th Kentucky Cavalry, about 300 men, together with the 21st Massachusetts Regiment, about 400 men, were stationed at Mount Sterling, a small and friendly village with a population of 754 according to the 1860 census. During the Civil War, Union and Confederate forces took turns occupying Mount Sterling.*

Slavery was a delicate issue in Kentucky. Slaves, residing in the areas of Kentucky occupied by Union troops, were not included in Lincoln's Emancipation Proclamation, and the Union army was forbidden to interfere with any civil process in the state of Kentucky. Although all freed slaves were entitled to their freedom, Union soldiers were not allowed to aid or to abet the escape of slaves.

While the IX Corps troops offered at least the assurance of security to the harassed citizens of Kentucky, the New England soldiers were not cordially welcomed. There was a strong prejudice against "Massachusetts Yankees," including the 21st Massachusetts Regiment, that resulted in concealed displeasure and even open insults. These "abolitionists" were simply not wanted in the Kentucky com-

munities. These prejudices ameliorated when a regiment was garrisoned within a town. The Union soldiers changed the popular attitudes by their discipline, intelligence, general good conduct and the gentlemanly demeanor of their officers.

Augustus Woodbury, writing in 1867, identified the 21st Massachusetts Regiment as one noteworthy example:

> It was sent down to Mount Sterling, on the 5th of April, to hold the place and, with other troops, to secure the neighborhood against the occurrence of rebel raids, to which that section was peculiarly open. The regiment was very coldly received. It remained at this post for three months, and during that brief period, coldness was changed to cordiality, contempt to unwonted esteem, aversion to hospitality and kindness. When the regiment was to be ordered away, the inhabitants of the town actually petitioned the commanding general to allow the troops to remain for their protection. Two loyal cavalry regiments raised in the vicinity had been stationed near the town, and were still to hold the position. But the citizens were even more ready to trust themselves to the care of the Yankees than to the keeping of their own neighbors.

George Hitchcock personified the "Massachusetts-Yankee" soldier who impressed the people living in Mount Sterling, and this is the essence of his journal while posted in Eastern Kentucky.

* * * *

April 1, 1863—In the morning we marched through the village with flying colors, and camp on the Fair-grounds, a mile from town. After we had fairly pitched our tents, Co. A was detached from the reg't and sent into town to guard Col. Clark's Headquarters, a large, solid old house, the former residence of an ex-governor. There are several churches, three hotels and stores in abundance about the place. Attended a prayer meeting in neighboring chapel in the evening.

April 2—I was on guard at the stables last night. We have received orders to march tomorrow morning with three days' rations. Attend a Methodist prayer meeting again tonight. Suffered from teeth-ache.

April 3—Roused at five, and find the day pleasant. Packed up and fell in with the regiment as they came along. March out of town eastward, on a pike leading past the residence of Congressman Garrett Davis, as rear guard to a wagon train. Teams and horses were pressed into our service from the farmers to carry our knapsacks and luggage. After a weary march of twenty-one miles passing through only one small village of Middletown, we go into camp near a pleasant grove at dark, worn out and nearly every man of us foot-sore.

[*Garret Davis, a congressman from Kentucky, was elected to the United States Senate in 1861 to fill the vacancy caused by the expulsion of John C. Breckinridge. In 1856, he was nominated for president by the Know-Nothing Party.*

7. Spring and Summer in Eastern Kentucky   83

When most Kentuckians were undecided in their course of action in the Civil War, Davis came out for unswerving and complete adherence to the Union.]

April 4—Slept but little during the night on account of the cold. Our Brigade packed up and marched three miles through the village of Mt. Sterling and pitched camp two miles from the village on the Ticktown pike. A rebel guerrilla band had a running fight with our cavalry along here last week. I was on camp guard today. [*In 1890 Hitchcock added: "The result has been a very unsettled state of affairs throughout this thinly settled portion of the state."*]

April 5—Very pleasant and spring-like. Sunday—I have been washing clothes and cleaning streets!! Will these occupations come under the head of "If any of you have an ox or an ass that fall into the pit on the Sabbath-day? Inspection at half past ten. Two of the 10th Kentucky who came in from the mountains and report a rebel force in the vicinity.

April 6—Gen. Ferrero arrived here from Lexington where he has been Acting Division Commander. He has assumed command of the Brigade again. Several orders restricting the soldiers liberty were read at dress parade. Great caution is taken to guard against surprise from guerrilla bands which infest the country.

April 7—I was on guard near the residence of Col. Cluke of the Union Army, who was murdered by the rebels when they passed through here.

April 8—Col. Hawkes rejoined the regiment from Massachusetts. He brought me a bundle from home. Maj. Richardson drilled the regiment in the Manual today. Orders were issued instituting regular camp duties.

April 9—Spring-like, birds singing. Squad drill in the manual. Rations becoming scarce. Hard tack almost gone.

April 10—I am on picket with a half dozen others of the Jefferson Road a mile out from camp. The entire Army of the Union is to be mustered in today. Half-rations were dealt out to the reg't. The supply trains are eagerly looked for tonight.

April 11—Smoky and warm. The expected trains did not arrive till night so we starved through the day. Many of the boys have been off to the neighboring farm-houses foraging for food. A citizen who came in today reports that five Union men were carried away by guerrillas day before yesterday, eighteen miles out.

April 12—Sunday. Inspection of guns and knapsacks at nine o'clock. A squad of men went down town to church carrying arms, it being considered more prudent for them where the country is so full of guerrilla bands. The camp has been swarmed with negro slaves, women and children mostly, peddling pies and cakes, Sunday being a sort of holiday for them.

April 13—Two guerrilla spies were found and arrested in a barn not far off by a squad of the 35th Mass. Their place of concealment was exposed by a negro slave belonging on the premises. Gen. Ferrero was present at Dress Parade with lady (?), music by the 11th N.H. Band.

April 14—After sleeping soundly a few hours we were roused up at midnight and ordered to pack up in light marching order. Started off at one a.m. with 51st N.Y. for Sharpsburg 13 miles away. Marched swiftly along through the darkness halting a few moments for rest occasionally, at which times sleep would overcome most everyone, making it lively work for the officers to rouse us at each start. As the light began to dawn in the east we approached the town and the object of our visit became apparent. Quietly and quickly half the troops were drawn off to the right and left, each detachment making a half detour of the place and formed an unbroken skirmish circle around the town. As soon as the circle was complete, the remaining half of the force marched into the village. The town was taken completely by surprise and no one escaped. As we marched through the main street, people look out with wonder-eyes on the apparition of an army rained down. We were invited to breakfast—by ourselves—with the rebellious inhabitants, squads of men under an officer being sent around to different houses. At some places, the snapping, fiery rebel women proposed to doubt the propriety of this summary self invitation by forcible acts. Having never had the experience of a large hostile army invading and desolating their homes and property, as has been the case in many and most places in the border states, their looks of amazement and disgust could easily be accounted for as the men politely went from garret [*attic*] to cellar and appropriated whatever delicacy could be obtained. Those places where we met with civility a request was made for food to the amount desired which could be spared. John Wallace and a squad of Co. A under Lieut. Lawrence were sent out to surround a house and search it for a hidden rebel but we found the bird had flown.

During the morning about a dozen rebels were found and taken under guard and the remainder of the day was spent in arraigning and examining prominent citizens suspected of complicity of this model backwoods Jefferson Davis-worshipping place. Also visited the townhouse-college-academy-meeting house—whatnot where we remained during a hard shower till about half past five p.m. when we escort our rebel delegation out of town and march them back to Mt. Sterling, lodge them in a county jail and arrive in camp at ten in the night very tired and foot-sore.

April 15—In the morning went on guard with Lieut. Henry Hitchcock commander. The paymaster is here paying off the Brigade. Learned by home-letters of the death of Lyman Holt and Martin Gilson in Louisiana.

April 16—Our regiment signed the payrolls today. Gen. Ferrero's farewell address was read at Dress Parade, the command of the Brigade now devolving on Col. Hartranft of the 51st P.V. rec'd orders at night to march immediately to Winchester fifteen miles distant. [*In 1890 Hitchcock added: "Ferrero was a dashing officer of rather small stature whose appearance reminded me of pictures I had seen of Bonaparte. We were always proud of him as a show commander for his fine military appearance but his habits of dissipation and immorality were such that he could not command the respect which an officer of his rank ought to have."*]

April 17—Very warm finds us still in our Mr. Sterling camp but the remainder of the Brigade left during the night. The 21st marched into the village and we learn we are left to guard the place, and the 9tsh Army Corps has been scattered about Kentucky to guard important places. We occupy the Court House which stands in the center and on an eminence overlooking the town. Four companies occupy the lower floor and six companies the upper. The line-officers have tents pitched on the green surrounding the court house. The regiment was paid off, after which I was detailed with six others in charge of Lieut. H.S.H. to go out and picket the Paris-pike a mile from town. The regiment is required to throw out pickets on all the roads leading out of town of which there are the "Paris-pike," "Winchester-pike," "Lulebegruel dirt-road," "Ticktown-pike," "Sharpsburg-pike," "Owingsville-pike," "Maysville-pike," "Hinkston-pike." The day is beautiful and our post is in the shed adjoining the Toll-House. Our duties are light during the day, simply to demand a written pass from everyone going <u>out</u> of town. And in the night two men are placed, one a few rods out beyond the Toll-House, the other a quarter of a mile away at the gate opening to a private road which guerrilla bands have several times succeeded in passing into town. We have to demand the countersign from everybody we see or hear, and in case of refusal powder and ball are to be given. We stand our silent night-watch with wide-open-eyes straining out into the darkness, for the creeping-crafty treacherous bushwhackers have within a few days, laid more than one man outs in cold blood on these very picket posts but I was not disturbed during the night.

April 18—We were relieved at half past ten. Cincinnati papers inform us that Gen. Cox takes the Dept. of the Ohio and Gen. Burnside takes the field. There is considerable drunkenness in quarters tonight.

[*Major General Jacob Dolson Cox, who on the death of General Reno led the IX Corps during the Battle of Antietam, assumed command of the District of Ohio and the Third Division of the XXIII Corps (Ohio) on April 16, 1863. He was Governor of Ohio in 1866–67.*]

April 19—I am on picket on the Ticktown pike near our old camp-grounds in charge of Lieut. McKabe of Co. B. A rebel bushwhacker who murdered a Union citizen a few miles out was brought in by us during the day. When we are off duty we have opportunity to out to the neighboring farm-houses for milk, eggs, poultry and when we can we get the negro women to bake biscuits for us; and as the weather is beautiful we are unanimously of the opinion that this is really "parlor soldiering."

April 20—The Brigade Band left us today. District or County Court is in session under our quarters. Lieut. Parker returned to Co. A and Lieut. Valentine of Co. F has returned from Washington.

April 21—The Provost Guard are very strict, arresting every man caught outside the court-yard without a pass. Many are confined in the jail (which is used as our guard-house) for drunkenness. Henry has been assigned to Co. K till further orders.

April 22—I am on picket on the Winchester pike in charge of Sergeant Gethings of Co. K. A spy came by our post into town and we were notified to be on the watch for his return but he went out across the fields, behind the hills and escaped. A squad of cavalry was sent out to catch him.

April 23—And succeeded for in the morning the spy went out by us again in irons with the dozen fellows brought from Sharpsburg some time ago. They were all under a sufficient guard en route for Cincinnati. Today has been one of changes. Col. Clark returned from Cincinnati with his resignation accepted.

April 24—His farewell address was read at Dress Parade and he returns home. In him we lose out most efficient, our finest-looking and most highly cultured officer. Col. Hawkes assumes command of the Post and Capt. Clark takes the regiment. All but two of the Captains have resigned, also several Lieutenants. [*In 1890 Hitchcock added: "It is rumored that they received hints that they were not wanted longer on account of their complicity with the rioters in Columbus, Ohio. They were certainly not in harmony with the present commander on the temperance question. This action on their part was wise, if not patriotic."*] Company A takes possession of one of the jury rooms, a high light airy room shut out from the rest of the regiment. Received papers from home.

April 25—I am on picket under Sergeant Koster of Co. H on the Winchester pike. A squad of our men were sent out on the Sharpsburg road to hunt for some rebels concealed about there but returned unsuccessful.

April 26—Sunday. Attended Episcopal Church in the p.m. Captain Saunderson, Hill, Wheeler, Walcott and Aldrich have been honorably discharged. Capt. Saunderson came in and bade us good bye tonight and starts for Lexington tomorrow morning at four.

[*Three of the discharged captains received commissions at a later date: Charles F. Walcott, colonel of the 61st Massachusetts Regiment; William T. Harlow, major in the 57th Massachusetts Regiment; and Asahel Wheeler, captain in the 61st Massachusetts Regiment.*]

April 27—A deserter of the 14th Kentucky, who was caught burning the house of a Union man and stealing a negro was brought in to jail. The 14th

Kentucky was raised from this vicinity and are a wild, reckless, unsoldierly set of men stationed a mile from town good for nothing but to bushwhack their hated neighbors. Adjutant has been put under arrest for drunkenness.

April 28—I am on picket on the Lulebegruel road under Corporal Humiston Co. I. As this is an unimportant road, only three men and a corporal are stationed here, which today are Lem Whitney, Jack Reynolds, the corporal and myself. During the night a shot was fired nearby rousing every one of us, but on investigation it proved to be a negro shooting his dog for killing sheep, and we return to our post relieved.

April 29—Citizens came in from Sharpsburg this forenoon bringing the news that a force of rebels entered that place and drove out Union men. After much excitement on the street among citizens and soldiers, Major Williams of the 10th Ky. Cavalry started off with four hundred horse-men to change the tune. The force was made up entirely of citizens as the regular cavalry were off scouting.

April 30—I was roused up in the night and with nine others under Lieut. Howe went out scouting in a suspicious locality a few miles from town but returned at daylight without finding anything to reward us. Two Union families came in from the mountains driven out by the rebels, in a state of great destitution. We have received orders to march to Columbia 150 miles south in the wilderness of America. We are to start tomorrow.

May 1, 1863—The marching orders were countermanded, through the exertions of the citizens who hastened a petition to Gen. Burnside urging the need and importance of our stay here. I am on picket on the Ticktown pike under Sergeant May, Co. D. Many of the boys are on a high spree tonight over milk-punch, egg-nog and the "undiluted" large numbers have been put into the guard-house.

May 2—News was brought in that our cavalry had met and were fighting fifty rebels, seven miles out and reinforcements were sent to them.

May 3—The cavalry returned this morning. I am on picket on the Ticktown pike under Sergeant Curtis, Company E. The regiment rec'd orders to be ready to march at nine o'clock tomorrow morning so we came in from picket at dark.

May 4—The marching orders were again countermanded. The 10th Kentucky Cavalry passed through town for Owingsville with two mountain howitzers. A rebel spy and a female mail-carrier were found

May 5—Two howitzers, belonging to the 10th Kentucky, passed through town today. The criminal court commenced session today in the Presbyterian Church.

May 6—I am on guard in the rear of the Court House. News from Hooker's says that he has captured five thousand prisoners and gained possession of Fredericksburg.

May 7—Today brings news that Sedgwick has fallen back from Fredericksburg Heights and the enemy again hold them.

May 8—Today brings news that Hooker has recrossed the Rappahannock and that the slaughter on both sides has been terrible. I went down town on a pass.

[*Battle of Chancellorsville on May 1 to 4, 1863, was General Robert E. Lee's greatest military victory but came at great costs—"Stonewall" Jackson was mortally wounded and could never be replaced and the Confederates suffered irreplaceable casualties (12,821 killed, wounded and missing that was 22 percent of the Army of Northern Virginia. The Union's casualties were 17,278—13 percent of the Army of the Potomac).*]

May 9—I am on picket on the Maysville pike under Sergeant Miller of Co. E. Hooker has again returned to his old Falmouth Camp-grounds. Gen. Stoneman made a circuit of the rebel army and joined Gen. Dix's forces two miles from Richmond.

May 10—Sunday. Attended Episcopal Church in the afternoon and the Methodist in the evening. Some of our good singers of the 21st assisted the parson's pretty daughters in the musical branch of the service.

May 11—I went out on a pass and visited the MacPhelah Cemetery, half a mile north of the village. It is situated on a high hill overlooking the place from which we have a fine view, not only of the town, but of a large stretch of beautiful farms and farm-houses. This borders on the region known as "the Blue Grass Region," and is consequently very fine fertile country. John Wallace has been appointed sergeant and returned from the provost for duty in the company. Although the reported capture of Richmond is not credited, the citizens have been celebrating the supposed victory by firing sky-rockets.

May 12—I am on picket on the Paris pike under Corporal Dyer of Co. K. Col. Hawkes visited the post during the afternoon.

May 13—News of the death of Stonewall Jackson and Van Dorn, in the late fighting in Virginia. [*During the early evening on May 2, 1863, after his masterpiece at Chancellorsville, Jackson was accidentally mortally wounded by his own men and died eight days later. Major General Earl Van Dorn was murdered at his headquarters in Spring Hill, Tennessee, on May 8, 1863, by a resident of the neighborhood, Dr. Peters, who stated that Van Dorn had "violated the sanctity of his home."*]

May 14—Col. Hawkes has gone to Lexington on official business and Maj. Williams of the 10th Kentucky is in command of the post.

May 15—I am on picket on the Paris pike under Sergt. Sperry of Co. C. Lieut. Hayward has been dishonorably discharged from the army for drunkenness and left for Massachusetts.

May 16—Lieut. Fuller, Quartermaster, started for home on a fifteen days furlough. Col. Hawkes returned from Lexington. Discharged pieces today.

7. Spring and Summer in Eastern Kentucky 89

May 17—Attended inspection at eight, church in the forenoon, dinner at noon, church in afternoon. Dress Parade at five when Rev. Mr. Tompkins addressed the Reg't and church in the evening.

May 18—I am on picket on the Owingsville pike under Sergeant Cummings of Co. D. Several rebel soldiers and two officers were brought in past us under guard.

May 19—I have been calling on Henry who has command of the Provost Guard, a detail of fifty men from our regiment. They have to guard the county jail and various public buildings principal to keep order through the town and prevent soldiers from disturbing the peace. Their Quarters are in the same building with the posts-headquarters on Main St. News that Vallandigham has been sentenced to imprisonment on Fort Warren during the war.

[*Clement Laird Vallandigham, a prominent "copperhead," was a controversial Democratic congressman from Ohio who symbolized "peace at any price" opposition to President Lincoln. In 1863, he denounced the government for refusing to end the war by mediation. He was tried by a military tribunal and banished within the military lines of the Confederacy in May 1863. Vallandigham's comment that "he did not want to belong to the United States" prompted Edward Everett Hale to write "The Man Without a Country", which appeared in the Atlantic Magazine in December 1863. This fictitious story stimulated patriotism more than any other wartime writing.*]

May 20—Had a pass and went outside of town, bathing. A number of hospital bummers returned to the regiment from Lexington. Our Brigade is at Lancaster seventy miles south of here.

May 21—I am on picket on the Ticktown pike under Lieut. Goodrich of Co. D. A citizen came in and reported the rebels in force about forty miles from here.

May 22—Very sultry and warm. Spent time reading.

May 23—"Ernest Linwood." [*1856 novel by Caroline Lee Hentz*] Attended a singing meeting at the Episcopal Church: Rev. Mr. Tompkins' daughter playing the organ, Officer Hawkes, Davis, Hitchcock, Goss, Valentine and private Carruth male singers with a complement of female voices.

May 24—I am on picket at the Sharpsburg Toll Gate under Sergeant Wilder of Co. A. Spent most of the day in writing letters.

May 25—Received a pass and went out bathing near the house of the "swamp angel," a notorious character. Reports received that Vicksburg has been taken after a severe battle.

[*Vicksburg did not surrender until July 4, 1863, one day after the Union victory at Gettysburg. After a long Union campaign, Vicksburg was under constant shelling with a critical shortage of rations and almost fifty percent of the Confederate troops sick or wounded—General John Pemberton surrendered his garrison* to General Ulysses Grant. The capture of Vicksburg was one of the most important Union strategic victories of the war.]

May 26—Very warm and dusty. I have been down to Henry's rooms.

May 27—I am on picket on the Owingsville pike under Sergeant Wallace of Co. A. Our Drum Corps, which is composed of considerable talent, held a concert in the Court House hall.

May 28—Col. Hawkes has gone to Cincinnati. I went out on a pass tonight. The "New England Minstrels" repeated their concert to accommodate the yesterday pickets, which I attended. It consisted of comic and sentimental songs, dances, jigs and witty dialogue accompanied by an excellent orchestra of violins, guitars, flutes and bones.

May 29—Dress Parade was omitted on account of rain and I have spent the day in reading. [*In 1890 Hitchcock added:* "These occasions have become the great attraction of social life of Mount Sterling. All the elite turn out to honor us with their presence; multitudes of negroes and backwoodsmen make up a great crowd which inspires the 21st to do their best, and it seems as if they had become perfect in the manual."]

May 30—I am on picket at the Sharpsburg toll-gate under Sergeant Curtis. Col. Hawkes returned from Cincinnati. Rumors that Gen. Burnside has been relieved.

[*General Burnside was not relieved. He did resign on December 11, 1863, after the successful termination of the siege of Knoxville.*]

June 1, 1863—Regimental inspection of knapsacks and equipments this afternoon. Twelve rebel soldiers came in and gave themselves up to the 10th Kentucky Cav. Quartermaster Fuller returned from Mass. Received papers from home.

June 2—I am on picket at the Sharpsburg toll-gate under Sergeant Muzzy of Co. F. Several have gone home on fifteen day furloughs.

June 3—A Grand Match Game of Base-Ball was played outside of town on the Ticktown pike.

[*Baseball originated from a game the English called "rounders," and after considerable modification the Americans called the game "town ball." In 1845, the Knickerbocker Club of New York provided a rule book for the game; the Knicks' Louis Fenn Wadsworth has received belated credit for his innovations. However, the popularity of baseball really dates from the Civil War, during which it was played with enthusiasm by Union and Confederate soldiers. Nevertheless, Alexander Cartwright and Abner Doubleday should not be credited with inventing the game.*]

June 4—Lemuel and I received passes and went out two miles on the Lulebegruel road, had an interesting tramp, stopping at several farm houses and going in swimming. Orders were received in the evening from Gen. Hartranft for the 21st to report to Paris tomorrow, and it is reported that we are to go down to Vicksburg with the 9th Corps. Rev. Mr. Tompkins preached a sermon in the evening. [*In 1890 Hitchcock added: "He has become a great friend of the regiment; he is a staunch Union man, and being a person of great influence, it is believed that he will succeed in keeping us here."*]

June 5—Our marching orders have been countermanded during the night. I was on guard at the courthouse. A negro who had been convicted of trying to kill his master was taken from the jail this morning and after much delay, caused by difficulty in securing a guard (Henry was called upon and requested to furnish escort which he refused to do considering the trial a farce and illegal). By noon a portion of the 14th Ky Cav. escorted the convict out of town and hung him. The entire proceeding was a disgrace to a Christian country done under the name of the "law." A small drum-cord was used which broke, of course and the strangled man was kept alive till a stronger rope was procured from town after a delay of some half an hour. Although many of the regiment witnessed the scene I had not the heart to go. The paymaster has arrived with payrolls.

June 6—Twelve rebel prisoners were brought in today. Went to a Choir meeting at the Episcopal Church this evening.

June 7—Attended church in forenoon at which the Lord's Supper was administered. In the afternoon three or four of us went down to the negro church, which was not profitable to us for worship. the comical and ridiculous ceremonies and language of this semi-barbarous race which, to them make up true worship to us seem like the plays of a first-class Minstrel Troupe. The army telegraph arrived today connecting immediate communication with the rest of the world.

June 8—I am on picket on the Hinkston road under Corporal Goodness of Co. H. This is a quiet romantic road leading away through the hills to the north and we saw hardly any passing except a few Negros during the day. The regiment was paid off today. Eight prisoners were sent to Cincinnati today.

June 9—Received two months pay of $26 twenty six dollars.

[*On August 6, 1861, the United States Congress established pay of $13 per month for three years for privates in the Regular Army and Volunteers in the service of the United States. On June 20, 1864, the pay was increased to $16. Soldiers were scheduled to be paid every two months in the field, but frequently the pay was received at four-month intervals and some soldiers had to wait six for eight months between payments. In 1861, lieutenants were paid $105.50, captains $115.50, majors $169, colonels $212, and brigadier generals $315 per month.*]

June 10—We learn that the 9th Corps and a part of the 23rd have been sent to Vicksburg, and that we are to remain in Kentucky for the present, though it is feared that the drawing away of the army from Kentucky will open it to the roving guerrilla bands of East Tennessee which have constantly disturbed our outposts in the south eastern part of this state.

June 11—I am on picket on the Hinkston road again, under Corp. Barney McNulty of Co. C. The 10th Ky Cavalry passed through town from Owingsville to Lexington. Cole returned to the company from provost duty.

June 12—A grand match game of base-ball, Adjutant Parker leader of one side and Lieut. Kelt leader of the other. They play for a supper which Parker's side wins and a grand carousel they have at the Sterling House in the evening. I sat for an ambrotype [*on front cover*].

[*Ambrotype: A photograph on glass, with lights given by the silver, and shades by a dark background showing through.*]

June 13—I was on picket on the Owingsville pike under John Wallace Co. A. At noon I went into town on an errand and as I was returning to the post the startling news was brought in that the scouting party composed of a portion of the 14th Ky. Cav. had been attacked by superior force of a guerrilla band a few miles out. When I reached the pickets, there was wild excitement. Large numbers of stragglers and cowards of the 14th were galloping in bringing the most improbable and conflicting reports, that they were all cut up and the enemy was momentarily expected. Our whole picket guard of eight men was formed across the road with fixed bayonets and for a short time found pretty lively work in keeping the increasing crowd of poltroons from rushing past us into town. Our post was in a sightly place commanding a view of more than a mile of the pike beyond and the clouds of dust from the retreating cavalry as they "hove" in sight, kept us in suspense for a while thinking it might be the approaching rebels, until the 21st came hurrying out at double-quick and I confess to a feeling of pride as I saw the growing confidence and courage which the sight gave to the weak-kneed 14th stragglers. Before going out far it was ascertained that the enemy was in considerable force three miles from us and were supposed to be making a feint to draw our force from the village and then enter by some other road.

The regiment was then drawn in, and each company posted at commanding points just outside the town, where they could easily concentrate in case of a surprise at any given point. The raiding party is variously estimated, some setting the number above a thousand. Nothing was heard from them during the remainder of the day and strong pickets were thrown out in all directions at dark and the whole force lie on arms. All citizens are ordered in doors under penalty of being shot if not obeying.

June 14—The night passes away silent as death, nothing occurring to break the stillness except the barking of hundreds of dogs which may be heard miles around at the farm-houses. I was on picket two hours in the night in a corn-field from which the slightest sounds could be heard on two roads. Sunday morning finds us bivouacked four companies, in a large cherry orchard, a quarter mile from the court house. We lie on arms all day, spending time in playing cards, dominoes, reading dime novels and picking the ripe cherries. Sergeant Wallace and Lem Whitney went out with a flag of truce on the Owingsville road fifteen miles and could find no force. They found seven of the 14th Ky. murdered by the side of the road and five wounded. They make extensive inquiries at the houses in the vicinity but could not gain any information which direction the force came or went. they were told that no quarter was given. When a Ky. man was caught he was instantly shot or bayoneted. Major Williams was shot but not killed. The 10th Ky. came in from Richmond [*Kentucky*] this evening.

June 15—We remain in the orchard all day. Two field-pieces were put into position on a hill near the Hinkston road where they command three pikes leading into town. Two new mounted regiments arrived during the day, the 8th and 9th Michigan. Maysville is reported burnt by the raiders which shows the direction they have taken. Several families have been ordered to leave town within twenty-four hours for "Dixie," being implicated in assisting and giving information to the raiders. The scare is about over.

June 16—I went out on picket on the Ticktown pike under Lieut. Bean of Co. H. The regiment moved into a locust-tree grove near the Court House. The 8th and 9th Mich. and parts of the 10th and 14th Ky. have gone out to the mountains to trap guerrilla band on their return from Maysville.

June 17—I pitched my tent alone today. The rebs went right into the trap set for them and lost nearly all their horses and stolen plunder, the enemy taking themselves to the woods. But twenty-five were caught and brought into town and confined in the court-hall where I am on guard tonight. Henry has charge to them.

June 18—Twelve more prisoners were brought in today and one of them killed by a Co. K man for trespassing beyond bounds. This act makes the others very peaceable and quiet. They are a very rough and ragged looking set but nearly all look wide awake, daring and determined. Read news that Lee's army is moving into Maryland and Hooker's stores and supplies all moved from Falmouth where they have been for the past six months. This indicate an offensive move on the part of the enemy and a defensive move on our part.

June 19—The cavalry have relieved the 21st of picket duty for the present and we are detailed to work on fortification. I am on prisoners' guard tonight.

June 20—Court Martial has been held at the court house to try the Co. K man for killing the rebel prisoner but he was discharged unblamed.

June 21—Sunday morning inspection at nine. Soldiers are obliged to go to church under guard with an officer to prevent interference from provost guard. Rev. Mr. Tompkins spoke to the regiment at dress parade. He appears to be a staunch Union man and takes great interest in the regiment.

June 22—The prisoners were sent to Lexington and the New England Minstrels held another concert in the hall before a crowded house.

June 23—I was on guard at headquarters. I heard Bramlette, Governor elect, speak in the court hall in the afternoon. Another minstrel concert again tonight.

June 24—Col. Hawkes is sick. Rev. Mr. Tompkins spoke to the regiment and offered prayer at Dress Parade.

June 25—A general inspection took place today by Lieut. Col. King of the 35th Mass. who is on Gen. Sturgis' Staff.

June 26—Received news that Lee's army is on the north side of the Potomac advancing into Pennsylvania.

June 27—I went out with Cole beyond the picket post on the "Paris dirt road" to Mr. Fergerson's Farm House, where we bought butter for ten cents a pound and eggs for five cents a dozen, the regular price among the farmers. We talked politics a while and then return to camp. Henry was tried for a furlough and been refused as no more furloughs are to be granted.

June 28—Attended Episcopal Church in the morning and Presbyterian in the evening. Also heard preaching in the court house.

June 29—Heavy thundershower. Lee's army is moving on Harrisburg, having occupied Carlisle, York, Chambersburg and other important places. This is turning the tables on us with a vengeance.

June 30—Regular monthly inspection and muster in under command of Capt. Davis. A Lieutenant of the 14th Ky. who was wounded in the late fight and belonged to town, died and was buried this afternoon. The 21st escorted the body to the grave and fired a salute over is grave; a large number of young ladies in white scattered flowers over is grave.

July 1, 1863—Nine men from the 21st were detailed for picket. John Wallace was detailed for provost duty.

July 2—The regiment drilled one hour in the manual. A guerrilla band destroyed a train of cars between Frankfurt and Louisville last night.

July 3—John Morgan is advancing with a large force into the state from over the mountains. Received news of fighting in Pennsylvania.

[*John Hunt Morgan was a Confederate general and cavalry raider. Morgan's Raiders, officially organized as the 2nd Kentucky Cavalry and calling themselves the "Alligator Horses," attained legendary fame raiding, skirmishing and fighting battles in ten states—especially in Kentucky and Tennessee. Morgan was captured near New Lisbon, Ohio, on July 26, 1863, but escaped from the Ohio State Penitentiary on November 26, 1863. He was killed at Greenville, Tennessee by Federal troops on September 4, 1864.*]

July 4—The citizens of Mt. Sterling held a picnic on the Maysville pike in honor of the "Glorious Fourth." Henry has gone to Sharpsburg to spend the Sabbath.

July 5—I was on guard at headquarters. Flying rumor about Morgan during the day and at seven in the evening orders arrived for the regiment to make all haste and march to Lexington to which place Morgan appears to be heading for. After great hurry and excitement in which many of the citizens join, we get started a little past midnight saying good-bye to large numbers of citizens whose interest in the regiment kept them up till this late hour. Great fears are expressed for Mt. Sterling as the people have taken a very avowed stand for the Union and they are now left exposed to the tender mercies of all the wild rebel hordes occupying the mountains of Eastern Kentucky.

July 6—With the usual slim judgment of our leader the regiment, which has become tender and unfit for campaigning after a few months of quiet and ease, is started off at a very quick step, almost double-quick, for its march of thirty-six miles. Presuming he has never attended horse-racing or any other human race, we give him proper credit, feeling that simply common sense would teach anything but a grown-up baby that the best way to get over the road in good condition would be to begin "easy" and work into a livelier step afterward. We hurry on in this manner about three miles without a single stop. When many of the men show signs of giving up, the leader consents for a few moments to halt and away goes knapsack and overcoat. If I'm to die like a mule I prefer to dispense with all unnecessary trappings. We continue our tramp through the night and at sunrise reach Winchester where the regiment is halted a few hours for rest. Starting off again at almost a double-quick we become convinced that the horse which carries the leader must have been wound up too tight or else have forgotten that he is the honored leader of a pack of mules which are unable to keep pace with him. Before the middle of the afternoon several large blisters came out on my feet, so barefooted I trudge on alone a few miles further until I give out entirely and am picked up by a baggage wagon and carried into Lexington reaching there at midnight.

July 7—All the detailed men are returned to the company and we pitch camp by the side of the Lexington and Danville R.R. right under the guns of Fort Clay, a strong fortification commanding the railroad approaches to the city as well as the main pike from Danville. Barricades have been erected on all the roads leading southward from the city. We are in sight of the great Henry Clay monument. The colossal statue on top can be seen for miles around. The 48th Pennsylvania Reg't of the 1st Division 9th Corps comprises the only troops which are in the city.

July 8—Received news of the Surrender of Vicksburg and at noon the heavy guns of Fort Clay sent out their stunning salute of thirty guns over our heads to celebrate the event. Morgan has passed by us toward Louisville and is supposed to be aiming for the free states on a daring raid to secure horses and other plunder, knowing the scarcity of troops in this state. Lee has been repulsed in Pennsylvania [*Gettysburg*] after heavy fighting and is retreating into Virginia.

July 9—Adjutant Parker arrived from Mr. Sterling and Henry has returned from provost duty to Co. I. There was a picket detail from our regiment tonight. Lee has been blocked in Maryland and is preparing to give battle on the old Antietam ground. [*false information*]

July 10—I am on camp guard. Lieut. Valentine arrived from Massachusetts. Morgan has crossed the Ohio into Indiana and advancing into the interior.

July 11—Received a pass and went into the city and out to Henry Clay's monument. Henry is officer of guard today.

[*The Henry Clay Monument is located in the center of the Lexington Cemetery. This magnificent monument to Kentucky's famous senator and three time presidential candidate was erected in 1857 after Clay's death in June 1852. The monument was built using native limestone and consists of a 120-foot-tall Corinthian column surmounted by a statue of Clay. Henry Clay was best known for his attempts to secure a compromise between the states on the issue of slavery.*]

July 12—Sunday. I am on camp guard today. There has been a blind violinist in camp making fun for the boys. The 12th R.I. nine months regiment passed by on cars en route for home. Inspection this morning. Col. DeCourcy was here today.

July 13—I went into the city on a pass. A battery passed through town to Cincinnati.

July 14—News of the Great Anti-Draft Riot in New York in which many persons have already been killed. [*In 1890 Hitchcock added: "Foes without and foes within.' This is a big job we have on our hands but we must spit on our hands and take a new 'bolt.'"*]

July 15—News of the capture by our troops of Morris Island and fighting in Charleston. Lee has crossed into Virginia.

July 16—Left our old camp-ground and moved over a mile into the old Convalescent Camp Ground back of the Cemetery and near the Frankfort pike half a mile from the city and in sight of it. Our camp is a beautiful grove of lofty maples and whitewood, near the residence of the owner Mr. Lee. His place is a handsome aristocratic mansion with extensive grounds surrounding, laid out tastefully with great profusion of flowers. I am on guard at headquarters. Received news of capture of Port Hudson with seven thousand prisoners. Signed the payrolls and received two months pay.

[*After a lengthy siege, Port Hudson, Louisiana, finally surrendered on July 9, 1863 (five days after Vicksburg)—there were 3,000 Union casualties while Confederate losses were over 7,200, including 5,500 prisoners.*]

July 17—Cole and I have been into the city on passes.

July 18—The Draft in Ashby has been completed without any riot and the one in New York has been subdued. [*In 1890 Hitchcock added: "Draft Officer in Ashby was George Loring Hitchcock—my father."*]

July 19—I attended church in the city, the Presbyterian which appears to be a wealthy one. Fine toilets and fine singing and fine equipages, preaching rather dull and heavy.

July 20—Major Richardson's wife arrived from Mt. Sterling.

July 21—I went into the city and bought boards for a bunk and now have my tent arranged in fine comfortable manner. Morgan has lost two thousand men since crossing into Indiana and is returning through the center of Ohio.

July 22—Sergeant John Wallace has gone to Camp Chase, Columbus [*Ohio*] with a squad of men in charge of some rebel prisoners.

July 23—I was on guard today.

July 24—Went into the city visiting stores attempting the onerous task of exchanging greensbacks for reading matter. Col. Hawkes went to Cincinnati.

July 25—John Wallace returned from Columbus and Hawkes from Cincinnati. There were services held in camp by a volunteer preacher of the Christian Commission and tract [*pamphlets*] distribution which we are sadly in need of, as the camp is filled with novels and reading trash.

July 26—I was on guard.

July 27—Mrs. Hawkes and sister Mary arrived from Massachusetts via Cincinnati.

July 28—I called on the Mass. ladies at the Broadway Hotel. A raiding band of guerrillas under Pegram have crossed the Kentucky River fourteen miles from here and are making for Paris; it is supposed to cut the railroad. The 21st was sent over by Fort Clay to defend it in case of attack.

July 29—Laid on arms all night and till evening of today when we returned to camp and were immediately ordered to take the cars for Paris, where we once marched. The orders were countermanded before the train was made up and we returned to camp again.

July 30—I was on guard today at the gate near the R.R. Learned that the rebels attacked our force at Paris but retreated without damaging the R.R. or succeeding in making much trouble, going back by way of Winchester. It is also reported that Mt. Sterling Court House has been burnt by them.

July 31—Regimental Monthly Inspection in the afternoon. The companies were drilled this morning the first time for three months. Troops have been coming in from the south on the railroad all day.

August 1, 1863—Very hot. Rev. Mr. Tompkins and his sister visited our camp from Mt. Sterling. Sid Haywood has returned to the company from the Quarter Master Department.

August 2—I was on guard at headquarters and at noon while on my beat a heavy thundershower occurred which soaked me completely. Four hundred prisoners were brought from Lancaster today. Our whole regiment is detailed for work tomorrow.

August 3—A large squad was sent out to Saundersville, a rebel hole seven miles southwest, to guard the polls at election. Sixty men were sent to Louisville with the rebel prisoners.

[*On July 31, 1863, General Burnside declared martial law throughout Kentucky to preserve the freedom of election, to prevent disloyal persons from voting and to silence any civil authorities who might be disposed to interfere.*]

August 4—The guards returned from Saundersville and Louisville. I went into the city on a pass.

August 5—Another squad was sent to Louisville to guard prisoners.

August 6—I am on guard in a large peach orchard adjoining the Lee Mansion. The trees hang loaded with luscious fruit and being only a few rods from our camp, in a sequestered place it offers a great temptation to our fruit-loving boys. The negro servants are instructed to give the guard a generous supply. A national thanksgiving today over the victories of Gettysburg, Vicksburg and Port Hudson is celebrated in camp by omitting drills and parade. I find much time to read. The 65th Illinois passed through the city for Hickman's Bridge [*Camp Nelson*].

August 7—Sergeant Major Lewis has gone out with a squad of men on a scout in the direction of Winchester and Sergeant Chamberlain has gone with another squad to Camp Nelson. Charles Wyman, who is employed at Capt. Hall's headquarters at Camp Nelson, called on me on his return from Cincinnati, where he has drawn fifty thousand dollars for government uses. Although passing through dangerous localities and among thousands of reckless soldiers, where a knowledge of his possessions would almost surely expose him to robbery, he passes unarmed even with a pocket pistol. With the unassuming haversack and a small bundle of private effects, he returns to Camp Nelson safely with his secret known only to a few.

August 8—General Burnside passed through the city today. Henry is boarding at a Mr. Hoagland's, a short distance from camp on the Frankfort pike. By invitation from Henry and wife I dined there and sat down to a civilized table and tablecloth the first time for a year. Here I witnessed the curious scene of a blessing asked by the host, a deaf and dumb man, and a lively conversation kept up throughout the whole by a family of five, all but one of which were deaf and dumb, it being carried on by use of hand-signs. The only one who had possession of her five senses compete was a daughter of about twenty-three years who was bright, intelligent and keen as a razor, who held her own opinions in regard to the propriety of the word "rebel" as applied to the people of the south, and of the impropriety of northern soldiers occupying this beautiful city and its suburbs. Her conversation was not in the least guarded or careful even though addressed to "Shoulder-Straps" yet withal she was polite and pleasant.

August 9—I attended Presbyterian Church today. Several ladies were present at Dress Parade. I called on Mary with Jonas Davis in the evening.

August 10—Gen. Burnside is in town today. Troops are continually passing to the front over the Lexington and Danville R.R. Col. Hawkes drilled the Battalion the first time since we left Newport News, chiefly for the benefit of the Massachusetts ladies, as it is remarked.

August 11—Gen. DeCourcy, who is in charge of the Department, was in camp today and consequently we received orders to march to Camp Nelson.

August 12—I guarded the peach orchard till afternoon when we packed up and marched a short distance. Fortunately the orders for marching were changed and we were loaded on to cars. Rode out of the beautiful city on a beautiful sunny afternoon out by the beautiful Ashland, the country-seat of Henry Clay's family, past large orchards of luscious peaches tantalizing the beholder, and through this American Eden, "the blue grass region," which not only gives bountiful harvests to the owners but enraptures the lover of the beautiful landscapes it lays out. The timber land can hardly be called forests for the trees which are all of hard wood, beach, maple and oak mostly, do not grow near to each other and underbrush seems unknown, but rich pasturage everywhere. It is not strange that Kentucky is world renowned for its fine horses and cattle and this is the very heart of the "horse" region. But the cars are bearing us quickly away from this to an entirely different aspect. We reach Nicholasville a rusty looking town of three or four thousand inhabitants, at dusk. Yet off the cars and after some delay in and about the streets we march off to the south-east on a broad dusty pike, five miles and camp in an open field by the side of the road at ten.

August 13—After a sound sleep under the canopy of heaven we take our coffee, brush up and enter Camp Nelson after a three mile tramp, with colors flying and drums beating. I was surprised to find the place of such activity. It has been for a long time a convenient base for supplies for our army operating in the south and eastern part of the state on the direct stage route to Knoxville via Cumberland Gap, lying near the Kentucky River and a place easily defended on account of its natural fortifications. The country about here as we near the river becomes very rugged and rough, and the pines and spruces and other evergreens begin to appear. As we enter the place, we pass by the numerous tents of Capt. Hall's headquarters and then pass large corrals of mules and team. Then we pass various camps of troops rendezvousing here and hospital camps. We go into camp in the edge of a piece of woods, mostly pine, on a slope facing another on which lies a large convalescent camp, and between the two runs the main road. Spend the day in laying out and pitching camp in the most approved style. Just before night we are notified that we are to receive a visit from Gen. Burnside, consequently prepare ourselves with unusual care and as we caught a glimpse of his cavalcade coming over a district hill the 21st did her best to show how well she could do. Gen. Burnside was accompanied by Capt. Hall and other officers, but these two men being the favorites of the regiment, we were anxious to do our best and after congratulatory remarks from them and the Dress Parade finished officers and men crowded around them to shake hands. I learn that Gen. Boyle is commander of the post here and that Gen. Fry has the Department. The pun is that if general boil and then a fry results in a burned side we had better have a Captain haul over the whole affair, which we understand is the case, as Capt. Hall is the main-spring of the entire place while Gen. Boyle has duties of inferior responsibility.

[*Camp Nelson was named for Major General William Nelson, who founded Camp Dick Robinson; for better protection from invading Confederate armies of Tennessee, the camp was moved to the Jessamine side of the Kentucky River and renamed Camp Nelson by Major General George H. Thomas. General Nelson was killed by a fellow general, Jefferson Columbus Davis, in a Louisville hotel on September 29, 1862.*]

August 14—I have been making a bunk for myself and arranging my tent in a very comfortable and cozy style. Freeman Cole has been detailed hustler for Gen. Burnside's private secretary. Several details have also been made for headquarter guard which has been established in a cottage house a quarter of a mile from camp. Col. Hawkes has been appointed Assistant Inspector General for Camp Nelson. During the day we learned of our proximity to the celebrated Boone Cave not a half a mile away, so a few of us of Co. A immediately after Dress Parade armed with candles and matches wandered through the woods till we come to a rocky precipice hundreds of feet in height over which we could look down into the rolling river. Clambering down over the rocks, with difficulty we find the entrance which is so low that we have to crawl several feet on hands and knees when at last we enter a lofty chamber. Here we light our candles and start on our exploring tour. This first chamber is large enough for a full regiment to be drawn up in line within. Then there are different openings, some of which we explore till we come to a terminus driving out multitudes of bats from their dreary homes. Finding the main passage to the heart of the cave, we grope along sometimes entering large chambers then small cozy rooms with only an outlet the size of a man's body. In nearly every part which we explored we found stalactites formed in fantastic and beautiful shapes. Sometimes we had to climb up over rocks twenty or thirty feet and crawl on hands and knees through some small aperture, over thick slime in order to proceed on our way. Having no guide but our own instincts we turned about after proceeding nearly half a mile fearing we might lose our way back. We conjectured that we were at that time, groping our way several rods down directly under various camps of busy activity. And although we kept up a continual chatter and jollification the thought would force itself in upon our minds, what if the immense stones held up by what seemed only a thread from completely blocking out exit! Imagination lent haste to our retreating footsteps and we were repeatedly laid flat with candles extinguished. Then with half-feigned, half-real fear we would yell out to the retreating comrades for assistance and when at last we reached the outside world we breathed freer, though the heated summertime air seemed as if blowing from an oven in contrasts with the cool even temperature of the cave.

The cave is said to have been explored to the distance of five miles in different directions. Here, it is said that Daniel Boone hid himself from the Indians and at various times made it his fortress from pursuing Indians. Return to camp well saturated with mud, and tired.

[*Daniel Boone Cave is located in Jessamine County, Kentucky, a half mile east of Camp Nelson near Hickman Creek. The hill between the village of Camp Nelson and the cave was the Civil War campground. As a boy in Ashby, Hitchcock was always investigating the Indian cave on Jone's hill. He had written that it was "a resort full of mystery for youthful imagination."*]

August 15—Water is very scarce here, nearly all having to be brought in barrels with army wagons for the distance of three miles. I was detailed with three others to guard the most important spring three miles from camp, our duties being to keep mules and horses and their drivers from stirring up the mud and to keep it clear. I learn that our 9th Corps has returned from Vicksburg and the 2nd Brigade is encamped near Covington.

[*Because the Kentucky River Palisades rise over 400 feet above the river, the water supply was initially a huge problem for Camp Nelson. However, the army solved this problem by constructing a powerful steam pump on the river which brought water up the palisades to a 500,000 gallon reservoir. This tremendous engineering feat supplied water for the camp with indoor running water faucets and water closets in the hospital and soldiers' quarters.*]

August 16—Weather cloudy. We were not relieved till afternoon and returned to camp at four. Saw Gen. Burnside leave Camp Nelson with his escort and a large body guard for East Tennessee. He strikes right out into the American Wilderness and will have to cross several large bridgeless rivers and over two or three high ranges of mountains. A very long wagon train loaded with supplies goes out with him. Charles Wyman has been to see us this evening.

August 17— I was on guard at the new hospital building. Major Richardson has been appointed Provost Marshal and Capt. Parker Assistant Quarter Master of the post so they have left the regiment for the present.

August 18—Col. Hawkes' wife, Major Richardson's wife and Lieut. Hitchcock's wife arrived from Lexington and took quarters at the cottage. A member of the Christian Commission spoke and prayed with the regiment at parade in the evening. I went down to the river in the afternoon, about a mile from camp. At this place the river runs through a narrow gorge, with high rocky bluffs on either side and is consequently quite turbid.

[*The Christian Commission was founded by YMCA leaders in November 1861 to provide blankets, clothing, books, and spiritual support to Union soldiers.*]

August 19—Frank Peckham has been detailed Ordnance Sergt. and Lem Whitney clerk at Gen. Fry's headquarters.

August 20—I was on guard at the Headquarter stables. Henry Colby of the 36th Mass. was here to see us. In the afternoon, the body of Gen. Nelson arrived from Louisville en route for interment at Camp Dick Robinson. It was escorted by a detachment of the 1st Division 9th Corps marching to the slow and solemn music (Death March in Saul by Handel) of the 48th Penn. Band, to the headquarters and the body remained over night.

[*Major General William Nelson, who commanded the Army of Kentucky and was organizing the defenses at Louisville, was killed by Brigadier General Jefferson Columbus Davis in a Louisville hotel lobby on September 29, 1862. Davis, who had been brooding over a rebuke from Nelson, was never punished and returned to active duty.*]

August 21—Gen. Fry and staff accompanied the corpse to Camp Dick Robinson today. Several members of the regiment joined us from Lexington.

August 22—Gen. Ferrero just returned from Vicksburg, Miss., was in camp with Capt. Hall. Ansel Orcutt returned to the company from Portsmouth Grove, R.I. hospital.

August 23—Sunday. Heard preaching at Gen. Fry's Headquarters this morning. Col. Hawkes returned to the regiment. Our quarters were inspected by the post surgeon.

August 24—I was detailed with twelve others in command of Capt. Barker of Co. B to go to Louisville with thirty or forty rebels prisoners. Marched to Nicholasville through the fine clay dust ankle deep and beneath a searching sun. Rode in cars to Lexington and amid a thunder-shower, deposited our prisoners in "No. 3 Jail." We then found lodgings at the "Soldiers House" next above the Broadway Hotel on Broadway. This place was the private residence of some rebel but has been confiscated for the use of detachments of soldiers passing through the city.

August 25—After looking about the city in the forenoon we take our squad of prisoners and at two in the afternoon embark on cars for Frankfort, which we reach late in the afternoon. We saw the public buildings, the Arsenal and passed directly by the Capitol, which is a beautiful structure, and crossed the Kentucky river which is very wide at this place. The 2nd Md. is doing guard duty at this place and we passed the block-houses along the railroad which they had thrown up in defense from John Morgan's raiders. Passed through other interesting places and at dusk we reached Louisville. For more than a mile the train moves at a horse-trot through a busy straight street, which from the appearance of the busy throng on either side and the numerous signs, proves to be the "German Quarter." Reaching the depot we march another mile across the city and surrender our prisoners at the Military Prison in the South Western part of the city. We cross the street and a short distance away we find the Soldiers Home and secure lodgings. This House seems to be the best conduct of any in my experience south of Mason & Dixon's line, planned and built for the purpose. Entering the yard by the sentinel we pass beds of plants and flowers into the building. We report at the office and then pass further on to the large reading room where we make ourselves thoroughly at home with all the conveniences. A well-filled large sleeping rooms with bunks to accommodate several hundred sleepers. Everything is kept in the most scrupulous neatness. We lie down to rest between white sheets with pillows for the head, a luxury which I have not enjoyed for more than a year. After a great many unnecessary blunders of pretended ignorance of the use to which to put our extras and much frolicking, sleep closes my eyes and senses soundly till morning.

August 26—After performing the morning duties I look out and find we are within a stone's throw of the Great Depot of the Nashville and Southern R.R. on Broadway. The street or avenue is the most superb of anything I ever saw of the kind. A hundred feet wide with side-walk a rod wide running as straight and level as an arrow as far as the eye can reach, with enormous shade-trees the entire length. For the most part this is the "elite avenue" of the city, elegant mansions on either side. Capt. Barker kindly allows us a day to look around so the forenoon is occupied visiting the Locomotive Works connected with the Nashville R.R. and going down to the Ohio and watch the steamers passing up from New Orleans and the Mississippi and down from Pittsburgh and Cincinnati. In the afternoon I strolled about the streets visiting several extensive flouring mills and tobacco warehouses, probably the largest in the world. Market St. is a scene of busy activity. At equal distances are built very long market houses where all kinds of produce are offered for sale. I saw immense quantities, the express offices were over-run with crates. At night after partaking of our supper which was well appreciated, I spent the evening in reading and retired early, feeling quite like sleeping after the day of sightseeing.

August 27—Started at five in the morning for Camp Nelson, reached Nicholasville at half past one in the afternoon. Preparations are going on very extensively and briskly here for the building of the Tennessee R.R. over the mountains. We had a very tedious tramp through the clouds of dust to camp where we arrived at six.

August 28—Col. Hawkes, Lieut. Lawrence and Sampson with six sergeants have gone to Massachusetts for conscripts. Mrs. Hawkes returned home day before yesterday having received a telegram telling of the sickness of little Mary. I have been furnishing my quarters with bunk, and table, including refrigerator, which is simply a hole in the ground with a covering of turf in which I place my butter, meat and milk.

August 29—I am on guard at the "prisoners pen," a place consisting of two large hospital tents enclosed in an imaginary square of several rods which is thickly guarded by us of the 21st. Sam Adams, a member of Co. A from Orange, Mass. who deserted from the regiment at Newport News more than a year ago, returned to the company having in the meantime enlisted in a Pennsylvania Regt. and become sick of it. Allen the 9th Corps Mail Agent member of Co. A has been in to see us. The scene as I started on my beat in the evening is charming, awakening the emotions and carrying my thoughts far away. It is one of those serene, mild nights lighted by a grand full harvest moon. From the elevated slope on which I stand, I look across the intervening quarter of a mile, up the opposite slope on which lies the white tented camps of the 21st Mass. and the 49th Ky. in the outskirts of the tall pine grove, the whole lighted by numerous camp-fires while further away in the background up in the pines on the crest of the hill are the headquarter tents of Gen. Fry, forming a camp of considerable size itself. Further still to the left, a mile away the extensive corrals and camps of cavalry. Turning half way round to the right, away down through the gorges and narrow rocky defiles, the deep sullen roar of the rolling Kentucky river resounds. Then as my eyes turn backward from all this beautiful night scene to the thickly packed camp of hospital tents my immediate neighbor-hood, I wonder what my future will open up to me, whether of an opportunity to explore the imaginary wilds far to the southward which may mean sickness, pain and death or possible a change of circumstances with these very prisoners, whether a wearisome guard duty in this place for months or whether the approaching happy termination of the war may come soon, and bring a blessed peace to all.

August 30—I left Massachusetts just one year ago today for the seat of war, a year crowded with severe experiences which far exceeds anything of former years. [*In 1890 Hitchcock added: "A year crowded with thrilling and severe experiences but none which I regret for the part I have taken in them."*]

7. Spring and Summer in Eastern Kentucky 105

August 31—Monthly regimental inspections and muster in was held in the afternoon in charge of Capt. Davis, Lieut. Valentine acting Adjutant. I called on Mary [*Henry's wife*] this evening and made the acquaintance of Mrs. Richardson.

September 1, 1863—Government issued to the regiment blouses, socks, shirts, blankets, and knapsacks. I am on guard at regimental headquarters. Allen has been returned to the company for duty. Jones is acting Sergeant Major.

September 2—I learned that Mary Hawkes died a week ago. Capt. Hall visited the regiment at Dress Parade. There were three commissioned officers only in line, owing to the large number of details.

September 3—I wrote to John Mayo of the 33rd Mass. in the Army of the Potomac. A large squad of negroes [*Hitchcock used word "darkies" in his 1890 diary*] were conducted into camp and reported at Gen. Fry's Headquarters for work on the railroad.

[*The prejudicial values of the 19th century toward African Americans are evident throughout the diary; however, words do not have the connotations or meanings that they have today. The word "darkies" is considered offensive today but not in the 1860s.*]

September 4—I am on guard at the Quarter Master's tent. Two large squads were detailed from the regiment to go to Louisville with prisoners. There was but one commissioned officer in line tonight. 30 is the full complement.

September 5—Our Sutler has been filling up with goods from Cincinnati. We learn that Gen . Burnside has reached and taken Kingston, Tenn. and thinks East Tennessee free from the enemy in any form.

[*Sutlers accompanied troops selling food, drink, and supplies. According to the Articles of War a sutler "shall supply the soldiers with good and wholesome provisions or other articles at a reasonable price."*]

September 6—I am on guard at the quarter master's. Charles Wyman has been down to see us. Orders have come for the 9th Corps to move. The regiment was inspected by the medical director of the 9th Corps.

September 7—Another inspection of the regiment today by the Inspector General. I received a letter from John Mayo, Bristol Station, Va., where his regiment is stationed guarding the Alexandria and Orange R.R. Another squad have gone to Louisville with prisoners.

September 8—I am on guard at the prison quarters The camp is excited over the report that we are to leave our comfortable quarters and follow Gen. Burnside over the mountains.

September 9—And today the orders <u>come</u> to report to our old Brigade which has already passed through here en-tramp for Cumberland Gap. The

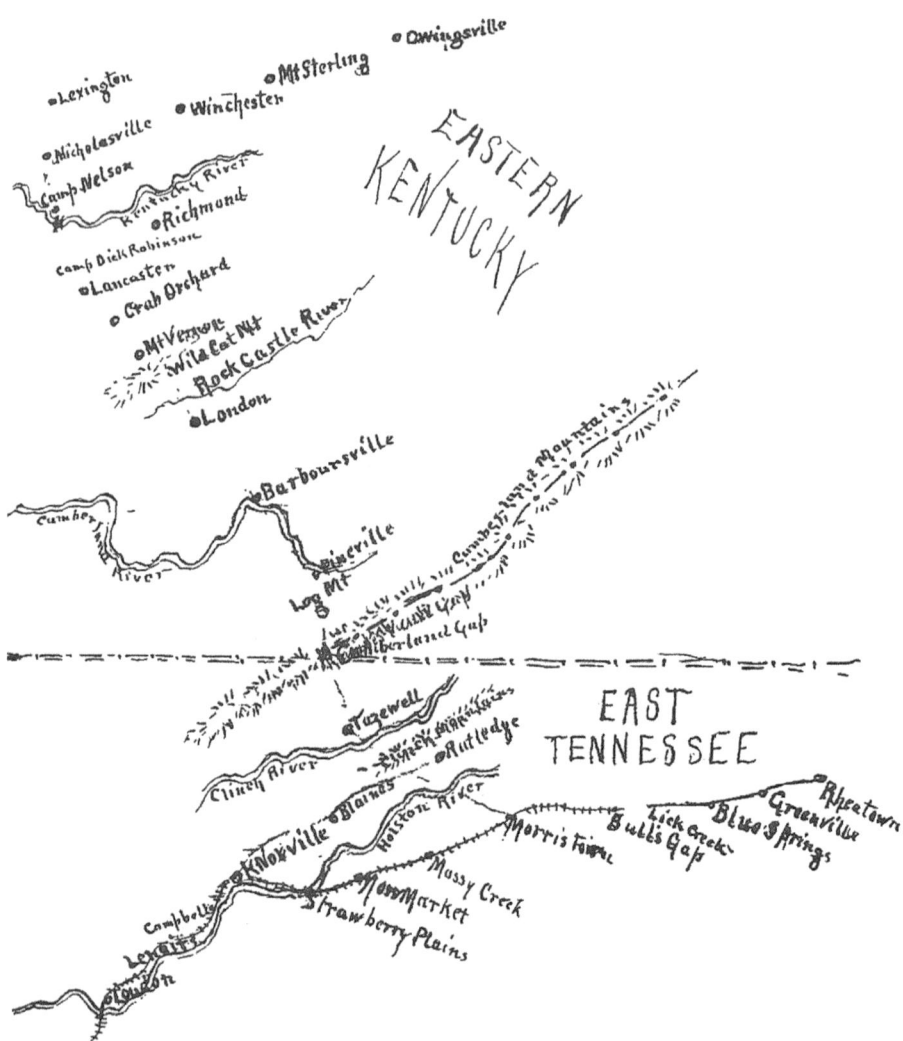

Map 2: Route of the 21st Massachusetts Regiment during the Knoxville Campaign in 1863. Drawn by George A. Hitchcock for his 1890 diary from his 1863 sketch.

51st N.Y. came and report to Gen. Fry for duty in our place. Asa Franklin Van Buren Piper and I called on Henry and wife in the evening.

September 10—Guard was mounted as usual. Great efforts are being made by Capt. Hall and our officers to have our marching orders rescinded as it was understood by Burnside that we were to remain here through the winter and the change has been made by Gen. Potter, commander of the Corps, who wishes to favor his old regiment. Our old Brigade Band played for us tonight at Dress Parade. The capture of Cumberland Gap, Chattanooga and Morris Island is reported. Called on Henry again tonight.

September 11—I was on guard at prison quarters but was relieved by the guard from the 51st N.Y. early in the day and we are making all preparations for the long march. Lemuel and I visited the cave at night. [*In 1890 Hitchcock added: "We have no reason for complaint for the very pleasant summer's duties in Kentucky; the remainder of the day is occupied in preparations for the long march of two hundred miles away from civilization over the mountains via Cumberland Gap."*]

8

The East Tennessee Campaign

"My God! Hitchcock, you're shot!"
—Hitchcock, November 23, 1863

Knoxville was the major city of eastern Tennessee, the mountainous region for which Lincoln felt such concern as it was the center of Union sentiment inside the Confederacy. According to military historian, John Keegan, from the beginning of the war, Lincoln was anxious to bring it under Federal control.

With the Virginia and Tennessee Railroad providing an unbroken connection for the Confederacy between Maj. Gen. Braxton Bragg's army in the west and General Lee's army in the east, East Tennessee was an important strategic region with its valley of the Tennessee and Holston rivers, located between lofty mountain ranges. This was the only railroad linking the eastern and western parts of the Confederacy and was a very important priority for providing military supplies and transferring soldiers. Although the area was isolated from the North by natural barriers, many of the leaders and a majority of the people in East Tennessee supported the Federal government.

In early June 1863, General Burnside sent two divisions of the IX Corps to reinforce Maj. Gen. Ulysses S. Grant's army in Mississippi, where he was engaged in the siege of Vicksburg. The 21st Massachusetts Regiment remained at Mount Sterling, Kentucky. These divisions returned to Kentucky (First Division on August 12 and Second Division on August 20) depleted and exhausted. Since the Union army was recruited by the addition of new regiments rather than filling up the old regiments, the divisions of the IX Corps remained under strength.

On August 16, 1863, Burnside left Camp Nelson, a 4,000-acre depot located five miles south of Nicholasville, Kentucky, on the long-postponed invasion of East Tennessee. His army consisted of 15,000 men of the recently constituted XXIII Corps, led by Maj. Gen. George L. Hartsuff. The IX Corps would follow later. The army, due to the area's miserable road network, divided into five columns fanned out across a front of more than a hundred miles.

8. The East Tennessee Campaign

The Federals crossed the Cumberland Mountains by seldom frequented roads and by some that were deemed impassible by a large army. Soldiers climbed the rugged terrain with an indomitable persistence and courage. Horses and mules were tested to their utmost. The objective was to cross the mountains into East Tennessee, surprise the Confederates and capture Knoxville (thereby gaining possession of the entire region). Supplying the troops and securing the lines of communications were tremendous obstacles to this campaign's success.

Major General Simon Bolivar Buckner, who had assumed command of the Confederate Department of East Tennessee on May 12, 1863, was ordered by General Bragg to evacuate Knoxville before Burnside's troops arrived. On September 2, 1863, Col. John W. Foster's brigade of Federal cavalry occupied Knoxville without any resistance. General Burnside received an enthusiastic welcome from the 5,000 residents of Knoxville when he arrived the next day. The army had marched more than 200 miles in two weeks, and Knoxville was now firmly in Federal hands.

On September 9, Brig. Gen. John W. Frazer surrendered the Cumberland Gap to General Burnside without firing a shot. This important and easily defensible pass was one of the region's critical communication links. Although several hundred Confederate soldiers escaped, General Frazer and 2,000 Confederate soldiers were taken prisoner—including the 55th Georgia Regiment, and 62d and 64th North Carolina Regiments.

Burnside notified President Lincoln the following day that he wished to retire to private life now that East Tennessee was occupied. Lincoln, however, insisted that he needed the general until East Tennessee was secured, and thus denied the general's request. Burnside dispersed his troops to guard his line of defense that extended for 170 miles along the East Tennessee and Georgia Railroad and the East Tennessee and Virginia Railroad from Charleston to Carter's Depot, Tennessee. With the threat of a Confederate attack, Burnside directed the IX Corps to proceed to East Tennessee as soon as possible, and he ordered all his troops back to Knoxville and Loudon on September 18. The 21st Massachusetts Regiment left Camp Nelson for East Tennessee on September 12, passed through Cumberland Gap, engaged a Confederate force at Blue Springs on October 10. Hitchcock's regiment finally arrived at Knoxville five days later after having marched 185 miles.

Several important departmental command changes took place in mid–October. On the 18th, Maj. Gen. Ulysses S. Grant assumed command of the Military Division of the Mississippi, a large area composed of three departments: Ohio, Cumberland and Tennessee. General Burnside retained command at Knoxville, General Sherman assumed command of the Department of the Tennessee and General Thomas, who relieved Maj. Gen. William S. Rosecrans, was placed in command of the Department of the Cumberland.

The Confederates were also active during this time, using their advantage of interior lines to shift troops west from Virginia. General Lee sent Maj. Gen. James Longstreet's Corps with the divisions of Lafayette McLaws and John Hood to reinforce General Bragg in September 1863. The addition of these troops enabled the Confederates to defeat Maj. Gen. William S. Rosecrans and his Army of the Cumberland at Chickamauga on September 18–20. After Bragg squandered his opportunity to retake Chattanooga, Longstreet's 17,000-man force, including Maj. Gen. Joseph Wheeler's cavalry, was detached by Bragg on November 4 to engage and defeat Burnside's army and reopen direct rail communications with southwest Virginia. Eight days later, Longstreet's Corps approached Loudon. His troops were exhausted, hungry and ragged, and expected rations and supplies were not available. As Longstreet's Confederates approached, Capt. Orlando M. Poe, chief engineer, Department of the Ohio, fortified the heights on the south side of the Tennessee River, opposite Knoxville. Poe reinforced and enlarged the defensive forts and earthworks around Knoxville's eastern, northern and western perimeter while the Tennessee River protected the southern side of the city. Fort Loudon (renamed Fort Sanders in honor of the mortally wounded William P. Sanders), was located in the northwestern angle of the Knoxville perimeter. Its parapets were thirteen feet high and sloped forty-five degrees, and a ditch, which was six to eight feet deep and eight to twelve feet across, surrounded the fort.

When Burnside sent 5,000 troops toward Loudon to confront and to delay the Confederate thrust, Longstreet crossed the Tennessee River and headed for Lenoir's Station, eight miles northeast of Loudon. When Longstreet arrived on November 15, the Union troops were gone. "Old Pete" hastened toward Campbell's Station, intending to defeat the Union troops piecemeal. Following parallel routes, Longstreet's and Burnside's troops raced for Campbell's Station, a strategic hamlet 15 miles southwest of Knoxville, where the Concord Road from the south intersected the Kingston Road to Knoxville. If Longstreet took Campbell's Station, he would cut Burnside off from his Knoxville fortifications and compel him to fight unprotected by his strong earthworks. Union Col. John F. Hartranft's division of the IX Corps (including the 21st Massachusetts) with Col. James Biddle's cavalry were the first Federal's to arrive at Campbell's Station. The troops secured all the roads and allowed the retreating Union troops to pass through by 11:00 a.m. on a rainy November 16. The Federals formed a stout battle line with Hartranft's division on the left, Ferrero's division of the IX Corps on right and Brig. Gen. Julius White's division of the XXIII Corps in the center.

As the Union line was forming, Longstreet approached and ordered attacks against both Union flanks. Maj. Gen. Lafayette McLaws' Division launched a hard-hitting assault and Burnside's right buckled for a time before rallying to hold its ground. Brig. Gen. Micah Jenkins, a Longstreet favorite, maneuvered his division ineffectively as it deployed and was unable to turn the Union left. Burnside took advantage of the Jenkins' lackluster performance to withdraw his three divisions on the Kingston Road three quarters of a mile and redeployed them on a ridge. The Union force withdrew after dark and retired into the defenses at Knoxville. Brigadier General Robert B. Potter, commander of the IX Corps, reported that Hartranft's energy and prudence were responsible for the successful retreat. Brigadier General William Sanders, with fewer than a thousand men, met Longstreet's troops two miles from Knoxville and stalled the Confederate advance for hours. Sanders was mortally wounded, but the additional time enabled Engineer Poe to complete and strengthen the Knoxville fortifications. At Fort Sanders, the ditches were widened, trees felled and wires stretched from stump to stump. On November 17, Longstreet arrived and a quasi-siege of Knoxville began.

At 6:00 a.m. under cover of fog on November 29 with frost covering the earthworks, three brigades of McLaws' Division (William Wolford's Georgia Brigade, Benjamin Humphrey's Mississippi Brigade and Goode Bryan's Georgians) assaulted Fort Sanders. Without means to cross the ditch or to scale the icy parapet, the attack was doomed. Within twenty minutes, the attack was over. The Confederates lost 129 killed, 458 wounded and 226 missing, while the Union lost but five killed and eight wounded. "I know of no instance in history where a storming party was so nearly annihilated," boasted Captain Poe. Within an hour after the failed assault on Fort Sanders, Longstreet was notified by President Davis that Bragg had been defeated at Missionary Ridge on November 25 and that he should abandon Knoxville and rejoin Bragg's army. After consulting for three days with his senior officers and realizing that his tenuous supply situation prevented a march across the mountains to join Bragg in northwest Georgia, Longstreet decided to retreat up the East Tennessee and Virginia Railroad toward Bristol, Virginia. Meanwhile, on December 4, General Sherman with a 25,000-man relief force, which had been sent by General Grant from Chattanooga, had closed within two-days march of Knoxville. On the following day, Burnside's pickets discovered that the Longstreet's army had retired. Sherman arrived at Knoxville on December 6.

On December 11, Maj. Gen. John G. Foster assumed command of the Army of the Ohio, and General Burnside left Knoxville three days later. Confederate casualties in General Longstreet's Corps during the Knoxville Campaign (November 14 to December 4) were: 198 killed, 850 wounded and 1,296 captured. Total Union casualties for troops commanded by General Burnside during the Knoxville Campaign (November 17 to December 4) were 92 killed, 394 wounded and 207 captured. The 21st Massachusetts Regiment lost 4 killed, 11 wounded and two captured during this period.

The campaign of Knoxville, together with Grant's victory at Chattanooga, returned eastern Tennessee to Union control for the remainder of the war.

September 12, 1863—This morning was bright. We were roused up at five and after waiting till eight the 2nd Maryland and 48th Penn. came along when we joined them and took up our line of march. We now belong to the 1st Brigade 2nd Division. Pass through a fine farming region and soon after noon go into camp, nine miles from Camp Nelson, in Camp Dick Robinson near the grave of Gen. Nelson. Soon after we had pitched our shelters a deluging thunder shower came up which did not close till dark. We received pay in the eve.

September 13—Cloudy and good marching weather. Col. Sigfried of the 48th P.V. has command of the Brigade. Started at six and marched all day. Passed through Lancaster and camped for the night near Crab Orchard nineteen miles from our last camp.

September 14—In the morning we marched through Crab Orchard which appears to be a representative southern town and is said to be the constant scene of bloodshed and trouble. Marched four miles and camped in a rough field a mile beyond Crab Orchard. The 2nd Brigade is camped just across the road so we are formed into a Division again. Henry has been detailed Aide-de-Camp for Col. Sigfried and has now the privilege of riding horseback while we of the humble fellow regiment have to walk. My first battle (South Mountain) was just one year ago.

September 15—Capt. Davis inspected the regiment and five days rations have been issued which we distribute on various parts of the body, haversacks and knapsacks being overloaded.

September 16—Roused at five and started at eight. Had an easy march of eleven miles, halting two hours for dinner. The company cooks prepare coffee three times daily which is highly appreciated by every marching soldier in the line. Camp for the night two miles from Mt. Vernon having passed through a hilly region.

September 17—Passed through Mt. Vernon, a small dirty village around which are built fortifications. It being hardly possible that these works can be erected for the protection of such an unworthy object; we take it that they are intended for the protection of the outside world coming in contact with the God-forsaken place. We pass hastily through and find the country as wild. Just before noon we met the rebel brigade of prisoners, twenty-five hundred in number, which were taken at Cumberland Gap. A sorry-looking set they were, ragged and dirty. Gen. Frazer, the rebel officer in command of the Gap at the time, walked along several rods in the rear of the column looking very dejected. They are all under guard en route for Louisville. Late in the afternoon we toiled up the steep road to the top of Wildcat Mountain. Halt a short time for rest on the summit and the eye takes in a view as wild, rocky and to all appearance as uninhabitable as anything in the far West. Descending, we see the blue outline of the Cumberland Mts in the far east. Pass through scenes of Zollicoffer's battle of a year ago where immense trees were felled across the road—probably effectually blockading it for the time, though they have since been cut through. After a fifteen mile march we camp at dark near the banks of the Rock Castle River, by the side of the rough cabin of a lone settler in this wild country, from whom straw was procured for our use.

September 18—The night proved stormy and the marching was not improved thereby. After crossing the river at the ford we begin to ascend Rock Castle Mt., which was not very rough but one long, steep inclined plane of a mile in length unbroken in its ascent to the summit. For the remainder of the distance of eight miles of our todays tramp out route was quite level and densely wooded. We passed but one building in our entire route till we reach Loudon, our camping place. Here we receive rations of fresh meat which are cooked up. The 11th N.H. is stationed here, a lone outpost in the mountains.

September 19—The night was very cold and chilly. Marched through a more open and inhabited country than yesterday fourteen miles. Camped fourteen miles from Barboursville and forty miles from the Gap. [*In 1890 Hitchcock added: "We are now in the heart of the wilderness about a hundred miles from any railroad and each day getting further away from the paternal care of Uncle Sam."*]

September 20—The morning opened mild. Marched fifteen miles, passed through Barboursville and camped a mile and a half beyond, near the banks of the Cumberland River where three days rations were dealt out. In the evening I saw a signal rocket fired from a distant mountain-top.

September 21—Left our camp at seven and followed the course of the river, finding level and easy travel though closed in by lofty mountains. The river takes a very crocked course and although we march fourteen miles we do not camp more than half that distance, air-line from our last night's stop. Reaching the famous Cumberland ford, we strip off shoes and stockings, pull up pants and wade across and camp by the side of the river.

September 22—Col. Griffin of the 6th N.H. takes command of the Brigade. Take up our march and toil up over Log Mountain. After our dinner halt we come out of the mountains and at about two come suddenly in sight of the "Gibraltar of the South" five miles away in the southeast. We take our first view of the Cumberland Gap from a very advantageous point. From here it looked like an insurmountable wall shutting out all communication with the region beyond. The eye takes in a long stretch of the Cumberland range entirely destitute of forest or timber and unbroken save where we see the "slit" called the Gap, around which fortifications rise tier upon tier and rifle-pits running zig-zag in all directions over the mountains, the whole appearance giving one the impression of defiance to any force which might be brought against it. We plod wearily up the steep rocky sides and at four, find ourselves in the "Gap." Looking northward the eye takes in almost an unbroken view of wilderness and solitude. South into Eastern Tennessee, the prospect is more pleasing open cultivated tracts and fertile valleys. We were refreshed at a large spring of ice-cold water bubbling out of the rocks near "Corner Stone" which is a square block about two yards square. This is the boundary of the three states Kentucky, Virginia and Tennessee. Various members of the regiment, myself included, found great satisfaction in standing on this mystic spot feeling that we were in three large States of the Union all at once. After planting our colors on the rock and giving three lusty cheers, the regiment descended a few rods to the government buildings used for the posts, where we camped for the night, making a march of fourteen miles today.

September 23—Left camp at seven and march into a very different appearing country from that of yesterday's march, open and cultivated land all about us. We now take the direction of Morristown, a station on the Virginia and East Tennessee R.R., forty-seven miles from here. In the vicinity of the village of Tazewell we see the desolations of war, the fertile fields, whose crops are choked down with rank weeks for want of a tiller, appear on either side and even the native swine, of which the country seem to abound, are obliged to lean against the trees to support their emaciated forms!! The village of Tazewell, once a very pretty place, has been almost entirely burnt by the barbarous rebels and the naked brick walls of ruins tell a pitiful tale of trouble.

September 24—We camp just beyond the town thirteen miles from our last night's ground. Left camp at seven and march all the forenoon reaching the Clinch river at noon. We halt for dinner near its banks and afternoon cross the ford, which at present is quite deep, being up to our middles most of the way. The current was quite strong and we found difficulty in keeping our footing. Occasionally a man would upset and receive a sousing much to the amusement of those who had crossed successfully. We go into camp on the opposite bank eight miles from last night's camp. The afternoon was spent by the entire Brigade in washing clothes and bathing. As the roads have been dusty we all appreciate the opportunity. The trains have all gone on to Knoxville except the brigade supply and at night we receive five days supply the reason of which is that we are about to cross Clinch Mountain and the roads are considered well nigh impassable for loaded teams.

September 25—We arose this beautiful morning at six. A large portion of the regiment (myself included) was detailed to assist the trains in the ascent and descent of Clinch Mt. Our route in the morning lay along a beautiful fertile valley which is quite thickly settled with large rambling well-to-do farm houses which show more signs of thrift than anything we have seen south of

Mason & Dixon's line. the ascent of the mountain was accomplished with much difficulty until we neared the top when we encounter rocks. Rocks which appear to have no regard for the traveler are piled up all along the road till we reach the top and as the poor patient mules toil over them they seem to threaten instant destruction to both mules and wagons and contents. Reaching the top a short halt is made when we begin to realize the situation. A most glorious picture opens before us. Away up in one of the loftiest summits of the lofty East Tennessee ranges we look down into the far famed valley of East Tennessee, the section so remarkable for its mild temperatures, great fertility, constant verdure and excellent water privileges. This valley appears to be an isolated spot in the heart of the United States shut in on all sides by almost impassable mountain ranges, although the choicest spot. The manners and customs of the inhabitants are very backward and but very few of the modern improvements have yet found their way into the region. Away toward the east we discern the Smoky Mountains, the southern continuation of the Virginia Blue Ridge. Although standing out in bold relief are many prominent peaks yet they are only distinguishable as a pile of ethereal blue while in the intervening space, the eye detects several distinct ranges of less altitude. Almost at our feet the Holston winds along among the mountains to the southwest where, at a point some sixty miles below it changes its name for that of its mother state. The valley for a most part appears to be open and much cultivated, though but few settlements or houses can be distinguished. Through this valley runs the Virginia and East Tennessee R.R. The main artery of the Southern Confederacy (so called) connect Virginia with the head of the Gulf States, the body and heart of this sore monstrosity.

After due preparations, clogging and chaining wheels, fastening ropes to the ambulances, the sick being transferred to the backs of horses and mules "pressed in" for the purpose. The descent is slow and perilous. For a half mile the opening (for it cannot be called a road) is filled with jogged rocks and huge round paving stones. In one place a long unbroken steep or slide of rock extending two or three rods, and inclined plane of nearly forty-five degrees; where the teams were kept from destruction only with the utmost efforts, as it was one team was upset, completely demolishing the wagon and killing one mule.

We accomplish the task and reach the foot of the mountain at noon and halt for coffee in a romantic glen beside a musical little brook running down among the rocks. While eating our lunch and lolling about on the grass in the cool shade we can look back up the rugged heights we have just overcome and see the white tops of other wagons far up hundreds and thousands of feet running the same gauntlet we have just passed through.

In the afternoon we passed some celebrated Springs where were extensive buildings of brick for boarders. A constant thick cloud of dust fills the air along our route and it is impossible to see forward of us to the distance of two rods, so dense is it. This penetrates our clothing and covers everything with a thick coating so that we could hardly be distinguished from so many "gray backs." At night we reach the Holston which at this point is very wide, probably a third of a mile. Each man undresses and, throwing his clothes over his gun, wades the stream, which averages from three to five feet deep. Having effected a crossing we went into camp for the night near the banks, after a march of thirteen miles.

September 26—The brigade is roused, formed and put in motion by Aide-de-camp Hitchcock and after a march of seven miles reach Morristown a place of considerable size where there are shops for manufacturing rolling-stock for the Virginia and East Tennessee R.R. We halt for dinner and continue our march in the afternoon following the railroad. We reach Mossy Spring a station on the R.R., at night and go into camp after a march of nineteen miles. We had a comparatively level route. Soon after we had pitched camp, the 18th Kentucky passed us going toward Knoxville.

September 27—The dust continues intolerable. Left camp at six and after marching three hours, passed through New Market. Halted several hours for rest at noon near the railroad. Meanwhile a Brigade of mounted infantry composed of the 65th Illinois and 71st Indiana and a full battery passed us. By the middle of the afternoon we reached the bridge at Strawberry Plains, or where the bridge was destroyed by the rebels. A line of single plank had been put across on which the brigade filed across, each man singly, which operation took several hours. The wagons had to go around some distance below and cross at a ford. We went into camp at sundown. Several deserters from Bragg's Army passed us, going to their homes. Marched eighteen miles today.

September 28—March all the forenoon and at noon we reach the barracks and buildings known as "the Confederate camp of instructions and conscripts camp." We halt for dinner after which we proceed about three miles further when we go into camp just outside of Knoxville on the north bank of the Holston and in sight of the city. We have now accomplished the journey of two hundred and five miles and are all in pretty good condition with the exception of being very dirty. James Carruth, who was detailed as hostler for one of Gen. Burnside's staff, came out to see us.

September 29—Major Richardson and Capt. Clark arrived today direct from Camp Nelson. Cleaned up gun, equipments, camp streets and washed in the river. Gen. Burnside came down to camp at evening like a good father to see how his boys had borne the march. Of course he was received with three times three and a tiger. Half rations were dealt out to us tonight for the first time. We learn that transportation of supplies is very uncertain and great economy will have to be used.

September 30—I received a pass and visited the city; saw Parson Brownlow's home. The city is situated on very hilly and abrupt ground. The appearance of the place is very dilapidated and unlike most of the southern cities and large villages which are usual of brick, this is mostly of wood. It is at present transformed into a military beehive and but very few citizens can be seen. Regimental monthly inspection by Maj. Richardson in the afternoon. Our regimental sutler arrived. I called on Henry in the evening at the brigade headquarters.

October 1, 1863—Received rations of softbread. The sutler opened his goods. It is reported that three loads of mails have fallen into the hands of the enemy between here and Cumberland Gap.

October 2—An afternoon company drill was commenced today. Several promotions were read at Dress Parade: Ed Lewis to 1st Lieut. and Adjutant Henry S. Hitchcock to 1st Lieut. Co. I, Lawrence 1st Lieut. Co. A, Lieut. Barker Capt. Co. A. I saw a black bear which was captured lately in the Smoky Mountains.

October 3—A part of the 1st Division has been ordered back to Tazewell.

October 4—Received orders to leave our camp standing and march to the depot at nine. We pack into cars and ride back over the same road we have just marched over. Disembark at Bull Gap six miles from Knoxville and bivouac in a very rough field. The night was cold and we find but an hour or two for sleep most of the time spent on the windward side for a fire. A large force of the enemy is reported coming near here from Virginia.

[*The railroad leading southwest from Knoxville is the East Tennessee and Georgia Railroad, while the line running northeast is the East Tennessee and Virginia Railroad.*]

October 5—We marched through the Gap and then five miles further halt near Lick Creek. Co. A which number about a dozen men build a shelter of rails covered with brush which we all share in common. With a large rail fire on the open side we manage very comfortably. The rebels are five miles from here. We receive a ration of meat.

October 6—Lemuel and I were sent out on picket and were on a post with a 48th Penn. corporal. [*In 1890 Hitchcock added: "As the enemy's outposts are now within two miles of us, our watching was no sinecure—silence and vigilance of the strictest sort all through the night. It appears that our force is inadequate to meet the enemy; we are therefore awaiting the expected arrival of General Wilcox, who is coming over the mountains with several thousand Indiana troops."*]

October 7—We were relieved from picket by the 8th and 9th Michigan Infantry. Rations are all gone and poor prospect for any more except by foraging on the country. Another reported battle by Rosecrans.

[*There was no mention of Maj. Gen. William S. Rosecrans in the 1890 diary. At the Battle near Chickamauga on September 19 and 20, 1863, Rosecrans was unequal to the crisis—fleeing the battlefield while Gen. George H. Thomas, "The Rock of Chickamauga," stayed and fought valiantly and successfully against Maj. Gen. Braxton Bragg's Confederate Army of Tennessee. After the battle, Lincoln considered Rosecrans "confused and stunned like a duck hit on the head."*]

October 8—Our foraging brought in some flour which was confiscated from the citizens. A capture of a few prisoners with horses and weapons were brought in at night. The 8th Brigade of the 1st Division arrived. Dress Parade was held.

October 9—Laid about taking matters easy till toward night when affairs began to take a turn. The expected brigade of Indiana men "hove" in sight from Cumberland Gap and about the same time our wagon train from Knoxville with our tents and supplies arrived. In view of our expected move tomorrow, we are inspected in arms by companies.

October 10—Packed up at seven and filed out on the road going toward Blue Spring. After an hours delay in which we have opportunity to see what our strength is, we begin our move. Several regiments of cavalry and mounted infantry passed by us and take the lead while our Division of some three or four thousand men brings up the rear taking under our protection several batteries. The Generals commanding in person are Burnside, Wilcox, Potter and Ferrero. As they are all fighting men and the troops are tried veterans we have all confidence. After marching four or five miles we found the enemy prepared to give battle just beyond the small village of Blue Spring. The infantry make a short halt while the mounted men and cavalry made an effort to dislodge them, but without success. At noon we hurry through the town and our Division is divided up and sent forward to support the batteries. As the land is quite hilly it affords a good chance for that branch of service to be quite effective. Yet as the enemy had the cover of some dense woods they held us at bay for several hours, when late in the afternoon, our 1st Division was sent forward, which charged upon them, driving them through the woods and out of their good position with considerable loss on both sides. Night closed down upon us finding the 21st comparatively unharmed, only two or three having been wounded although we were under fire several hours while in support of Capt. Benjamin's battery. [*In 1890 Hitchcock added: "Night closed the conflict with considerable loss on both sides but the prestige of winning the first battle in the campaign gave our troops great confidence."*]

[*At the Battle of Blue Springs the Confederates lost 66 men killed and wounded and 150 taken prisoner. The Union lost 100 men killed and wounded.*]

October 11—Laid on arms all night and the enemy finding our force too forcible stole away during the night. We were brought out early in the morning and after yielding the road for Gen. Shackleford's Division of Cavalry to pass, took up the pursuit at nine. Then began a chase, which for our regiment was without a parable during the war. We hardly halt for rest for the next six hours and much of the time we took the double quick step. Passing the farmhouses we are constantly informed that the enemy was but four or five miles ahead, going at the top of speed. Occasionally we pass a fallen horse which shows us that the chase is a hard one even for horses. At three in the afternoon we go racing through the streets of Greenville, much to the bewilderment of the good people who are just coming out of church, this being the Sabbath day. When dusky night throws his mantle over the scene, thoroughly exhausted we camp for the night just beyond the village of Rheatown and give up the chase. The distance traveled is estimated at about thirty three miles.

October 12—Orders came for us to march at six but Gen. Burnside having decided to give up the pursuit, they were countermanded and we rest for the day. A very large mail came in at night, the first received since we came over the mountains.

October 13—Commenced our return tramp, following the wagon train. Passed through Greenville at noon and go into camp by the middle of the afternoon, making eighteen miles tramp. Quite a number of Co. A boys, myself among the number, slept in a barn in a pile of chaff and found very comfortable quarters.

October 14—A portion of the 1st Division were taken on board the cars during the night and sent down to Knoxville. Col. Hawkes and Capt. Sampson came up with the regiment having just returned from Massachusetts via Cumberland Gap. Started at seven and marched to Bull's Gap Junction where we pitch camp. We hardly get our fires to burning when Burnside came down on the cars and ordered us to continue our tramp. During our shortstop here we witness the working of the triangle which the backwoods customs of East Tennessee do not allow to be superseded by the more convenient and less expensive turn-table commonly used by railroads for reversing an engine. March twenty miles and camp a few miles from Russellville.

October 15—March through Russellville, a rebel hole, and reach Morristown, nine miles, where we take the cars and carry them to Knoxville (sarcastic). Reached Knoxville late in the afternoon and reaching camp find to our discomfiture all Co. A tents lost and gone. To add to our troubles the rain began to descend. Dr. Clutter lent us the fly to his large hospital tent which afforded shelter from rain from above, but as the rain continued pouring all night we laid in a running stream of cold water all night. I received a letter from W. Lamb, Rodman's Point, N.C.

October 16—I arise in the morning feeling much demoralized. My past few days experience of hardship and exposure has thrown a <u>deep-tinged blue</u>

over my feeling. A change of officers has been made, assigning Capt. Barker to Co. B and Capt. Parker to Co. A. The boys of Co. A find a vacant chamber in a neighboring dwelling house where we take up quarters and it a desirable change from the soft mud which has been our lot for the post two days.

October 17—Cleaned up gun and equipments for inspection.

October 18—Inspection this morning. I went into the city on a pass.

October 19—I was detailed to go out with Sergeant May to hunt up a rebel spy, who was supposed to have joined one of the raw Kentucky regiments which are encamped at the Fairgrounds three miles, whither we proceeded. We looked through several regiments until we alighted in a company where the man had been, a short time before, but probably having "smelt the cat" he had disappeared. Not gaining any further clue, we returned into the city and reported at Gen. Burnside's headquarters and then returned to camp at dusk.

October 20—The 1st Division have moved, gone southward in the direction of Chattanooga, and we are also under marching orders for tomorrow. Distant heavy cannonading can be heard in the direction of Loudon which apprises us that our neighbors on the south are becoming too familiar. The prospect is that detachments from Lee's army in Virginia will close in upon us on the north and from Bragg's army on the south, while guerrilla bands will shut off communication on the east and west. The old 2nd Brigade has just arrived from over the mountains.

October 21—Drummed up at four with orders to start at six. After waiting till eight, the orders were countermanded and we set to work and pitch tents again. Heard that Wolford's cavalry had a fight with the enemy yesterday.

October 22—With true soldier style, the Company A boys, having secured a fine lot of boards, set to work and in spite of the immediate prospect of moving, we have some very fine comfortable quarters, completed just at noon. I sit down to enjoy the fruit of my labor and eat my dinner under "my own vine and fig tree." When after fifteen minutes repose, orders come for us to march at two. After loafing about the depot through the afternoon we pack into the cars at eight in the evening. After innumerable delays we find ourselves at Loudon bridge twenty eight miles south of Knoxville at half past one in the morning.

October 23—More asleep than awake, we tumble out of the cars and drop down by the side of the track when sleep draws oblivion over us, but at early day light a royal thunder shower succeeds most effectually in withdrawing oblivion and sleep from us. So thinks Capt. Davis who in a profound slumber was lying half under water when Col. Hawkes suggesting it as a labor-saving method of washing his face, draws away his rubber blanket and receives the full benefit of a shower bath. The shower settles down into a cold storm and we stand around fires several hours awaiting orders and receiving none. The Loudon bridge which crossed the Tennessee was a very large structure over which the East Tennessee and Virginia R.R. passed, and consequently a very important point. When Gen. Burnside first came over into East Tennessee, the enemy retreated and burnt the bridge, thereby severing the link which joined Virginia to the Gulf States. The river at this point is wide and the massive stone piers stand as monuments to the wreck. Toward the middle of the afternoon, the entire brigade without the aid of orders broke up into small squads and took to woods nearby and made shelters. Co. A at present consists of twelve men, Jonas Davis, Orderly Sergeant and commanding the company, Albert Osgood, Charley Wilder, Wilbur Potter, Sam Adams, Jack Reynolds, Charley Blackmer, Marcus Gould, Lemuel Whitney, Frank Peckham, Asa Franklin Van Buren Piper and George A. Hitchcock. We build a shelter of rails over which we cover rubber blankets. For a fire we pile rails around a large oak and as we lie down to sleep with our hot fire working into the heart of the oak, we take turns watching it in case it should fall in an unexpected direction.

October 24—But morning comes and finds us all safe. The 2nd Brigade with Gen. Burnside and Potter came down from Knoxville last night. In exploring the woods we come upon a deserted camp of log huts which are appropriated by the 2nd Maryland and the 21st Co. A secure s a hut by itself. Cannonading may be heard a short distance below us down the river.

October 25—Gen. Burnside pitched his quarters some twenty rods from ours, so the Co. A detailed orderlies have been in to see us. Numerous reports are rife that the rebels are very active in an offensive movement upon us.

October 26—Called on Henry at the Division headquarters. We learn of an order just issued by the War Dept. for reenlisting volunteers into veteran regiments with a bounty of $452.

October 27—The day has been spent by the 21st in pitching over its camp. They have now pitched in and concentrated its companies.

October 28—This morning we aroused at four, struck camp and at daylight march down to the river where the pontoon bridge is laid. We learn that a portion of Bragg's army is working its way toward us with the object of taking us on our flank and go into Knoxville. The only force which we have on the south of the river is mounted which will not do to combat with infantry. so the forenoon is spent in drawing them back to the north bank. At ten A.M. they are all across.

We had all been aware for several days that a locomotive and several cars were in our possession on the south side and now as we heard the distant whistle, a general stir ran through the army which laid along the edge of the river, and which could see the line of the railroad on the opposite side for more than a mile. The track was clear and uninterrupted up to the first pier of the destroyed bridge and from that point down to the river surface the distance was about seventy-five feet. As the rumble of the train became distinct, every member of the army foreseeing the fate of the approaching train, secured good points of observation. Soon it came rushing in sight. With breathless excitement we watched to see if the engineer had got off. Approaching within a quarter of a mile we saw the train slack a little and two men jump off. simultaneous with the movement, the train began to increase its speed, showing that they had put on all steam as they cleared the locomotive. On came the doomed train with great velocity and with a terrific bound the entire train was hurled down into the river. The boiler of the engine exploded with a deafening roar throwing off clouds of steam and spray far out on the river. And all the cars disappeared immediately beneath the water, showing the great depth of the river. As soon as the last man had crossed the pontoon, the 21st went to the further end of the bridge by single-file and returning, each shouldered a plank and deposited by the side of the trains in waiting. Just before the final loosing of the pontoon some panic stricken darkies rushed up by the further side and begged leave to cross, which was granted and as they reached the shore, gratitude and happiness shone out from every particular pore of their faces, for their deliverance. The further end was then unloosed and the current swung the boats around to our side where they were dragged ashore to await transportation.

About an hour after the bridge was up, we distinctly saw a horseman ride up on to the opposite heights more than a mile away. He appeared to be watching our movements and after a few moments, galloped away. Nervous with anxiety, we laid about the banks all the afternoon. expecting each moment to see a rebel battery open up on us who are in easy range. At about five in the afternoon, a rebel officer was seen riding down to the banks of the stream with a flag of truce who requested a communication. Adjutant Gen. McKibbin of our division answered the call by sailing across to him, but the meaning of which was unknown to us. At dark, the division went back out of range of rebel artillery and camped for the night. There is much surmising what we shall do next.

October 29—Aroused at light and head toward Knoxville. The mud in the roads is very deep from the heavy rains of the past week. After a tramp of six miles we pitch camp near Lenoir's Mills, a station on the R.R. twenty three miles from Knoxville. The 1st Division camp on the northwest side of the railroad and the 2nd Division on the southeast side.

October 30—The Holston River runs parallel with the R.R. a quarter of a mile in the rear of our camps. Gen. Burnside and staff went up to Knoxville. We heard cannonading at dark, up the river. Piper and Adams were detailed to assist in laying the pontoons, so we surmise that we are in a position where we can resist a large force and if obliged to, can retreat to Knoxville without danger of being cut off. I was detailed to guard regimental headquarters at night, which sets in with very hard rain and intensely dark. When I go onto my beat at nine all fires are out and as <u>watching</u> is out of the question, I <u>listen</u> with all my five senses combined in the ear. After accustoming myself to the suspicious sounds in the vicinity and the distant reports of scout and picket firing, and satisfying myself that my body is actually present with my faithful old "Enfield," both tightly grasped under my rubber (for I cannot discern the faintest outline of either). The rain pelting in torrents, not feeling that I can justly be court-martialed for deserting my post, I take a rapid flight (in mind) and with one bound I have crossed the Holston, Clinch, Cumberland, Allegheny, Blue Ridge and many other deep rivers and lofty ranges and find myself in the quiet home of my boyhood, nestled away up among the New England hills far away. Contrasting the two pictures, one where war's desolating hand has never been felt and being away from any thoroughfare where a soldier's uniform may be seen, and where the terrible conflict is only understood when read from the news-papers, even then the fact does not seem more of a present reality than the story of the "Revolution." The other picture, seen only by the mind's just now. The blackness of night, the bivouac exposed to the inclemency of approaching winter, shut up by impassable barriers of nature on all sides, the formidable army of Lee standing between us and our forces in Virginia, and the well-known fighting Corps of Longstreet closing in upon us with Gen. Bragg's army to back it, living on half-rations, tents lost—"Halt! Who comes there?" "Corporal of the guard with the second relief." "Advance."— O, Well! Boy perhaps you haven't seen all sides of army life yet. Suppose you crawl in and catch a nap before you go on post again; in the meantime, go to sleep and dream of mother, you great nineteen year old baby.

October 31—Regimental monthly inspection. Company A squad is feasting today, for, in addition to our half rations, we have a sheep which the foraging brought in. The enemy tried to cross the river at a ford nine miles above, but were repulsed. Henry was down to see me. Had a letter from home.

November 1, 1863—Heavy frost last night. I was the only man of Co. A on inspection as the rest were all either on duty or sick. At about noon Jonas [*Davis*] hands in a written order to me detailing me as member of the division provost-guard, so I pack up and report at once and find quarters with a Scotchman, a young man of the 7th R.I. from New Bedford, Mass, native of Glasgow, Scotland.

November 2—I have taken an extra duty to perform as hostler for Henry.

November 3—I rode down to Lenoir with my horse and had him shod at the Division wagon camp. It is reported that Lee's army has suffered defeat between Bull Run and Alexandria.

[*At the engagement at Bristoe Station, Virginia, on October 14, 1863, Lee's total losses were about 1,900 while the Federal casualties were 548.*]

November 4—Capt. Davis has been appointed Provost Marshal on the 2nd Division Staff. There seems to be a lull in affairs about here affording us a chance to rest a little, but whether it is the lull that precedes the storm, the future only can tell.

November 5—Commissary continues to issue but half rations which seem light for hearty men, but I am favored in receiving an extra half ration as hostler for the staff.

November 6—I have been on guard at headquarters. Last night was very cold.

November 7—Charley Blackmer came over here on detail as hostler for division surgeon. Willcox's brigade has been driven back from Greenville and the Third Brigade of the 1st Division has been ordered up to help them. They left during the night. I received a letter from home.

November 8—Another very cold night. I went over and had my descriptive list made out at the company. The provost guard was inspected this afternoon by Lieut. Dillenback.

[*Whenever enlisted men or volunteers are separated from their company, on furlough, on attached service or in the hospital, descriptive lists are prepared by the commanding officer of the company indicating all data that will affect their pay.*]

November 9—Our clothing and supply train is expected tonight. Flour was dealt out as a ration today.

November 10—I was on guard at the big corn pile which feeds all the horses and mules connected with the Division. Corps commissary arrives with the long supply trains just over from Kentucky. The mules and teams look rough from their long tramp. Our Division have received orders to march tomorrow morning.

November 11—A large detachment of the 2nd Division laid the pontoon in the rear of their camps not far from here. The Provost guard received clothing and were inspected by Provost Marshal Davis.

November 12—I was on guard at the forage pile near Corps commissary tent. Stood four successive hours during the night. I received my blanket which was left at Camp Nelson. When we came away, it was sent with officers baggage and just arrived in the train.

November 13—Capt. Merritt's train from Kentucky came in tonight loaded with clothing. Our Army is being inspected by Gen. Grant's Inspector General. My tent-mate and I went out this evening and secured an armful of boards which we intend to improve our quarters with.

November 14—Stormy. As we laid in our comparative shelter early this morning, half awake and planning how fine we would fortify ourselves from future storms, Henry hurriedly thrust his head into the tent and says, "Make all possible haste and pack up and then come and help us at the headquarters," for news has just arrived that Longstreet, who has been quietly gathering his forces for the past few days, has very quickly thrown a large force across the river during the night only two miles below and was pushing in our outposts intending to attack our main army which is much inferior in numbers. In less than fifteen minutes, the excitement produced in the camps is intense; the long-roll could be heard from all directions. A large force was sent immediately on double-quick to destroy the pontoons just finished. As there was no time to be lost, the planks were thrown into the river and the boats stove in pieces by the axes of the pioneer-corps, which sound we hear and increases the excitement. In a very few minutes our headquarters were packed, loaded and on the move, hastening at double-quick on the road toward Knoxville. We pass long lines of troops, all headed toward Knoxville, but none toward the enemy. After marching a couple of miles near the railroad track we hear the whistle of an approaching train and down from Knoxville comes a locomotive and one passenger-car on the platform of which stands Gen. Burnside. I never saw a train dash along at such speed before and from the appearance of Burnside as he shot past us, knew he meant business. The army was made to "about-face" and new confidence seems to inspire the troops as they found that Gen. Burnside had no idea of allowing Longstreet to pass into Knoxville without some trouble. The wagon trains were hurried along toward Knoxville. Consequently I, as one of the provost guard, went along to guard the train, a proceeding quite unusual for me, it being the first time I have been away from my regiment in any campaigning. We march all day and late in the evening, park our wagons in a large level field. During the night the weather changed, the wind arose, and a hurricane passed over camp tearing down tents and scattering campfires.

November 15—Soon after light we start with the trains. News came in during the night that the enemy was slowly pushing back our troops, that our army had taken advantage of the ground as they retreated and given battle till nearly flanked when they would retreat in good order till a new vantage ground was secured. Learn that Col. Hartranft has taken command of the Division. Reach Knoxville just as the people were coming out of church from the afternoon service, it being the Sabbath. As we march through the streets we hear the report that the army is fighting desperately and the dull heavy roar of artillery confirms it. There is also sharp and brisk cannonading going on across the river in the southeast about four miles away showing that the attempt is being made to cut around our army and get into the city, by the enemy.

November 16—The day is dark, damp and chilly. Fearing the possibility of drawing fire from the enemy's artillery or an attempt to capture our train, we move out on the Tazewell road half a mile from the city, on the north and temporarily park the wagons in a secluded place where remain all day and night. Our entire force under command of Gen. Willcox came in from Bull Gap and are massing on the south side of the city. We learn of the battle at Campbell's Station [*thirteen miles from Knoxville*] which was a general engagement, fought yesterday afternoon. Also hear that our 9th Corps is just outside the city.

November 17—The day continues dark and chilly. The twenty-four hours commencing this morning have opened up to me a new experience of army campaigning. Our Corps arrived in the city this morning and from our points of observation, we see the troops massing in strong lines on the heights which lie on the north and west of the city, and forming a semi-circle around it. The land appears to lie in such a way that our forces have the advantage of safely protecting the city in case of a siege, which seems to be our lot now. After moving about from place to place behind the hills to keep our teams concealed from the enemy till the middle of the afternoon when all the detailed men are ordered to join their regiments and every bummer and negro is set to work immediately digging fortifications. I find the 21st posted on a prominent hill overlooking the city at its back and a ridge extending over a mile along in a southwesterly direction, along which we can discern the enemy busy fortifying, and along the intervening wooded flat we see the flashing of the skirmishers' guns of both armies. This point is used by the Generals for observation and a staff officer of either the corps or a division is kept continually posted here with field-glasses to watch operations.

Every man of the brigade either officer or private was set to work at dark digging on fortifications and by midnight, the 21st had made a comparative shelter for its men. We were then ordered to go out on our left to support a battery just planted and to dig fortifications for the protection of its gunners. For a long distance in each direction of our line the stillness of the night is broken by the sound of pick axe and shovel and the tearing down of houses and buildings in the vicinity and all fences and obstructions which would hinder the progress of a line of battle. Sounds which portend a desperate resistance.

November 18—After daylight we caught a little rest. Several of Company A found an undisturbed spot in the kitchen of a house in the rear of our earthworks. In the afternoon we were kept in the trench under arms to be in readiness in case of a sudden assault. At dark I was detailed with about half of the regiment to go on the skirmish line. As we reach the line about a quarter of a mile in front, we use the greatest caution in relieving the old relief. Even a loud whisper is instantly checked for fear of disturbing or arousing the vigilance of the enemy's line who are but a few rods in front.

November 19—We suffered severely from cold all night as we had to stand perfectly still in an open field within sound of the enemy's voices. At daylight the skirmishers concealed themselves behind hillocks, trees or buildings. Half a dozen of our regiment found protection behind a barn. The rebel skirmishers kept up a lively firing on us whenever they thought they saw a movement and we were not backward in doing the same. During the forenoon the rebel line of skirmishers was pushed forward, driving in ours several rods. Several of us rallied behind a large brick house and effectually checked the line in front keeping a pretty content fire all day making any organized movement impossible. Skirmish firing was very rapid all around the line all day but without any result as the enemy did not make any forward move. The bulk of Longstreet's Virginia Army is probably opposite us encircling from the Holston on the north around to the south within a radius of five miles. Wolford's cavalry and mounted infantry hold the enemy in check on the south bank. If Longstreet can trust his army to sit down here with Gen. Grant between him and Bragg and several hundred miles away from Lee, he may starve us out in a short time as supplies are very low, but time only can tell the result. [*In 1890 Hitchcock added: "On our side, the supplies of food for man and beast are very low but our fighting spirit is very good, so it is a question of endurance."*]

November 20—I was relieved at dark and laid in the trenches all night and day. At dark the enemy fired a few shell over our heads into the city. New fortifications are being constantly thrown up and a very formidable continuous line confronts the enemy all around. We feel confident of resisting very great odds. After dark the skirmish line in front of us was illuminated by the burning of several houses between the lines. They were burnt by our men to prevent the enemy securing a foot hold in or about them. A detail of men is kept in all such buildings, the houses being packed with inflammable stuff and their orders are "to hold on till they are sure of an attempt by the enemy to get possession and then touch a match to it and run." Hence the burning of these houses. I was detailed to go on the line as relief near one of the burning buildings. When we relieve the old picket we have to creep stealthily around behind fences and buildings and when in the vicinity of our respective posts, crawl on hands and knees under cover of darkness only out on the open field to the rough rifle-pets formed of piles of rails. There are from two to six men on a post according to the importance of the position, and at a distance apart of about five rods.

November 21—Rained all night and all day without intermission. Our condition can be better described than understood. A pool of water settled all around and in our rifle pit, which defense being so shallow, we have to hug the ground to be shielded from observation and yet constantly watching the state of affairs in front. Occasionally changing position to rest our sore limbs, a head or an arm is exposed to the ever watchful rebel picket, when "whiz" comes a "minie." Wet to the skin and not a wink of sleep for nearly thirty six hours. Darkness throwing over a shield and the new relief taking our places, a better state of affairs might be questioned when we return to the damp trenches to eat our half ration of bread, and the weather having cleared up cold my prospect for making up lost sleep in my wet clothes is certainly not very flattering.

November 22—Permission was given to the regiment to quarter in some dwelling houses in the rear of the fortifications providing half the reserve force remained continually in the trench. Quarter rations only were issued, showing clearly that we must be starved out by inches if Longstreet would take the city. A few shells were fired into the city which met with an exchange from our batteries apparently with great effect. Another house was burned on the picket line tonight. I am again on the skirmish line tonight and in a more exposed post than any on the line. Samuel Adams and myself are together in a pit hardly large enough for two standing upright. Know by the lay of the land that daylight will expose us to a flank fire from the enemy. We begin enlarging the pit by turns, first one watching and the other meanwhile digging, loosening the clay soil with bayonet and throwing it out with hands.

November 23—It was very slow work but by daylight we had made an excavation large enough to conceal our whole bodies beneath the surface. The dirt was thrown up in front on the top of which we placed small pine boughs through which we peer quite secure from observation. Yet hardly can I say this, for during the day the picket firing from the rebels was very vigorous and from one point not more than a dozen rods in front, a rebel sharp shooter was posted behind a tree, apparently doing great execution firing up to our fortifications. From two or three of our posts we had made repeated endeavors to hit an exposed limb, when just as I rose up to point my gun through the mask, "Zip!" A flash, a duck of the head, and a twig fell into the pit, cut off exactly in a range with my head, a smarting sensation on the top of my head as if a ball had gone through my scalp and I clap my hand to my head. All done in the space of a second and Adams cries "My God! Hitchcock, you're shot!" It takes several moments to convince myself that I am unharmed. The concussion of the ball as it whizzed through my hair caused a smarting for several minutes.

Toward night the firing of the rebel pickets increased to a regular crack, crack!, but with hardly any effect except a man of Company I being shot in the arm. At dark, suddenly all their firing ceased and the noise of the axe from their fortifications which had been heard continually of late ceased entirely, and for an hour and a half a suspicious, ominous stillness rested on the scene. Awaiting impatiently the coming of the new relief till after nine. Capt. Samp-

8. The East Tennessee Campaign

son came along and said, "The enemy are preparing to charge on us. Stand firm and give them two good volleys." With our guns full-cocked and pointed directly in front, we had but a few moments of this terrible suspense after he had passed on, when suddenly the wild rebel yell sounded out on our right which was caught up all along our front accompanying with a heavy volley. Adams and I waited till we saw all our posts on our right abandoned. Then came a line of flashing fire out of the woods on our left front a dozen rods away. In a moment more as the sound died away the yell broke out and headlong came the rebel line, toward us. We both fired into them and then retreated down the level slope to the railroad, the bullets whistling all about us. We reached the protection of the railroad where it is built up above the level, safely here has been the "inside line of pickets," but now it is entirely abandoned. Just at the juncture of the flames began shooting out from extensive railroad shops and mills between the picket line and the fortifications. We retreat inside the trenches where we find every one prepared for an attack but the enemy had halted at the railroad and by this time nearly every building and dwelling house in the vicinity of the railroad was in flames. The fire spreading soon reached the arsenal and its stores when pandemonium seemed to be let loose. Large quantities of ammunition which proved to be of a kind not serviceable for our army was so arranged as to be destroyed, creating an incessant rattle. This was followed by an explosion of large quantities of shells. At last the powder magazines were reached and as each explosion followed quickly, one after another, fragments of timbers, iron and bricks were thrown hundreds of feet into the air with showers of sparks making the surrounding blackness seem grim indeed. The most sublime of all was the burning of the saltpeter stores, which sent clear blue flames nearly a hundred feet into the air, lighting up the country around with a weird light. The troops were all on "qui vive" for an expected attack. Burnside stood nearby us looking through his night glass for a long time, surrounded by his staff. Over thirty houses were burned aside from the arsenal and railroad buildings and flouring mills. A regiment of South Carolinians, Palmetto Guards, was thrown against our picket line where I had been, as was afterward ascertained by prisoners who were taken by the 48th Penn. which was sent out and forced back the rebel line till they took possession of the houses and began a fire from the doors and windows.

November 24—After another night of watching we were aroused before daylight and the 21st Mass. and 48th Penn. under command of Col. Hawkes filed off to the front down among the railroad buildings, out on the open stretch of land intervening these and the buildings beyond which were filled with rebel soldiers and sharpshooters. Hastily forming in line of battle, just at daylight we charged in among the houses, meeting a brisk fire from the enemy which was posted in the houses and behind fences. Several of our boys fell but we pressed on and reaching the houses we had the satisfaction of seeing the rebels skedaddle pell-mell, leaving everything, knapsacks and blankets, haversacks and rations. Several prisoners were taken in the houses. After following the skedaddlers as far as the Kentucky railroad about a quarter of a mile beyond, we were ordered to halt. Being right under the enemy's fire, it was deemed imprudent to push further and we had also a slight shelter under the low embankment of the railroad. Here we kept up a brisk firing till every "Johnnie" was back in his picket hole, in the original line. There here we were right in the jaws of the Secession serpent. The fortifications of the enemy frowning down upon us and their rifle pits scarcely a dozen rods away in our front. But the slight shelter of the railroad tracks saved us from these and up the railroad a short distance was a large rifle pit filled with the enemy who were troublesome for a while, but keeping sharp watch on this place sending bullets at the slightest sign of a movement were soon silenced. After lying in this position several hours, orders were sent down from the city for us to fall back, orders which were more easily given than obeyed.

In retreating, we must either run the gauntlet of the entire line of rebel fortifications and rifle pits up a steep bank about five rods to the protection of a house, or crawl flat on the stomach for more than twenty rods with the simple shelter of the railroad sleeper and tracks where we would reach a basin out of which we could retreat with comparative safety.

After a long hesitation, Major Richardson, finding none ready to choose, leaped up and rushed up the bank followed by more than twenty bullets. He reached the shelter in safety, the bullets all striking too low. Soon a second man followed him in safety, but the bullets intended for him struck a poor fellow of the 48th Penn. where he lay partially concealed behind a stump, hitting him in the head and he rolled out in plain view of us all and died.

Most of the 21st chose the safer route which was very fatiguing as I found by experience, at last reaching safety, completely saturated with clay mud. In this uncomfortable plight, a sorry looking sight, I plodded up into the fortifications and was joyfully greeted by Henry who had been anxiously watching for me. Our loss is not yet accurately known. Several were wounded and two of the 21st killed outright while the 48th suffered severely. Our little German cook of Company E was shot while he lay concealed in a hand car which stood upon the tracks. He laid groaning all day and after dark he was brought in by two of his comrades and died during the night. November 25—I was roused up before light and detailed with others to reinforce the picket of the second Brigade. Traveled over the same ground we charged yesterday morning. In our rifle-pit today we watched an officer of the enemy ride out of the woods on a milk white horse. Stopped very coolly and viewed our lines. Several of our pickets sent him "lightning dispatches" when he prudently turned and galloped out of sight. Later in the day musketry and cannonading was heard across the river where Wolford is holding the enemy in check. Ripley of Co. K was shot dead by a rebel sharpshooter while standing on the breastworks in the afternoon. At night we were relieved from picket and set to work digging rifle-pits further in advance which took us very near the rebel line of pits. Through the cold dim, starlight night we ply the pick and shovel till nearly daylight working very slowly and silently knowing that if discovered by the rebel pickets they could cover us easily. We dug one pit in the front yard and another in the back yard of a very tasty modern built house, ruthlessly tearing up beautiful shrubbery of choice kinds. All the furniture was strewn about the yards, some of which was very costly. I confiscated a fine map of North America which laid in the wet grass detaching it from the rollers, folded it and sent it home. We returned to quarters before daylight.

November 26—Thanksgiving day at home, and how shall we spend it here? For we ought to be truly thankful that our lives have been spared through these severe hardships and dangers. As food has become so scarce we have but one meal today. That consisted of roast beef. No side dishes of bread, potatoes or else, and the beef was the result of a rebel heifer confiscated on the picket line. "Jule" our cook <u>confiscated</u> some barley which he burnt and made into coffee. Afternoon I went down into the city to Division Headquarters and saw the provost boys who remained when I returned to the company. We are under orders to be prepared to move at a moments notice as the enemy is expected to be preparing to attack us and break our lines.

November 27—We stayed in the trenches all night and nearly all day waiting for the expected attack which has not yet come. The enemy is feeling our picket line endeavoring to find our weakest point so we look for them with a tolerable degree of certainty. During the night as one of our videttes [*mounted sentry*] was standing in front of the rifle pit in the shadow of a large tree, he heard the rustle of leaves near him and watching closely discovered the form of a man worming himself along within a rod of him. As he had not discovered the vidette, he continued to move till within arm's length when he received the whispered order "Halt." He was relieved of his arms and brought into camp as a spy.

November 28—Went out on picket before light in the rifle pit near the ruins of the brick mansion. Rained hard all day and notwithstanding rubber and woolen blankets, I became soaked to the skin. At about nine in the evening the firing suddenly increased until a whole volley from an advancing line was heard about a quarter of a mile down the line in front of the 1st Division accompanied with the wild yell of the enemy. After a few minutes the firing diminished and we knew nothing of the result. Wait anxiously watching about an hour lying in the mud when another volley and another yell and this time nearer than before, several of the spent bullets striking about us. As before, the firing gradually ceased but our batteries have discovered something through the impenetrable darkness for first one entire battery opens its thunders and then another and another till all the line of batteries on this side of the city are belching forth from their lurid sheets, shot and shell uncomfortably low, over our heads.

November 29 [*Confederates assaulted Fort Sanders at 6 a.m.*]—Musketry was incessant. As the center of attraction was on this fort the key of all the other fortifications, we were kept in our trenches knowing we could best take them in their rear to advantage. But the desperate conflict is over by broad daylight and our brave boys have held the "key" and down past our street comes a long line of rebels. Not finding it necessary to carry arms they travel along as captives instead of victors. The result is at last ascertained. The enemy threw his picked forces massed against the fort [*Fort Sanders*] which was filled by one or two veteran regiments and Capt. Benjamin's battery. The "Burnside Wire" created great confusion among the enemy throwing them pell-mell in great heaps into the ditch when our boys tossed lighted hand grenades among them making their rout complete. But as the remnant was retreating down the hill, the 2nd Brigade charged on them and took a large number of prisoners. Their loss was estimated at seven hundred.

An armistice was granted till five in the afternoon for the enemy to carry away its dead. Throughout the day brisk conversation was kept up between the picket lines until the signal gun at five proclaimed hostilities opened.

November 30—Our ration is today a quarter ration of wheat bran which will not sustain life long. I went on picket this morning near the brick house by the railroad. Positive information has been received of a large reinforcement enroute for our relief.

December 1, 1863—Off picket this morning and on again at night. Surely this is a good deal of a good thing, but I am one of the healthy ones yet and the silver lining of this cloud is growing brighter so I live in the future somewhat.

General Burnside issued orders among the troops praising them for their fortitude and giving account of a great victory by Grant's army at Chattanooga. He received the news by couriers who ran the enemy's lines. Before going on picket at night I accepted an invitation from Henry to tea at a citizen's house where I find some folks have enough to eat if soldiers do not. Henry also makes one a most acceptable present of a cavalry overcoat which meets a great want of mine as the wintry weather comes on. Truly a "friend in need, is a friend in deed."

December 2—Our picket post is at a brick spring-house, the rendezvous of the officers of picket, and although the nearest point to the rebel line, we have had a much easier day than for several days past, less watching and more chances to exercise our limbs. Our boys have been holding conversation with the Johnnies throughout the day although contrary to orders. Each side have agreed to withhold firing on each other without due notice. Consequently the day has been quite still. We learn that the 6th South Carolina regiment are picketing in our front.

December 3—We were kept in the trenches most of the night expecting an attack while our artillery kept up a desultory fire the while. It is rumored that the enemy is leaving.

December 4—No firing on the line where I spent on picket. But one shot from the rebel battery (for fun probably). Much amusement from the contraband conversations is created for our poor starving boys will have fun even in their misery. A young heifer had been coaxed out in front of the lines by some shrewd rebel, where she was shot by him, with the intention of hauling back for their use, but not being badly disabled, she ran away from her would-be murderer directly into our lines when Harper of Company K finished her, in plain sight of the opposite party, and dragged her into the shelter of our rifle pit. Then began a series of altercations, entreaties and persuasions from the rebs to have us give up their rightful booty, but as the point could not be distinctly seen, they proposed to trade something to secure a morsel of meat which they were ardently longing for. Then the Yankee propensity for a bargain overruling the dictations of a hungry stomach, propositions were made and accepted, exchanging a small piece of meat for rebel news-papers.

[*Richmond Examiner, December 1, 1863—Editor John M. Daniel wrote: "It appears that Grant is doing his best to fulfill the arrogant orders of his masters, and that Bragg has been getting himself whipped again near Ringgold. Never, perhaps, in history, has the consequence of incompetent generalship, and want of confidence between commander and troops, been more manifest than at present in northern Georgia. We have no doubt that General Bragg has done the best that he could, and for all the ill that has befallen him and us, Mr. Davis alone is responsible. It is clear, that if he persists longer in the pitiful perversity which has retained Bragg in the command, in spite of remonstrance, in spite of facts, in spite of common sense and duty, that the army of Georgia will be disorganized and lost.... There are many good officers, and any of them is better than a general who has always been favored by his Government and always frowned by fortune."*]

The joyful intelligence has come that Gen. Sherman fought a battle at Loudon, broke the enemy's lines and forcing them northward, has large reinforcements just below the city, while he himself has arrived at Gen. Burnside's quarters. A large body of rebel prisoners has already been brought in. Twenty two thousand prisoners from Bragg's Army have been captured.

December 5—During the night watching was kept up as strictly as ever but toward morning a staff officer of the Division came down to our post and said it was thought the enemy's picket line had been abandoned about an hour and he requested some man to volunteer to go out toward their lines till he ascertained whether it was true. Now we had heard the conversation of their picket, and seen their fires as they replenished the fuel up to three o'clock, and although it seemed probable that they had gone, it was a hard thing to undertake and as no one seemed inclined to go, Corporal Harrington of Company K, who was on duty at the time, was sent out. With a solemn face he gave up his watch and other valuables and started out into the darkness. He went down as far as the creek on hands and feet. Then crossing over he wormed himself up very carefully toward the nearest pit and hearing no sound, he grew bolder and with a leap bounded over into the pit, finding it empty. When he returned with the joyful intelligence to our anxious group who were waiting in the darkness, and told his story, which was immediately made know at headquarters and before day had fairly broken, Wolford's boys were seen galloping out on the Jacksonboro road to worry the retreating enemy. We at last breathe freer and dare to get out on the breastworks by daylight without fear of molestation. Later in the day our line of pickets which had been the scene of so much intense and painful watching for three weeks was abandoned. Our Brigade was sent out to reconnoitre the rebel camps and works. We met scores of ragged, miserable looking rebel prisoners coming in. Nearly all appeared glad to have fallen into Yankee hands. After a tedious tramp through mud and through woodlands and over hills, we came into Knoxville on another side of the city, having found no force. Though very formidable preparations to lay siege to the city had been made. We walked ten miles. Pay-rolls were signed after we returned.

December 6—I wrote home and received pay from the government. Toward night we were favored with a call from Generals Sherman and Burnside with their staffs, who came up to view the vacated works from our fortifications. Gen. Sherman is a plain looking man but smart, with heavy light brown whiskers. He wore an undress military suit with a civilian overcoat.

December 7—At four this morning orders came for us to march at seven with three days rations which being interpreted meant only one day's ration for three days use. As we marched out of the city toward the north we passed by Parson Brownlow's house where we saw his family standing outside witnessing the passing troops. Among the group was a rebel Colonel, brother of the parson's wife, who is held as prisoner. From a commanding eminence on the road we could see it filled with troops for miles, the entire 9th and 23rd Corps being on the move. Sherman's men remain in the city. After a brisk march of twelve miles we halt for the night.

December 8—As we do not hurry off on the march I went off among the mountains foraging for something to eat. Found meal and dried peaches which we confiscate, finding that the surly owners do not hold a proper respect for the Old Flag. At ten a.m. we take up the line of march with the enemy about a dozen miles ahead, and Gen. Sherman advancing on the opposite side of the river. We are on the road to Bean's Station. March eight miles.

December 9—Started at half past seven. Our route lay along a valley between two ranges of mountains running north-easterly about two miles apart. The lofty Clinch range on the left. Fires are burning in woods all along the sides of the mountains, probably signals of the enemy's. Our supply of rations is exhausted and we are now living on parched corn. We go into camp near the village of Rutledge at noon. Made a march of thirteen miles.

December 10—Laid in our bivouac all day. The boys have instituted general foraging and as parties of them return from time to time laden with pigs, turkeys, and chickens, considerable interest is created by their raffling them out to lovers of the game. Our hearts were gladdened with the sight of John Wallace, just arrived from Cumberland Gap. He came through with the first squad that has been through since the siege was laid and say that large mails are waiting for us at the Gap. We received two days rations of corn meal tonight.

December 11—No movement of troops today. Gen. Foster has arrived and taken command of our department at Knoxville. Although foraging seems to be the order of the day, yet no breadstuff can be found. A train came in from the Gap at night.

December 12—Our sutler came in with it and says he has three loads of stuff at the Gap for us. A large detail for a provost guard to protect citizens from the ravages of the troops was made from the regiment. [*In 1890 Hitchcock added: "Hunger makes a brute of a man and therefore is somewhat excusable."*]

December 13—Regimental inspection of arms and equipments was held at ten o'clock. The boys foraged a large lot of eatables for the company consisting of chickens, biscuit, beans, dried apple and peach, cabbage and pork.

December 14—Change of weather during the night to very chilly and cold. Orders came at midnight to march at seven in the morning, which were countermanded. Half rations of sugar and coffee were dealt out, a rare luxury to us. Large mails from the north have arrived and I received a large bundle of papers and letters.

December 15—Orders again came for us to be ready to move at a moments notice, so we struck tents and laid in line of battle through the day. It is known that the enemy has been reinforced from Virginia and are pushing us back fighting at Bean's Station. Under cover of darkness we file out in line on the backward track and march over one of the roughest roads I ever saw, fording streams. The order of companies and regiments was entirely broken and we all pushed along crowding and hustling like a pack of sheep though each man for himself. After about six miles of this kind of traveling we halt unmix and build large fires of rails, lie down on arms for the remainder of the night.

December 16—Started at nine in the morning, again on the retreat and after about six miles we are about-faced and drawn out in line of battle. The enemy have pressed in so closely that our cavalry have fallen back with us, skirmishing as they retreat.

December 17—Our Division is drawn out in one long line of battle extending across the valley and immediately throw up a barricade of rails. The cavalry dismounts and their horses taken to the rear out of range. They then form another line few rods in front of us and lie down flat. "Now is your time. Come on Johnnies we are ready to receive you." Soon the enemy's line of skirmishers are seen advancing out of the woods far up on the sides of the mountain on our left. Our cavalry falls back in our rear and our line of skirmishers is out and Benjamin's battery on an eminence just in our rear opens its fire on the advancing line which forces them to take cover in the woods again and as night soon comes on we conclude they dare not attempt a general attack. General Granger arrived with his 4th Corps which has just come around via Chattanooga from Mississippi. So we again take courage and are ready to meet the enemy. During the afternoon we hear heavy cannonading, very brisk and incessant across the river which is telling the story of death which is making over there. With Sherman's and Granger's and Burnside's armies we shall soon be able to withstand all that Lee can spare. Commenced raining at night and rations were given out so I with others of the company sat most of the night in the rain cooking them. toward morning it cleared up cold.

December 18—This morning as the enemy does not make an appearance; the 21st is ordered out to relieve the picket line of skirmishers. We find they are advanced two miles and the enemy is about a mile further. Brother Henry and another staff officer were sent out to place the foremost picket while we deployed out, the main line resting at a large farm house. We form a new barricade of rails but hardly is it finished when we are drawn back a mile nearer our main force at dusk and a straight unbroken line is established from summit to summit across the valley. Company A was placed across the creek on a post by itself where we kept a strict watch all night.

9

Winter in the Mountains

"They find but little sleep or rest in the bitter cold, for nothing short of constant motion could keep them from freezing."
—Hitchcock, January 9, 1864

A small Union force, including the 21st Massachusetts Regiment, trailed Longstreet's Corps as far as Rutledge, thirty miles northeast of Knoxville, but it was deemed inadvisable to attack the larger Confederate force. Longstreet's troops remained in East Tennessee until the following spring, causing considerable annoyance to Union troops by threatening their supply lines. The Southerners experienced extreme hardship during the winter in their camps around Russellville and Morristown with only shelter tents for protection, inadequate clothing and a critical shortage of food. The weather was bitterly cold—the worst winter in decades.

By December 27, 1863, two-thirds of the 21st Massachusetts Regiment, including George Hitchcock, had reenlisted for three additional years of service. On January 6, 1864, the reenlisted soldiers received orders to march to Camp Nelson and proceed by train to Covington, Kentucky, in preparation for their return to Massachusetts and a thirty-day reenlistment furlough. The regiment left Blain's Cross Roads on January 7 with 200 Confederate prisoners, starting their miserable trek back without sufficient food and clothing while having to endure severe winter conditions. The veteran Bay Staters arrived at Camp Nelson during the early evening of January 18. The men reached Cincinnati by train eleven days later on January 29, and arrived at Worcester, Massachusetts, on the early evening of January 31. They received a huge public welcome the following morning.

On January 28, 1864, the United States Senate and House of Representatives approved a resolution thanking Maj. Gen. Ambrose Burnside, and his officers and men "for their gallantry, good conduct, and soldier-like endurance." There were only four joint resolutions approved by Congress during the war that thanked an individual for great service to the nation.

* * * *

December 19, 1863—At night we are relieved and find the 21st has gone into camp near some woods. We pitch tents and finding the sutler with his stock of goods I buy a pair of boots which I stand in great need—my shoes are worn out and the approaching winter makes this a necessity for me.

December 20—The weather is growing very cold. Mud has frozen stiff. Regimental inspection by an officer of the Brigade staff. I went on picket at five at night. The nights are very long.

December 21—Laid on picket all day with Whitney and Wilder. Two more loads of sutler's goods with our knapsacks arrived.

December 22—Mended clothes. All detailed men have been ordered to regiments. I went on picket.

December 23—Cold and cloudy. At light our picket lines were ordered to advance and being deployed about a rod apart, we could sweep the whole valley from ridge to ridge—the object being to find whether we had any enemy in front of us and to catch any guerrillas which infest these mountain holds. As my post was up on the side of the Clinch range, I found a very rough route, at times almost impassable, up steep pitches and then down into ravines, then around some precipice and through almost impenetrable underbrush. Our greatest endeavor all the while was to keep pace and proper distance to my right guide and in passing through one dense thicket I lost sight of my guiding man Bailey of Co. I. When I closed in with the man next below him, he was missing and was not seen after that. After traveling about six miles in this manner, we halt and not finding any signs of the enemy, we return to camp by the main road. We passed several farm houses whose owners were all very loyal, some of them too much so, but one old man standing in front of his house showed all the fire of real hatred and exasperation, exclaimed, "Kill every mother's son of them, my rascally tory neighbors. I have four sons fighting them and if Government would take me I would go too."

December 24—Very cold last night. An order was read for reenlisting veterans. Cannonading was heard in the direction of Morristown.

December 25—Christmas Day. Had goose for breakfast. Charles Blackmer and Jack Reynolds returned from Knoxville, went there to see the provost guard at division headquarters. Tonight I went on picket. My post is on the top of a high hill overlooking our whole picket line and camps.

December 26—Rained all day, we made a shelter of a fly and kept "decently uncomfortable" until relieved at night. As we return to camp we found great enthusiasm over recruits enlisting as veterans. Dr. Cutter was making a speech upon a large stump showing the advantages of reenlisting and urging every man to do so. According to a promise from the Government of a furlough of thirty days and large bounties about three-fourths of the regiment have reenlisted, myself with the rest for the prospect of a thirty days rest at home is too tempting. [*In 1890 Hitchcock added: "But the government knew the importance of holding these veteran regiments, and the spirit of patriotism was surely at the bottom of the enthusiasm. Of course I joined the new recruits."*]

December 27—The report of our reenlistment has already been sent in to Corps Headquarters and it is thought that our regiment is the first one to have responded to the call from East Tennessee, though a Michigander regiment is nearly even with us.

December 28—Two obstinate birds of Company A have yielded and reenlisted with the rest of us, Samuel Gould and Reuben Mann.

December 29—The reenlisted of the 21st and 48th Penn. were sworn into a new service by a regular army officer. I went on picket on the front line in the woods.

December 30—Colonel Hawkes has received orders to report his 21st regiment to Governor Andrews in Massachusetts, and we are to leave here as soon as we can get ourselves ready. We are to go by way of the Gap with four days rations. [*In 1890 Hitchcock added: "We do not anticipate as easy a march as we found on coming out."*]

December 31—Commenced to rain at night. The regiment was mustered in for pay and the non-reenlisting ones are to join the 36th Mass. I went on picket at night, on the "side hill post" which lies in an exposed position. I did not sleep at all and so watched out the old year and the new one in.

January 1, 1864—Toward morning the wind changed and commenced snowing, growing very cold and before daylight it had become sleet but at daylight the storm ceased and the sun came out of a bitter cold sky. By the help of enormous piles of rails for fires, we roast one side while the other side freezes or constantly changing position we manage to keep from becoming "baked ice." We learn that the mercury fell to several degrees below zero. At night we drew rations of hardtack, sugar and coffee.

January 2—Cloudy, very cold, no thawing all day and all nature frozen stiff. Henry has come back to the regiment and has been assigned to Company A as commander. One hundred and seventy rebel prisoners came down from Knoxville whom we are to guard en route for Camp Nelson. Half the regiment has been detailed to guard them so no picket detail from our regiment has been made. [*In 1890 Hitchcock added: "Much interest is taken in our new allies—the graybacks; most of them are very ragged and barefoot."*]

January 3—The weather moderated at night and rain began to fall. I have been on guard over prisoners. Piper the only Company A man who does not reenlist left us, on a detail as teamster. Capt. Clark returned from Knoxville with orders for us to draw pay at Camp Nelson.

[*Asa Piper, resident of Templeton, Massachusetts, was killed on May 6, 1864, at Battle of the Wilderness.*]

January 4—Our ration today consisted of two ears of corn to a man. I fear we shall rob the poor mule. But our Johnnie friends seem well contented with our treatment of them, so I think their appetites may be of a more ethereal nature or else their idea of the Yankee ration is more exalted than mine.

[*In 1890 Hitchcock added: "As we sit gazing in awe and wonder at these emblems of a peaceful bucolic life, we are puzzled to know why the little boy in the reading book called for "only three grains of corn, mother." Perhaps his teeth were poor and he couldn't chew any more. But our rebel friends do not exhibit any unusual surprise at the "hog's food" and seem well contented to fare as we do."*]

[*"Give me three grains of corn, mother, Only three grains of corn. 'Twill keep what little life I have—Till the coming of the morn." This is the first of nine verses of the song:* Give Me Three Grains of Corn, Mother. *This story about a starving boy was printed in school readers during the mid-nineteenth century. According to Carl Sandburg, the 1848 version was long and "it prolongs desolation beyond endurance or healthy art. The latter quality is not found in the variants known among midwest pioneers." The verse mellowed and sweetened as it was passed on over the years and was sung in new ways.*]

January 5—A mild winter day and a very quiet one for me. I assisted Henry at building his eleventh-hour chimney and pitching tent. The boys are very anxious waiting for the order to move, and we all look forward with the brightest anticipations to a present relief from this season of hardships in the isolated country.

January 6—My turn comes again as guard over the rebel prisoners. In conversation with one of the prisoners I learned that he belonged to Longstreet's army and fought us at Fredericksburg directly opposite our regiment, also at Antietam opposite the bridge. He has since been in the Battle of Chancellorsville and in the battles around Chattanooga. Our orders have come at last and we expect to start in the morning.

January 7—We are up betimes and packed but do not hurry off till afternoon; began snowing early in the day. We distributed all our extra clothing and shoes among our rebel friends and at two p.m. file out of camp with them between two lines of our boys. In high spirits we bade good bye to our auld comrades and passing the Division and Corps headquarters we cheered our Generals who saluted us; then setting our faces "Northward" struck out into a blinding snow-storm and left our army behind. Passed Baines Crossroads and camp about seven miles from our old campground on the opposite side of the Clinch range. Company A made a fine shelter of rails and our fly pieces outside. Sam Gould returned to the Company so I bunk with him. We sat up till quite late, being in fine spirits, we enjoyed ourselves around enormous camp fires while the snow fell fast all night. (We have some curious feelings as we realize we are now cut off from our army and have no knowledge of the whereabouts of the enemy.)

January 8—At light the clouds cleared away and we started out through the snow which began to melt early in the day. By the middle of the forenoon we passed the headquarters of Gen. Willcox, who commands the new Indiana Brigade which is posted along the road to the Gap. He warned Col. Hawkes to keep a strict watch for guerrillas who are very troublesome through this region. During the afternoon Capt. Davis and Lieut. Walcott passed on horseback bound for Camp Nelson. By sundown we reached Clinch River and were put across in a ferryboat [*Walker's Ford*], straggling into camp a mile beyond. As the sun disappeared the air grows cold. We marched twenty miles.

January 9—Fair and cold. The prisoners now march in the rear of the regiment and today I march as guard with them. Passed through the village of Tazewell and camped a mile south of the Powell River after a march of seventeen miles. Reuben Mann came up with the regiment at night and says the 8th Michigan Infantry are a few miles in our rear bound for home. As the sun sinks out of sight it grows bitter cold and as there is a scarcity of rails in the vicinity, the boys demolished an old log house and soon have monstrous hot fires going. The prisoners were permitted to go and find rails which were discovered and quickly transferred to camp. I stood guard four hours during the night by one of the rebel fires. They find but little sleep or rest in the bitter cold, for nothing short of constant motion could keep them from freezing.

[*In 1890 Hitchcock added: "The prisoners give us no trouble and nearly all seem quite contented to be with us and share our comfort."*]

January 10—I caught an hours sleep just before daylight by the big log fires of our own camp. As it comes light we are convinced that we have passed through the coldest night of the winter! The frost work on the hair and beards of the men give us a venerable look. We are off by light and with light hearts soon become warmed into a brisk walk which soon brought to the river [*Powell*] which we cross over a new large bridge guarded by block houses and a fort on the north side. Guerrillas are hovering near so that our men dare not leave the command for much distance.

Reached the Gap at noon where we find a sutler and began filling our lean haversacks. Company funds are brought into use and we are feasting on a limited scale. Boots and shoes find quick sales with the half clad and half shod rebels who have the "simon pure" gold and silver as well as stacks of confederate bonds. Reaching the cornerstone we cast a look away back over the country which has been fraught with so much hardship for the last few months. Then turn forward into an unbroken wilderness of forest and mountains. We push ahead and reach Log Mountain where we camp for the night after a march of sixteen miles. Here we found a supply train toiling up the mountains, which was an inclined plain of glare ice. We drew rations of hardtack and "sow-belly," coffee and sugar—full rations for the first time for over three months.

January 11—Thawing. I guarded prisoners. The 8th Michiganders, unencumbered with Johnnies like us, passed us this morning. Congratulations passed between the two regiments over our future prospects. We started near noon and marched seven miles to the [*Cumberland*] ford which we crossed on a pontoon, and camped on the side of a mountain over-looking the river. We met two long trains going out to Tennessee. My post guarding the prisoners during the night was by a large stump which I set fire and as it made so comfortable a position for me, I remained by it all night When off duty I went to sleep and rolled into it, caught fire and burnt my overcoat and blanket quite badly before I realized my situation.

January 12—We were obliged to wait for our wagon train to come up and did not start till noon. Marched through Flat Creek and camped for the night about eight miles from our last camp. We again drew rations of hardtack and meat from a supply train which we met. We met three long trains and large droves of cattle going over the mountains.

January 13—Started before light and marched eight miles to Barboursville [*Kentucky*] where we halted to buy shoes which we all stand in great need of. My boots have given out about the toes so that they afford no protection except against the rough broken stone of which the pike is made. I carried the kettle today in the rear of the regiment which favored by feet in traveling.

January 14—Started at light and marched nineteen miles to Camp Pitman. Passed through London and was on prisoners guard till night.

January 15—Chilly and cold. Started before light on the Richmond Road but my feet becoming so sore I was obliged to give up at last and was piled into an old rickety cart which Dr. Cutter had pressed from some farmer. [*In 1890 Hitchcock added: "We went into camp near Big Hill after a march of fifteen miles on a side hill in deep snow. I am twenty years old today."*]

January 16—A beautiful day. Our soft beds of snow, we found somewhat settled this morning on rising. At nine commenced the ascent of Rock Castle Mountain and all the day we kept our course along a ridge of mountains known as the "Hog's Back" overlooking the surrounding country. At night as we near our journey's end we begin to see more cultivation and we descend "Big Hill," a very long and steep one. Camped in the valley near the camp of the 47th Kentucky. I made me a bed of fence-rails and laid me down and slept.

January 17—Started before daylight in a drizzling rain on the Richmond Pike, which we soon left and took a very poor circuitous route. Rain fell incessantly through the day. Toward night we struck the Lancaster Pike and went into camp about ten miles from Lancaster making about fourteen miles. I rode most of the way in an army wagon; my feet are very sore and swollen, threw away my socks as they gathered more grit and sand than they kept out.

January 18—Another stormy day. Started before light and reached Lancaster at ten a.m., pushed on to Camp Dick Robinson reaching there at noon and halt for coffee. Took up the line of march early in the afternoon. The men kept giving out along the march, so severe was the tax on sore feet. As I was unable to keep up with the main body and the wagons were all filled I received permission to "struggle." As I neared the river, my feet became very painful and it is with the greatest difficulty that I drag them along through the soft "pudding" mud which covers the pebbly bottom of the pike. I reached Camp Nelson during the evening where I found our good friend Capt. Hall busily engaged in getting the regiment into a comfortable condition. Loads of straw were sent in to us and we were quartered in a large new building prepared for government wagon building. Our prisoners were turned over to the Provost Marshal and sent to the Military Prison. We march twenty-five miles.

[*In 1890 Hitchcock added: "Our rebel friends, in whom we had become quite interested by our mutual hardships and contact, were turned over to the provost marshal and sent to the military prison."*]

January 19—Very pleasant and cold. Woke up and found a deep snow on the ground. The detailed 21st boys who were left here came in to see us. Clothing was given out, and I drew a new suit throughout. I bought a respectable dinner at a saloon. I feel thoroughly used up.

January 20—We were generously treated to a ride to Nicholasville. The entire regiment being carried U.S. Transfer Wagons, thanks to Capt. Hall. Quartered in the Court House several hours until three in the afternoon when we took cars for Covington. Reaching there at midnight, we got out and found quarters in barracks outside the city, a mile from Cincinnati.

January 21—Drizzling rain throughout the day. Our officers set to work immediately making out our discharge papers and others for making the muster-in-rolls. Charles Hayward came over from Cincinnati to see me and I went down to Covington with him. Examination of the regiment by Dr. Cutter.

January 22—The 6th N.H. Regt. another veteran regiment was paid off today. The 50th Penn. came in tonight.

January 23—Drew clothing and shoes today. The 100th Penn. came in tonight.

January 24—As our barracks are getting full the 100th Penn. was sent over to Cincinnati for quarters. Cole and I went over to the Eleventh Street Hospital to see Lem Whitney but could not gain admission. I again signed the enlistment papers. Red Tape, Red Tape.

January 25—Succeed in gaining admission to see Lem Whitney, find him suffering excruciating pain from a lame leg. The 16th N.H. started for home tonight.

January 26—Today we begin to appreciate the crowning glories of an efficient commander. I have just found that recruits of less than two years service cannot reenlist on the same conditions as <u>old</u> soldiers, consequently that I must turn about and go back to East Tennessee. We reenlisted in East Tennessee with the explicit understanding that the recruits of July 1862 to the Massachusetts Regiments held all the privileges of the regiment to which they joined, the great inducement held out to fill up the skeleton regiments of Virginia campaigns. With this understanding clearly approve by all the Commanding Departments and Corps officers in East Tennessee, we were allowed to reenlist. And now our far seeing, influential regimental commander allows himself to be bamboozled into the belief that he knows more than government itself, but such are the intricacies of human government. Maj. Richardson has been sent down to Lexington to see if extra furloughs may not be granted to us unfortunates, ostensibly to calm our troubled minds. The regiment was mustered in today and at night the 48th Penn. arrived from Tennessee.

January 27—Major Richardson returned from Lexington with orders for recruits to report at headquarters of the department in that place. So after all this painful, long tramp in midwinter over this mountain wilderness kept up through all its vicissitudes by the delightful prospect of a short rest with dear home friends, we are fully entitled to the pleasures and privileges in store for the rest of the regiment. A sorry disappointment and a "madder" set of fellows than we "raw recruits" can hardly be conceived. Who blames us? Time will yet unravel the befogged brains of higher officers. The regiment was paid off in the afternoon and the men mostly scattered off into Cincinnati to get rid of the pocket-burning greenbacks, leaving the barracks at night almost deserted, a relief to the ears of those who remained, as the past few days of noise in this crowded bedlam has testified. As but few returned during the night we apprehend turbulent times tomorrow when the drunken set return. As I was returning from the spring during the evening I was suddenly taken sick and fainted away. I had almost reached the barracks when I fell down and for a few moments became unconscious. Recovering somewhat, I dragged myself into the barracks and to my bunk and by morning I felt better.

January 28—During the forenoon I went downtown and received two months pay, crossed over to Cincinnati, called at Mr. Holden's place of business and rode out to Mt. Auburn with Mr. Charles Houghton and dined with Mrs. Hayward at Mr. Holden's. Returning I made a few purchases including a nice thick rubber blanket. [*In 1890 Hitchcock added: "R. A. Holden and Company* was owned by Reuben A. Holden and Charles E. Houghton, who were wholesale dealers in feathers, ginseng and beeswax."]

January 29—At five in the morning I packed and went down to the depot to meet the train to Lexington but missed the train so went over to Cincinnati, got a shave and bath. Returned to Covington in time for the two o'clock train for Lexington where I arrived at seven in the evening and found lodgings at the Soldiers Home on Broadway.

January 30—I went out in the morning to Fort Clay where I found the remainder of the regiment (those who were rejected for reenlistment) situated very comfortably in barracks clean and warm.

Comment in 1890: When Dr Cutter examined the regiment, he found quite a large number of men whose dissolute habits had brought on loathsome diseases, and he very wisely cut them off from the privileges of reenlistment. These are the comrades with whom my lot is cast and the stigma of disgrace as well as the association I must endure with them—surely "when it rains, it pours."

January 31—Sabbath day, which is my first one since last summer. Attended the Presbyterian Church in the morning and the Methodist in the evening. Wrote letters home and had roast turkey for supper.

February 1, 1864—I was detailed with nine others to report to the Provost Marshal in the city. We were instructed to make ourselves scrupulously neat for the Commanding Officer of the Post, Col. William S. King of 35th Mass., was ambitious to have his Massachusetts boys look more soldierly than the average Western soldiers who were about town! I was posted at the market and had orders to preserve order in the streets in that vicinity. the 18th Kentucky passed on the cars.

February 2—I saw Capt. Hall on board the train bound for Cincinnati. More of our boys came down from Cincinnati just recovered from the effects of a spree.

February 3—Went on guard again today. My post in front of Col. King's residence on East High St., the most fashionable street of the city, on which is John Morgan's home. My principal duty while on my beat walking back and forth was to salute all officers passing according to rank. This red tape is what is commonly styled "parlor soldiering." One of the "left behind" was shot in the head while on guard down at the Market. He was engaged in stopping a row when a policeman fired into the crowd hitting him. It is thought not to be a serious wound.

February 4—A disagreeable, squally day. In the evening I saw Tom Thumb and Commodore Nutt with their ladies at Melodeon Hall. The 116th Indiana passed through the city.

[*Melodeon Hall was a former performance hall in downtown Cincinnati,*

Ohio—replaced in 1901 with 17-story building. Tom Thumb was a character in English folklore. The History of Tom Thumb *was originally published in 1621— first fairy tale printed in English. George Washington Morris Nutt, better known by his stage name as Commodore Nutt, was a 19th century dwarf (36" tall), who became famous working for P.T. Barnum and traveling the world with a performing troupe.*]

February 5—This morning the 117th Indiana passed through for home. These are Willcox's six months troops whose time has expired.

February 6—Commenced snowing in the afternoon. I was on guard today on Mulberry St. above the Market. In the evening I found a drunken man making considerable disturbance, and arrested him and took him to the Provost Marshal and from there down to the No. 4 Jail.

February 7—Sabbath. Cloudy and cold. Attended church at the Presbyterian. Descriptive lists for Company I boys arrived today.

February 8—We boys got up a petition and sent it to Gov. Andrew [*Massachusetts*] with the approval of Col. King praying to be allowed to remain with the old 21st instead of the 36th Mass.

February 9—On guard again at Col. King's house. He came out on the steps at evening and told me he had received orders to send us all home to join our old regiment. How about two year recruits? We have just heard that communication has been cut off from Knoxville, the enemy having sent a raiding around to capture our trains.

February 10—Our forces have fallen back from Blaines Cross Roads into Knoxville.

February 11—A beautiful day warm and spring like. Cole and I walked out a few miles on the Georgetown Pike and visited a hemp factory. In the evening went with Samuel Gould two miles out on the Frankfort Pike and called at a fine farm house where he had already made himself acquainted. These pikes make some of the most beautiful drives in the world. They are very wide and well graded though most of the way nature has made them level, then the pike bottom covered with this white Kentucky soil renders it as hard as a floor.

February 12—I was on guard at a large wholesale whiskey store which, being filled with confiscated whiskey, has been closed by the Government. It is on Water St. nearly opposite the police station. A grand dinner to the Kentucky Veterans was given by the Soldiers Aid Society in the Masonic Hall to which all the soldiers stationed here were invited which invitation I accepted and enjoyed very much. The tables were spread with every delicacy and in a beautiful hall. The post band furnished music.

February 13—Took another walk out on the Louisville R.R. about three miles a nutting. Found many butternuts. Do not wonder now why such quantities of "Butternut" clothing abound in Kentucky. The 129th Ohio passed through town for home.

February 14—Sunday again. Attended Presbyterian church in the morning and Methodist in the evening. Several long freight trains passed through to Camp Nelson tonight.

February 15—I am on guard at Col. King's house. Our quarters are changed to the headquarters building where we have coal and gas to burn. Our descriptive lists came today and requisition make for clothing. Three men who have been detailed at Newbern two years joined us today.

February 16—This morning while I was on guard at three, the wind took a sudden turn to the cold corner and blew very piercing. As I came from very warm quarters without extra clothing, I think I have taken a severe cold as I feel strangely about my bones. We pack the stoves and keep them red hot but the intense cold is not driven out of the barracks. Our requisition for clothing has been denied for want of a commissioned officer [*all in Massachusetts*] to sign it and the men are growing mutinous under these repeated injustices. They cannot remember that they are nothing but privates, not men. These Kentucky boys who are generally of the ignorant class naturally depend on others and make far better disciplined men than our Massachusetts boys who think they know as much as their officers. So think the officers. Tonight the Allegheny Bell Ringers gave a concert at the Melodeon.

February 17—Continues very cold. The guard was taken off and the new one detailed refused to do any duty till clothing was furnished them. I am down sick with cold and headache. Sergeant Fox left for the hospital.

February 18—Clear and cold. Capt. Hall came up from Camp Nelson and procured the necessary clothing for us. Here is a "shoulder strap" that is worth having and a faithful friend he is too.

10

Hospital Life

"This is the first sickness of my life when I have been confined to my bed."
—Hitchcock, March 3, 1864

George Hitchcock recovered from "remittent bilious fever" and "dropsy" (edema) at the general hospital in Lexington, Kentucky, and spent additional time recuperating during a medical furlough in Ashby.

On February 29, 1864, President Lincoln signed a bill that revived the rank of lieutenant general and nominated Ulysses S. Grant for this position. The United States Senate confirmed the appointment on March 2, with an annual salary of $8,640. On March 8, Grant arrived by train in Washington with his 13-year-old son Fred. After checking into the Willard's Hotel, the new lieutenant general walked two blocks to the White House, where in the Blue Room he met President Lincoln for the first time. Grant returned to the executive mansion the following day to receive his commission as lieutenant general and assumed his responsibilities as general-in-chief.

On March 10, Grant met with Maj. Gen. George G. Meade at Brandy Station. Grant retained Meade as commander of the Army of the Potomac and appointed Maj. Gen. William T. Sherman commander of the Military Division of the Mississippi. The Illinois general planned a spring campaign involving the simultaneous advancement on several fronts against the South's two principal field armies: Gen. Joseph E. Johnston's Army of Tennessee, which was defending Atlanta from its position in North Georgia, and Gen. Robert E. Lee's Army of Northern Virginia, which was defending Richmond while dug in along the Rapidan River.

After traveling west for discussions with Sherman and after deciding to accompany the Army of the Potomac, Grant established his headquarters on March 26 at Culpeper, Virginia. A critical decision was made in April that would have a direct effect on tens of thousands of lives—including George Hitchcock's.

10. Hospital Life

On April 17, Grant halted all exchange of prisoners until the Confederates: (1) agreed to release a sufficient number of officers and men as were captured and paroled at Vicksburg and Port Hudson, and (2) accepted that no distinction whatsoever will be made in the exchange between white and colored prisoners in the military service of the United States.

On May 4, Grant and the Army of the Potomac crossed the Rapidan River and plunged into the thickets of the Wilderness, where Lee's army attacked and brought him to battle. Three days later, Sherman's troops advanced toward Rocky Face Ridge, Georgia, the first barrier on the long road to Atlanta.

* * * *

February 19, 1864—This morning the orderly came to me and advised me to be taken down to the hospital which advice I, of course, rejected as I expected to be up again in a day or two and also from a natural horror of hospitals in general. But as others advised me to go, fearing the small-pox which is prevalent, I consented and was taken down in an ambulance to the General Hospital on the farther side of the city. The building used are called the Transylvanian University. I was given into "ward one" a large airy hall formerly used as the College Hall but now filled with nearly seventy-five iron hospital cots. Before night however, I began to anticipate a serious time for me, fever having set in. [*In 1890 Hitchcock added: "My nurse is a man of about thirty years, a sergeant in some western regiment: A very quiet, calm fellow—cheery and faithful, one whom I love to watch as he goes about his duties so ready to respond to the constant calls both day and night and always an encouraging word for his various patients. This is the first sickness of my life when I have been confined to my bed, and the doctor calls it 'remittent bilious fever.' I am very weak and continue to have returns of the fever."*]

[*Transylvania University has a beautiful campus located three blocks from downtown Lexington; it was founded in 1780—16th college to be founded in America. During the Civil War the school struggled to survive and for a time its stately Old Morrison building was used as a hospital for troops on both sides of the conflict.*]

March 3—For two weeks my army diary has been necessarily a blank but today the doctor tells me my fever has left me. This is the first sickness of my life when I have been confined to my bed. Got off my bed for the first time and with the help of my nurse (who is, by the way, a most excellent one who knows his duty well) drew on my pants and wrote home giving an account of myself. My fever has left me very weak and I am having occasional fever turns which the doctor calls Remitten Bilious Fever.

[*Civil War Medical Terminology: "Bilious fever is caused by liver disorder and if remittent the fever drops, but does not altogether disappear." It is a common form of fever prevalent in the middle, southern, and south-western sections of the*

United States. Individuals coming from cooler sections of the country are particularly liable to be attacked. Later the doctor identified Hitchcock's illness as dropsy(edema).]

March 4—Our pay-rolls came today and are being signed.

March 5—We were mustered in for pay.

March 6—I saw a patient who has been sick in the second cot from mine breathe his last. . Rather hard lives for us who are weak and sick to have to see these sights.

March 7—Signed the payrolls. Tonight has brought me a treat from home in form of letters. Father sent me a "printed order" issued by Government which explicitly states what I have fully believed all the time, namely that we, the recruits of July 1862, are entitled to all the privileges of our old regiment.

[*In 1890 Hitchcock added: "It is a publication issued from the War Department at Washington explicitly stating that in order to keep up the old fighting regiments of Massachusetts to effective numbers, Governor Andrew was authorized to solicit recruits with the inducements that they should be entitled to all the privileges and standing as those who originally enlisted. Although having served less than two years, they could reenlist just the same as the veterans, but this was "applicable to no other state but Massachusetts." This order was countersigned by Governor Andrew with instructions to commanders of regiments to govern themselves accordingly. This fully puts the poor private in the right and leaves the enlisting officers of our regiment responsible for a great injustice done. Although impossible to correct the mistake in full, it relieves me and the rest to know that we shall not be sent back to the 36th Mass. We are still members of the brave old 21st."*]

March 8—I received a call from Samuel Gould. Stepped out of doors for the first time. I find that my descriptive list has been sent on to Massachusetts by mistake, which means that I was left in Lexington by mistake. Oh dear, dear, these long, long weary days!

March 12—I cannot sit up but a few moments at a time and although I am suffering no pain I am very weak. The surgeon pronounces it a case of dropsy. Our ward is filling up with sick, seven new cases arrived tonight.

March 13—Sunday. Weather changed to very chilly and cold. Our hospital chaplain held services in our ward at ten o'clock, very acceptable were they to me. Frank Burpee came down to see me.

March 14—Clark and Cole came down and brought letters from home to me; also one from Whitney. There were several admissions today including a case of small pox which is kept downstairs. I managed to go downstairs for the first time to dinner. Find my appetite growing keen.

March 15—Snowed in the afternoon. I was fortunate in securing a can of oysters which I relished hugely. I saw another man die tonight.

10. Hospital Life

March 16—A man was brought in by a carless ambulance driver to our ward, who had broken out very full with the small pox, but he was immediately carried out and the cold air striking him, he died in a very few minutes. Called into Ward Five and saw Sibley.

March 17—Saint Patrick's Day. I do not feel as well today, though the bloat is not as full in my feet. [*In 1890 Hitchcock added: "My feet and limbs have been swollen almost out of shape—some of the time extending as far up as the body."*]

March 18—Today's paper says Gen. Burnside is to take command of the Department of the South. I have applied to have my descriptive list sent for as I cannot draw pay without it.

March 19—Witnessed another death tonight. These sights seem very hard, with the thought that loving friends cannot be here to say the last good bye.

March 20—Services were held in our ward to ten. Feel very sick again having taken more cold, but am hopeful that I shall be up again.

March 21—Received precious letters from every member of the family, with bundles of papers and pamphlets and money. My sickness has not made me the only sufferer, my poor mother had an anxiety which only a mother can know for her boy. Henry has been appointed a recruiting officer at Mass. establishing his office in Worcester.

March 22—Sam Gould who was here today says that a captain is in town collecting all the detailed men of the 9th Corps and our squad expect to leave soon. They were paid off today.

March 23—Feel decidedly better, the swelling of my limbs has gone down so much that I can get on a pair of shoes.

March 24—The swelling continues to go down though my feet are quite sore. I have traveled around the hospital a good deal today.

March 25—Snowed in the night. The boys expect to leave on Monday. Burnside's 9th Corps is to be taken out of this department and again transferred to the Army of the Potomac. Received news of a rebel raid into this state.

March 26—The 21st Regiment has gone to Annapolis where the 9th Corps will rendezvous. One of our female cooks died tonight.

March 27—Received letters from home. Cole and Burpee brought up my knapsack to me. It is reported that this hospital department is to be transferred to Camp Dennison, Ohio.

March 28—Received a pass and went down town. Our squad left tonight at six. News of a fight at Paducah of this state and place burnt by the rebels. The commander Gen. Thompson was killed.

[*Confederate Colonel Albert P. Thompson commanded the Third Brigade of General Nathan Bedford Forest's cavalry when he was killed at Paducah, Kentucky, on March 25, 1864. Although the Confederate troops occupied part of Paducah, two attacks were repulsed at Fort Anderson, and they withdrew on March 26th. However, this raid alarmed the Ohio River valley.]*

March 29—Sam Gould brought down my rubber blanket. He leaves tomorrow. I employ my time in sewing, reading and writing.

March 31—Do not feel so well. The Copperheads of Southern Illinois are rising and five thousand troops are called for. The <u>core</u> of the 9th Corps is expected to pass through here tomorrow enroute for Annapolis.

April 1, 1864—Taking books from the hospital library. Have read the "Life of Martin Luther" and "Life of Gen. Havelock." [*Sir Henry Havelock (1795–1857) was a British General who united the graces of religion to the valor of the soldier.*]

April 2—Today have read "Exposition of the Knights of the Golden Circle" and "Travels in Egypt and Palestine." I entered my name for a furlough though I have a poor prospect for one at present as there are many applications ahead of mine and but few granted each week. The furloughs all have to travel to Louisville, Cincinnati and back before they are good.

[*Knights of the Golden Circle, which first appeared in 1855 after being known as Southern Rights Clubs with the desire to reestablish the African slave trade and acquire new slave territory, was a secret order in the North of Southern Sympathizers who disapproved of the war.*]

April 3—Sunday, services and inspection as usual. These long, long days drag heavily.

April 4—I received a pass and went into the city and over to Fort Clay which made me very tired. I saw a dwelling house burn up early this morning. I changed quarters and went into the convalescent ward.

April 5—I learned that my furlough had been sent in to be signed. At noon an alarm of fire was sounded and again at night—the last one was a very heavy one.

April 6—I was examined by Dr. Meacham. Others have been examined and sent away. New arrivals of sick. The hospital is filling to overflowing. I had a sick turn in the afternoon caused by taking cold.

April 7—Sergeants Fox and Irish were sent away to the regiment. While laying on my cot, I was startled and agreeably surprised at hearing the Surgeon's orderly call my name and tell me to walk down to the office and receive my furlough, which has returned duly signed. So a visit home is yet to be a reality. Although I am feeling better, I shall not start till Monday—today being Thursday. How can I wait four days?

April 8—Over thirty patients came in tonight who were spread out on the floors of the halls and in all available places for want of room. Two full regiments of Cavalry passed through the city and encamped just outside.

10. Hospital Life

April 9—Over one hundred convalescents were transferred to the barracks today. I secured my furlough and transportation at the Post Quartermasters and am now ready for my journey.

April 10—Sunday. I walked out about the city [*Lexington*] taking a farewell look at scenes of interest to me which I may never see again. I packed my knapsack and prepared for an early start tomorrow morning.

April 11—I laid down to sleep early but excitement drove sleep from m eyes. I roused up at four and hurried away to the depot not caring to linger about my old prison quarters till the half-past-five train should start. Before I was half way there I found my boasted strength had left me but by resting on the sidewalks in the cool air of early morning, I reached the depot nearly a mile away in time for the train. After a delightful five hours ride through a magnificent country we come in sight of the circle of bluffs surrounding Covington, all of which are fortified for the protection of the city of Cincinnati. Landed at Covington at eleven and crossed immediately to Cincinnati and stopped at the Soldiers Home on East Third Street. In the afternoon I went out to secure transportation home. After a long tramp I found the Post Headquarters and received order for transportation signed by the Post Commander. I then went out two or three squares and found the Post Quartermasters and after some difficulty I receive a package more of orders, then taking all these down to the Eastern R.R. Ticket Office, I secured tickets for seven separate roads. This being done, "red tape" was satisfied and I then went with Charles Hayward making a tour of inspection over the city, in the horse-cars. At eleven o'clock at night, I appropriated a seat in a fine passenger car of the Little Miami R.R. and rolled out of the city.

April 12—Riding all night brought before light to Columbus where we change cars and during the forenoon pass through Galion, Crestline and other places of smaller size and reach Cleveland in the afternoon. Change cars and go by the lake shore route, riding a long distance in view of the lake [*Erie*]. Through the cities of Erie and Dunkirk, reach Buffalo at dark, again we change cars on to the New York Central. And now begins a very severe headache which absorbs all my attention and keeps me awake through the night, and the continual rattle, rattle becomes torture to my brain.

April 13—I raise my head at light and find we have gone into a hilly country. Off to the distant South I can see the snow capped Catskills. Pass through Schenectady and arrive in Albany at nine in the morning. I bought a breakfast at the depot and cross the Hudson on a ferry boat. Take a direct south-easterly course and find ourselves in Springfield at noon. Change cars and now we begin to see snow all about. Reach Worcester at two and having two hours to wait for the train, I stretch my limbs with a stroll on to Main Street and almost the first persons I meet as I turned on to Main Street were

Father and Henry, a meeting entirely unexpected on both sides, and a very delightful one too. At four I went on to Fitchburg with Father. Had a sleigh-ride home in the evening and at nine was at the "home of my childhood" and in the arms of my mother, a complete surprise to her also.

April 14—I was thoroughly exhausted and did not leave the house. Received several callers.

April 15—I suffered a most excruciating headache all the afternoon, and fearing an attack of brain-fever, Dr. Emerson [*Dr. James Emerson—family doctor in Ashby*] was called and I found relief. I now draw the curtain and shut out curious eyes from the short three weeks delightful intercourse with friends and family.

[*In 1890 Hitchcock added: "The furlough on which I visited home was called a "sick furlough" because it was granted by order of an army surgeon. It was of the utmost value to me at this time to complete the recovery of an illness which was induced by the terrible strain upon my constitution in the march over the mountains upon half or quarter rations. When therefore the end drew nigh, I was feeling better than I had been for a long time, and although the partings from home friends were painful, I was enthusiastic to get back into the ranks of the 21st and have a part in the glory which we could begin to see was coming through a perfected Army of the Potomac."*]

Private George A. Hitchcock, photographed May 2, 1864, at his home in Ashby, Massachusetts, while on medical leave. He returned to his regiment on May 29, a few days before he was captured (courtesy of Martha Hitchcock Price).

11

Grant's Campaign

"In spite of the universal report of the past four weeks terrible campaign, I actually experienced a feeling of satisfaction and pleasure in returning to my old 21st."
—Hitchcock, May 29, 1864

On March 18, 1864, after a reenlistment furlough, veteran soldiers of the 21st Massachusetts Regiment left Worcester for Annapolis and joined a reorganized IX Corps, commanded by Maj. Gen. Ambrose E. Burnside. The corps acted as the army's reserve, reporting directly to General Grant until May 24, when it was assigned to George Meade's Army of the Potomac. The 27,000-man corps included 3,500 black soldiers in Brig. Gen. Edward Ferrero's division—the first colored troops to serve in the Army of the Potomac. The 21st Massachusetts Regiment, assigned to Col. Daniel Leasure's brigade in Brig. Gen. Thomas G. Stevenson's division, passed in review in Washington with the balance of the IX Corps before President Lincoln and General Burnside on April 25. The corps marched southwest and reached Bealeton Station, Virginia, on April 30. On May 5, Burnside's corps crossed the Rapidan River at Germanna Ford and joined with the Army of the Potomac, most of which had crossed the previous day. On May 6, while the Battle of the Wilderness was raging, George Hitchcock left his home in Ashby, Massachusetts, to rejoin his regiment south of the Rapidan.

General Grant accompanied Meade's Army of the Potomac in the field and made the army's strategic decisions. He planned to utilize his unlimited supplies and manpower to prevent Lee from employing the Confederacy's interior position to rapidly redeploy manpower elsewhere. Instead of Richmond, Grant viewed his objective as Lee's army, with which he sought to stay in constant contact. Through the use of protracted combat, Grant intended to bleed Lee through steady attrition.

Lee's three corps of 65,000 men faced Grant's army of 120,000 Union troops just below the Rapidan River in the Battle of the Wilderness on May 5–6. Grant planned to march rapidly through the Wilderness and gain the open countryside beyond Spotsylvania Court House, but Lee attacked the Union army in the brushed-choked thickets of the Wilderness—a bloody two-day battle. The larger Union army was neutralized by the densely wooded area that was traversed by narrow roads, rendering the artillery almost useless. The Union army suffered 18,000 casualties and the Confederate losses were estimated at 9,000 men in this savage, bushwhacking battle that ended in a stalemate.

Wounded Confederate soldiers were carried in wagons to Orange Court House and then transported by boxcars to the hospitals at Lynchburg. The Union wounded were transported by wagons to Chancellorsville and the next day wagons carried them to Fredericksburg. Lee's greatest loss was General Longstreet. Friendly fire by Gen. William ("Little Billy") Mahone's Virginia Brigade killed Gen. Micah Jenkins and severely wounded General Longstreet. A bullet entered Longstreet's neck and exited through his right shoulder; although the injury appeared to be fatal, Longstreet recovered and returned to active command in mid–October 1864.

The 21st Massachusetts Regiment was engaged on May 6. When Longstreet's troops in their slashing counterattack successfully turned the flank of Frank's brigade and rolled up Greshom Mott's division, precipitating a Union fighting retreat and redeployment along the Brock Road facing west. Maj. Gen. Winfield S. Hancock ordered Leasure's brigade to reconnoiter and to determine if any Confederates were forming for an attack. The brigade swept down the line across and opposite the front of Hancock's II Corps without serious opposition from the Confederates. During action in the Wilderness, the 21st Massachusetts Regiment suffered 18 casualties, including eight soldiers who were captured and later imprisoned at Andersonville.

During the afternoon on May 7, Union supply wagons moved to the rear, but rather than heading north, they turned south. This was the first time in Virginia that the Army of the Potomac continued an offensive after its initial battle. Grant moved Meade's army past Lee's right flank and was determined to reach Spotsylvania Court House first, positioning the Union army between Lee's army and Richmond. Determined Confederate troops, however, reached Laurel Hill first, checked the attacks of Maj. Gen. G. K. Warren's II Corps, and secured Spotsylvania Court House. Lee was able to use the watershed between the Po and Ny rivers as a bulwark for a twelve-day defense against Union onslaughts on May 10, 12 and 18.

On May 10, VI Corps Union-soldiers, led by Col. Emory Upton, briefly forced their way into the "Mule Shoe," a U-shaped salient bulging from the Confederate lines. On May 12, Hancock's II Corps succeeded in penetrating the salient, resulting in the fiercest and most deadly hand-to-hand fighting of the war. Eighteen hours of continuous fury ensued in violent rainsqualls for an area known as the Bloody Angle. In the end, the Confederate line pulled back and then held. It is ironic that the day before Grant's message to Washington stated that he "propose to fight it out on this line, if it takes all summer."

During the Spotsylvania campaign between May 8 and 20, the casualties were more than 18,000 for the Union army and more than 10,000 for the Confederates. The 21st Massachusetts Regiment was engaged at Spotsylvania on May 10, 12 and 18, suffering losses of 39 men, including two soldiers who were captured and later imprisoned at Andersonville. On May 10, General Stevenson was killed by a Confederate sharpshooter. The IX Corps lost an inspired and capable leader. Lemuel Whitney, who had joined and served in the Union army with George Hitchcock, was wounded in the arm on May 10 in a fruitless attack on Confederate entrenched positions. The Union campaign in the Wilderness and at Spotsylvania, between May 5 and May 21, was a strategic defeat for the Confederacy, because Lee's army was unable to prevent the Union army from penetrating further into Virginia and from bludgeoning its way closer to Richmond. The Union forces had suffered tremendous casualties, but in this war of attrition the Confederate losses were irreplaceable, especially the experienced officers.

Frustrated by the impossibility of penetrating the Confederate defenses at Spotsylvania, Grant initiated another jug-handled flanking movement twenty-five miles southeast toward Hanover Junction. Lee left Spotsylvania and entrenched along the North Anna River covering the vital railroad junction before the Union army arrived on May 23. After crossing the North Anna River and failing to breach the Confederate defenses, Grant recrossed the river on May 26–27 and moved twenty miles southeast, again turning Lee's right flank. The Union army crossed the Pamunkey River at Nelson's Bridge and Hanovertown on May 27–28 and closed on Totopotomoy Creek, where Lee's army again confronted the Union forces. In the movement from the North Anna River, the 21st Massachusetts Regiment took a circuitous route, while Lee's army marched half the distance.

The exhausted soldiers crossed the Pamunkey River at Hanovertown on May 29 during the early morning hours and continued for two miles before halting. Later that night, George Hitchcock rejoined his regiment.

On May 31, after the armies skirmished along the Totopotomoy Creek for three days, Brig. Gen. Alfred T. A. Torbert's cavalry division (Sheridan's Cavalry Corps) drove back a smaller force of Fitzhugh Lee's cavalry and seized the road junction at Old Cold Harbor. Both sides called up infantry, and on June 1, there was savage fighting in front of Old Cold Harbor. In the morning Sheridan's cavalry, fighting dismounted, repulsed Confederate infantry intent on recovering the key road intersection. In the afternoon soldiers of the VI and XVIII corps carried the fight to the Confederates. After the Union troops were initially successful, counterattacking Confederates closed the breach in their line. During the night of June

1–2, both armies maneuvered and redeployed, facing each other across a six-mile-long parallel-lines of earthen fortification from Topopotomoy Creek to the Chickahominy River.

There had been relentless and ceaseless warfare for four weeks. The casualties were enormous: 44,000 for the Union army and 25,000 for the Confederates. Grant attempted to maneuver Lee into open-field combat where superior Union manpower and firepower could destroy the Confederate army, but Lee's tactical skill, coupled with friction within the Federal command structure, thwarted Grant's initiatives, and the Union army was confronted by an entrenched defense at every new location. The conflict had become a war of attrition.

* * * *

May 6, 1864—With painful farewells I most ardently hope I may not long be detained from reaching my own 21st Regt. which I learn has joined Grant's Army of the Potomac and is now engaged in active operations. Met Henry in Boston and made arrangements with him to return to the front together. He returned to Templeton engaging to meet me at Worcester tomorrow. I hunted up Charles Wood [*former resident of Ashby and son of the Rev. Charles W. Wood; he was employed in Cotrell's bookstore on Cornhill*] and after tea went out to Dorchester Heights and had a magnificent view of Boston, its suburbs and the harbor by twilight.

May 7—Stopped over night with Mr. Severance on Charles St. and during the forenoon went out on the "Mill Dam" where are now the finest avenues of the city. In the afternoon, being unable for want of time to find my knapsack and haversack, I resolved to go along without them. Met Henry in Worcester who advised me to return and get them, giving me the right directions for finding. As they were both well laden with articles important for my internal and external comfort, it was best I should do so although I should lose the pleasure of his company. returned to Boston at half past ten Saturday night reaching there at midnight. Found very fine lodgings at the Soldiers Home, 76 Kingston Street. Heard of heavy fighting in Grant's Army.

May 8—Sunday. Rode out to Mt. Auburn in the afternoon. Was invited and attended the Old Colony Mission Sunday school Concert. Listened to pretty singing from the children and short speech from Rev. J.P. Bixby.

May 9—Went out after my baggage and at half past two P.M. left Boston on the Norwich Express. Reached there at sundown and being obliged to wait two hours for the steamboat train to New London, I went out into the city. Got supper and listened to some fine band music. At quarter past nine boarded the train and reached Allyn's Point, 14 miles at ten o'clock at night. Embarked on board the "City of Boston." After enjoying the calm beautiful starlight night on deck I went in to the main cabin at eleven and then retired to my berth.

11. Grant's Campaign

May 10—Woke at daylight, went on deck and find us sailing up New York Harbor or just passing Hell Gate. Drank in the view which will never cease to be interesting—approaching by water a large city. Landed at Jersey City, took breakfast and at seven started for Philadelphia, where we arrived at quarter past eleven. Rode across the city in horse-cars and at noon boarded the Washington and Baltimore R.R. train. Took dinner in the novelty of a dining saloon connected with the train which occupied two thirds of a common passenger car. Reach Baltimore at five and then on to Washington at seven and put up at the "Soldiers Rest." I found Dr. S. Hitchcock and Henry Goodrich of Fitchburg on the train before I reached Washington. They have been sent out to attend to the wounded of Fitchburg who fell in the last great battle of the Wilderness.

May 11—Left the "Rest" at nine and with a battalion of returning soldiers, boarded the cars in front of the Capitol. Rode across Long Bridge out to Alexandria from thence to Camp Distribution near Arlington Heights four miles from Alexandria. Here we are found quarters to await transportation to our regiments.

May 12—I was detailed for fatigue duty with a lot and went out and worked on the road near Fort Runyon. Worked until near noon when a heavy shower drove us back to camp. We are in a large village of barracks which are used for various purposed. The place is called Camp Convalescent. At night I drew a new haversack, canteen and shelter.

May 13—At half past four we were called up, went to the Ordnance Office and drew gun and equipments for I was obliged to give up my trusty old Enfield when the regiment left in Covington. Then amid a heavy rain which tested the qualities of my excellent rubber, several hundred of us started for Alexandria. This is the first time for five months that I have marched fully equipped. Marched to Alexandria through deep, slim, sticky clay mud, and after various ignominious falls and uncouth demonstrations on the "sacred soil" which it must be confessed is "slippery," we arrive at the levee, myself a pitiable looking object. My clean army-blue having become a rebel gray after my repeated contacts with mother earth. We embark on the "Steamer Swan" at noon and sail down the Potomac. Six miles below Alexandria we passed fort Washington situated on the Maryland side at a bend which commands the river for six miles below. Our course becomes due south where the river widens and we have a good view of the low Maryland shores on the left and the more uneven ragged shores on the right. We met a steamer bound for Washington whose decks were covered with wounded, just from the front. We give them rousing cheers which are answered only by the waving of a few hats. We passed in sight of Mt. Vernon having a good view of the surrounding buildings and land. As we near our landing place, ammunition is dealt out very bountifully to us. And that which we cannot dispose of in our cartridge-boxes we are ordered to pack into our knapsacks. Some men, having over a hundred rounds in disobedience of orders recklessly throw all but a few rounds into the water. Mine is consigned to my haversack which afterward becoming soaked with the rain, gives a peculiar, saltpeterish taste to my hardtack. Landed at Bell Plain on the Potomac Creek at a long wharf, where were several other vessels including a large Sanitary Commission boat. Here we witness a scene of confusion and bedlam rivaling pandemonium itself. This is the temporary landing place of supplies for the great Army of the Potomac at a narrow, winding cut in the line of bluffs. Along the shore are packed long lines of army wagons going in opposite directions. Thousands of straggling and wounded soldiers pressing down to the boats. Officers, quartermasters and wagon masters dashing back and forth in the thickest. Swearing mule drivers and the unmusical voice of the mule, calling for his supper. Then, away back on the hills, the evening retreat is sounding from the multitudes of camps. This is the Base of Supplies, but I prefer the Tenor. As we land and push our way up the hill we meet a long line of graybacks in the twilight, who prove to be the captured rebel officers just from the Wilderness among whom are Generals Steuart and Johnson. We bivouac in a rough field for the night.

May 14—And in the morning, move about a mile into camp and pitch tents. At noon I was detailed with a large sample from our battalion and sent down toward the landing where we come in sight of a large natural basin, a quarter mile in diameter filled with rebel prisoners, over nine thousand of Johnson's men captured at Spotsylvania, who are awaiting transportation north. We are put on guard over the. A large number of wounded came in from the front. They report that a heavy battle took place on Monday in which the 9th Corps was engaged [*Spotsylvania Campaign in Virginia from May 8–20, 1864*].

May 15—A very long wagon train came in from the front filled with wounded and multitudes are constantly coming in on foot, of those not so seriously wounded, all telling of the fearful slaughter that has taken place. New troops are constantly arriving from the north and tonight Corcoran's Legion arrived from Fairfax.

May 16—On guard again over the Johnnies. Three thousand were sent away, and six hundred more from the front brought in. A long train of captured artillery arrived. Grant has ordered all the "Parlor Soldiers" around Washington to be sent to the front, consequently a number of Heavy Artillery Regiments arrived en route for the front loaded with two or three woolens each, knapsacks stuffed to their utmost capacity, paper collars and white gloves, shining brasses and spotless clothing. Poor fellows, we can wish you a jolly time and a pleasant journey, but the prospect for the future is foreboding horrors which have before had no parallel in this war. How many may soon be laid low in death and others sent to starve in southern prisons. At night a German Band from Philadelphia played some very provoking airs to the Johnnies like "John Brown's Body" and "Down with the Traitors" which brought out hosts of groaning from the seething cauldron of graybacks.

May 17—Towards night I was told that a battalion of returning furloughed men like ourselves had arrived from Alexandria and thinking I might find Henry among them, I hunted them up and found Henry as I expected. They are in camp only a half mile from us awaiting orders. I saw a yesterday' Baltimore paper giving an account of the Spotsylvania battle.

May 18—About midnight we were aroused and startled with the report that a party of two hundred guerrillas were within two miles of camp preparing to dash in upon us and rescue the prisoners. Feeling that our thousands were able to cope with such a force and that such alarms were useless, we dropped to sleep again. But in the morning our battalion was ordered out to White Oak Church where we were divided into three companies and sent in different directions, ours moving off some three miles to the southeast. We then again divided into squads of a dozen men each and deployed a quarter of a mile apart. Our squad finds itself after a march of eight miles, away in the fields only about three miles from the Landing. A part of our number are Indians who belong to a company of sharpshooters, composed entirely of Indians of the Iroquois tribe. They are very reticent, talking in low tone in their own language. During the evening they sang some of the native songs. They are the men for picket duty and guerrilla watching and as vidette they find full scope for all their savage education.

[*Confederate Colonel John Singleton Mosby led 100 to 200 irregular troops or partisan rangers in Virginia. On May 17, 1864, Mosby, with about 200 men, attacked a detachment from Falmouth within four miles of Belle Plain. Union officials feared that Mosby would attack the depot or wagon trains on the way to the front. Therefore, Union supply wagons required heavy guard. Mosby's Raiders frequently operated in small squads of twenty to eighty men and attacked Union outposts, wagon trains and stragglers with such fury and efficiency that the whole area in northern Virginia became known as "Mosby's Confederacy."*]

May 19—Lieut. Sawyer passed by us from the front going to Washington with a squad of wounded men. He informs us that Lemuel Whitney has been wounded. In the afternoon we were relieved and march to White Oak Church, joining the rest of the battalion. We went on to Fredericksburg. By sundown we reached those great barren uplands which a year and a half ago were covered with the camps of the Army of the Potomac and passed the site of our old camping ground, when thrilling memories came over us. We descended the steep banks of the Rappahannock remembering the gloomy aspect of affairs when we last went over the ground. At nine in the evening we crossed on a pontoon into the city where we camped for the night. Marched eight miles.

May 20—Very warm in the morning. Commenced an investigation of the city and saw the awful effect of war upon this once beautiful city. The last time I passed through these streets it was on that cold winter's night when we were beating a hasty retreat from that "Aceldama" [*Reference in the Bible: Acts 1:18, 19*] of December 12th and 13th. Now the city is occupied almost solely by our troops. Nearly half the buildings are in ruins from that terrible bombardment and every building, every church and every available shelter is filled with our wounded. It is literally one vast hospital. The very few houses occupied by citizens were thrown open for the use of our wounded and the rebellious inmates ordered to assist in nursing and caring for our wounded. After a long hunt I found the hospital for the 9th Corps and the 21st boys in a church. The pews had previously been removed and the floors from basement to galleries and steeple were covered with wounded men, wounded in every particular part of the body. Some were quiet, others were crazy and others in agony made the sight most sickening. Those not severely wounded were acting as nurses, dressing wounds and helping the helpless. I found Lemuel Whitney acting in this capacity caring for a poor fellow with but one leg. As fast as the men died they were laid side by side in the church yard where there were long rows awaiting the "dead cart" which was constantly coming and going. In the afternoon I was detailed to go out on the old battle ground of Burnside and raise a hospital tent. At night a train of army wagons came in from the front bringing its freight of wounded, of last nights fighting. While they were unloading two were taken out who had died during the journey and among the number several rebel wounded who were cared for just the same as our own men. As I lie down to sleep, I cannot shut out the scenes of suffering I have witnessed in the last twelve hours and I am sure it is impossible to find anything to surpass it in intense bodily suffering.

May 21—Soon after midnight we were roused by the long roll. In less than five minutes we were in line, prepared to resist an attack, when we found we had been "done" by some frightened officers who had heard the report of small arms down in the city and which they supposed signified an attack from guerrillas, but was afterward ascertained to be the result of a drunken row. At about nine, wagons commenced moving out on the Bowling Green Road guarded by a considerable force of cavalry and infantry and for nearly ten hours this moving train was unbroken. The longest train I have seen yet and if the sound of cannonading a few miles out in the direction they have taken signifies a heavy force of the enemy they will find an excellent opportunity to cripple our fighting force.

11. Grant's Campaign 163

May 22—We moved camp down the Bowling Green Road a short distance out of the city. I was put on duty as safe guard at a house adjoining camp where I was furnished with meals. Two steamers have just arrived by the Rappahannock and a train of cars from Aquia Creek, the first since Gen. Burnside left here over a year ago. We hear that the army has moved again and that all communication has been cut off from it. [*In 1890 Hitchcock added: "Evidently Grant doesn't propose to advertise his movements for the benefit of the rebel government. Such audacity must doubtless throw our martinet officers into fits. The appearances indicate that 'popular opinion' has made and unmade commanders of the Army of the Potomac for the last time and that Government has decided to let the present commander 'run the shop.'"*]

May 23—I visited the battle ground and went over the very spots where we fought and charged in that awful butchery of eighteen months ago. In the afternoon I visited the 9th Corps Hospital and saw our wounded 21st boys again. Our wounded are being sent away very fast now, the worst cases are taken by the water route and the others by rail.

May 24—The monotony of the day was broken by arrival of a lot of refugees of the colored persuasion who with all their earthly possessions bound on their heads and backs were "bound north." The arrival of a schooner laden with supplies and the distant rumbling of cannon. At night I went on camp guard in the pouring rain of a heavy thundershower. Our army is at Hanover Court House.

May 25—Heard more cannonading this forenoon. Preparations for evacuating the city are being completed. At night a detail came for men to carry wounded to the boats and in another very heavy gale and shower I went off prepared for a night job. On reaching the hospitals we found other details at work and therefore did not have to stay very late. I carried several poor fellows onto the boats, each trip a half a mile in length, which drew the perspiration from me.

May 26—Very hot. I laid in my tent reading most of the day. A detail of one hundred men from our battalion is to leave here tomorrow morning, place and purpose unknown. I am one of the chosen ones. At night I walked two miles to the farther end of the city nearly opposite Falmouth and found Sawyer of Company K. Returning I found the city dark and desolate and nearly deserted. [*In 1890 Hitchcock added: "The city seemed like some vast charnel house which I shall be glad to leave."*]

May 27—Last night was very stormy. Was roused at three and at eight started for Bowling Green a guard for a train of medical supplies, in company of a squad of cavalry. Our road for several miles lay parallel with the river so we went over the battle ground of Franklin's Corps of December 1862 [*Major General William Buel Franklin commanded the Left Grand Division (I Corps* *and VI Corps) at Fredericksburg on December 13, 1862. He was blamed by the Committee on the Conduct of the War for the Union debacle.*] and past the boyhood home of George Washington of "hatchet and pear tree" fame. For a long distance where the river bends the southern bank slopes evenly back half a mile to where the rise of land gave the enemy all advantage for resisting an attacking force. The entire route lay through a rich and delightful country, highly cultivated, where the finest tobacco plantations of the South are situated. during the route we passed the celebrated "Pauline of the Potomac," McClellan's female spy [*Erroneous information—possibly Pauline Cushman, a former Union spy who had escaped execution and was traveling to Washington from Kentucky*]. About the middle of the afternoon some of our cavalry stragglers, who were out in the fields half a mile away, were fired at by persons on horseback in the edge of a wood, who instantly galloped out of sight. a squad of skirmishers were deployed and sent into the wood but as it was thought afterward that the party consisted only of one man, the owner of the house nearby where cavalry were depredating. The skirmishers were withdrawn and we continued our journey. Reached Bowling Green at five at night and went into campo twenty two miles from Fredericksburg. The village consists of only half dozen houses surrounding a large smooth lawn from which the place takes its name. The army passed through here yesterday morning and the temporary base of supplies is at Port Royal. The junction of the two roads is near our camp so there was constant travel past us while we were here.

May 28—In the morning a large party of negros passed us "bound for freedom" and after we took up our line of travel we were constantly meeting squads of them who were taking their first opportunity to escape as our army is going over a tract entirely new to them. We cross the Virginia Central R.R. and the Mattapony River. We now begin to keep a vigilant lookout, as news comes to us at noon that the portion of the train which left us at the Mattapony was shortly after taken by a band of guerrillas watching for us. We passed through Milford's and Morris' Stations, the latter place a complete and smoking ruins, passenger and freight depots, engine house and wood sheds. A short distance beyond we pass the burning ruins of a steam mill. We are now passing over the route which Gen. Sheridan has made memorable three weeks ago in his trip around Richmond. Hundreds of dead horses lie along the road just where they were shot down. For twenty miles we pass these loathsome carcasses, sometimes a dozen or more within sight of each other showing where the opposing forces made stands.

In the afternoon our commander became alarmed and took us off several miles around on a by road and through fields at last coming out on the main road near Hanover. We are hurried along, the cavalry riding most of the time at a trot and we are urged to keep up which at last becomes an impossibility ad men straggle along making our line extend a mile or two, when the commander rides back and drives the men forward at the point of the sword. We continue along at this rapid rate till late in the night. The lieutenant commanding our company of infantry at last exclaims, "Colonel may go to the devil with his body guard if he chooses, but I am going to take charge of these men, keep them together and in fighting trim and if we are to meet any guerrillas we can show fight." In pursuing our lonely way in the darkness, when near the edge of some woods we are startled out of our senses with the distinct order from some voice ahead "Halt" which is obeyed instantly, and then for a minute in the pitch darkness all was silent as a grave, except the almost audible knockings of each individual heart as the visions of guerrillas, ambuscade, Libby Prison, and starvation came with lightning rapidity before all minds. "Advance, one man and give the countersign" sends our lieutenant forward who finds the cavalry outpost of our own army to whom he explains our situation and we are allowed to pass. Another mile and we reach our infantry picket where we all tumble down, 30 miles marched, on the camp ground in sight of the camp fires of the main army two miles away, and soon I'm lost in sleep.

May 29—At light we start along (having lost our colonel) and march a mile and a half to the little village of Mangohick where we stop and get our coffee near the camp of Gen. Wilson's Cavalry Brigade. This is the rear guard of the army which pushes every straggler and hanger-on of the army before them. By noon we had reached Piping Tree Ford and overtook the wagon trains of the army and shortly after crossing over the river we find the army and our party separate, each man turning to hunt up his regiment. I passed the division of colored troops attached to our Corps on the north bank of the Totopotomoy Creek. Crossed on a pontoon bridge, passed a large camp of negro refugees. Steering in the direction of the artillery and infantry firing, I met Gen. Hancock at the head of his corps which was marching to take a new position our left. I marched two miles further when I found three Corps busily at work throwing up entrenchments with strong skirmishing engaging the enemy. In my quest for the 21st among the hundreds of thousands massed together, I found a busy and noisy army—the clatter of picks and shovels, the tramp of cavalry, the ringing orders of Brigade Officers, the hum of voices of the tired troops around the camp fires with their hard tack and coffee. It was sunset and the Brigade Bands far and near were taking up the "retreat," a thousand drums rolling out the different parts. The click of axes and crashing of falling trees and last and, certainly not least, the incessant rattle of musketry and occasional roar of artillery, all gave a most impressive sense of the active campaign of the Army of the Potomac. At dusk I found my 21st and was at once among the familiar faces of my old comrades and in spite of the foreboding aspect of all sights and sounds, in spite of the universal report of the past four weeks terrible campaign, I actually experienced a feeling of satisfaction and pleasure in returning to my old 21st once more. I was at once surrounded with a crowd of inquiring friends and was rejoiced to receive a package of home letters from Col. Hawkes which I had been deprived of for almost a month. I was considered <u>fresh</u> and better prepared, after my seventy mile forced march, for a night on the skirmish line, than any of the rest of the company. I was sent out at nine o'clock in front of the breastworks with the rest of the relief and deployed about twenty rods from the line where I kept step to the report of muskets from different parts of the line.

[*Black troops were added to the IX Corps and organized into the Fourth Division commanded by Brigadier General Edward Ferrero. They were the first colored troops to serve in the Army of the Potomac.*]

May 30—At light we received orders to move. after waiting for our turn till nine we marched about a half a mile where we halt in the road near Bethesda Church [*Shady Grove Road*] which Generals Grant and Meade occupy as headquarters. at noon we move a short distance toward the front, and through the afternoon we make but slow progress, moving short distances, then halting. At five P.M. Generals Burnside and Crittenden, our Division General, rode down to our Brigade and gave their orders for us to move forward. We push forward supporting the skirmishers which advance until each Brigade has taken its place in line of battle, under a brisk fire from the enemy. We halt and commence throwing up breastworks. I was detailed in the evening with a large squad to go back a mile to the Pioneer Brigade after shovels and picks. Returning we passed by the low breastworks of the Indian sharpshooters in some tall pines where the sight of Indians around their camp fires with the surroundings remind us of our schoolboy studies in history. We worked in the trenches till late in the night then laid down and prepared for a short nap, which is disturbed by an attack from the enemy in our front who tries to force back our pickets. Support is sent out and the attack repulsed.

May 31—By morning we had thrown up some very respectable works although the work had been carried on under difficulties of constant firing during the night. Just before noon our line of skirmishers advanced and were driven back. Then the first Brigade was sent out and repulsed with some loss in killed and wounded. Report came in that Corporal Lander of Company K had been shot on the picket line. So Dr. Oliver [*Surgeon in the 21st*] went out with two men and a stretcher and soon returned bringing the corpse of brave Lander. He was shot through the heart while going from our post to another performing his duties as a Corporal. The spot where he fell was in plain sight and but a few steps from the rebel line which rendered it perilous for anyone to go for the body. So one man runs out, grabs him by the heels and drags him to the nearest shelter. I went out at night with the relief on picket and am stationed at the same post where Lander was shot. Consequently I find myself in close proximity with the "Johnnies."

June 1, 1864—Opens very hot and at light the line was advanced about a dozen rods where we throw where we throw up a rail shelter and not quite so much exposed although right underneath the rebel post. A larger force occupy the places we vacated and put up some very powerful log breastworks connecting with the Third Division works. Early in the afternoon the rattle of musketry opened with a vengeance away two miles on our right, then the artillery firing increases until the sound signifies a general engagement. Just after we were relieved from our post at dusk, the rebel line advanced in our front. Capt. Howe immediately forms us in line and we take position behind the new entrenchments of the 103d N.Y. As the enemy advanced through the thick woods, they notified us of their approach in the gathering of darkness with a long sheet of flame from a thousand muskets and with their wild yell. Then Capt. Howe arose and gave the order to "Fire." As we were well protected, our aim was sure and effectively checked their advance, for they at once fell back out of sight and we returned to the regiment which had just returned from digging where they had received an attack in their rear, wounding several and killing Warren Clark of Co. K. Jack Reynolds was mortally wounded by a piece of shell fired from one of our batteries which was firing at short range. The piece entered his bowels making a shocking wound.

12

Captured at Cold Harbor

> "I raised my head and found to my horror the long lines stretched across the plain of graybacks sweeping up over my living grave."
> —Hitchcock, June 2, 1864

The Second Brigade of Thomas L. Crittenden's, which included the 21st Massachusetts Regiment, underwent a series of command changes during May and early June. Lieutenant Colonel Gilbert Robinson replaced Col. Daniel Leasure on May 14, and then he was replaced on June 4 by Col. Joseph M. Sudsburg. The confused state of affairs is evident by the fact that George Hitchcock believed that Colonel Leasure was still in command of the brigade on June 2.

On June 2, 1864, Ambrose Burnside's IX Corps was positioned on the far right of the Union army line. The left of Burnside's line was formed near Bethesda Church—three miles northwest of Cold Harbor and adjacent to Warren's V Corps. Since a one-mile gap existed to the left of the V Corps, General Meade ordered Warren to extend his troops to the left, closing the interval between himself and Maj. Gen. William F. Smith's XVIII Corps. General Burnside was ordered by General Meade to "move simultaneously with General Warren so as to keep massed in rear of his right," thus consolidating the Union line and preventing any flanking movements by the Confederates. Confederate troops from Maj. Gen. Robert E. Rodes' and Maj. Gen Henry Heth's divisions attacked the V and IX Corps during the redeployment, when Maj. Gen. Thomas L. Crittenden (who had succeeded General Stevenson as commander of the First Division of the IX Corps) prematurely recalled his pickets. Rodes' Division went into action on the right of Heth's Division. The Second Brigade of Crittenden's division, which was in the rear during the redeployment, was attacked by General Heth's troops.

Assistant Adjutant General Charles J. Mills, Crittenden's division, wrote to his mother: "Our Corps was on the extreme right, and the movement therefore should have been prompt and speedy, and the pickets not drawn in till we were well started. Instead of this they were drawn in before our rear had left, and we hadn't got more than half a mile, when the enemy came, right in our rear and we had a pretty sharp thing for about an hour; our Second Brigade [21st Massachusetts, 100th Pennsylvania and 3d Maryland regiments] got badly cut up."

Colonel Elisha Marshall, commander of the Provisional Brigade (later the Third Brigade) in Crittenden's division and the only officer in the division to submit a report, noted that before any troops could be put into position, the Confederates advanced rapidly upon the pickets, taking many prisoners. Marshall continued: "The enemy rapidly drove in our pickets, and owing to the fact that there was a gap between the Ninth and Fifth Corps on the left of the Second Brigade, the enemy flanked our lines, and consequently caused the retirement of the Second Brigade."

Lieutenant Colonel George P. Hawkes, 21st Massachusetts Regiment, wrote in his diary that the regiment "remained until 4 p.m. [the movement by the IX Corps commenced about one in the afternoon according to Colonel Marshall] when the 9th Corps was to change position in order to unite on the right and rear of Warren's Corps. The rebels took advantage of our movement and made an attack on our rear. We had the hardest shower here I ever seen."

In his memoirs, Confederate Lt. Gen. Jubal A. Early stated that in the afternoon on June 2: "Rodes' Division moved forward, along the road from Hundley's Corner toward Old Church, and drove the enemy from his entrenchments, now occupied with heavy skirmish lines, and forced back his left towards Bethesda Church, where there was a heavy force. Gordon swung round so as to keep pace with Rodes, and Heth co-operated, following Rodes and taking position on his left flank. In this movement there was some heavy fighting and several hundred prisoners were taken by us."

Confederate Maj. Gen. Henry Heth offered a slightly different version of the event: "Near Bethesda church I struck the IX and V Federal Army Corps. General Early was on my right." Heth told Early "that the enemy was withdrawing from my front, and that I had already given orders to attack. We drove the enemy to the entrenchments he had thrown up near Bethesda church." Heth also wrote: "But as Rodes failed to advance, my right flank became fearfully exposed and I gave orders to my brigade commanders to fall back."

Although the bloody little affair barely warranted mention by Civil War historians or in the official records, the 21st Massachusetts Regiment suffered 46 casualties that afternoon: 13 killed, 21 wounded and 12 captured. One of those prisoners was George Hitchcock.

* * * *

June 2, 1864—"O God the Lord, the Strength of my salvation, Thou hast covered my head in the day of battle. Surely the righteous shall give thanks to thy name."

All the earlier part of the day was unusually quiet for us, but the oppressive stillness was broken in the afternoon by orders for us to move out of the breastworks, crawling so that the enemy should not discover our move. After all the breastworks had been abandoned by our Corps, we were strung out in long lines half a mile back preparing to move to the left of our army in the plan to swing around Richmond. Here we halted for our skirmishers to be brought in. While waiting, a heavy thunder shower came up and in the midst of all, the cracking of musketry and whizzing of minies told us we were attacked in the rear. We were halting on a large open plain and a wooded chain of hills laid back of us a quarter of a mile where the enemy had occupied and were advancing in long lines to attack us. [*Two roads connect the Shady Grove Road with Bethesda Church. The road to the west intersects with the Shady Grove Road about one mile from Bethesda Church. At the time of the battle, the area west of this intersection was wooded and the area east, marked as the Bowles farm, was cultivated. This battle took place in these fields and woods near this intersection.*] In less time than it takes to write it the whole Corps had "about faced" and were swinging into lines of battle and charging into the woods. As we advanced a shower of bullets met us from our right front while a long line of graybacks were seen hurrying around our left with the intention of flanking our Brigade. The severe fire from our front checked us, so while we were putting volley after volley into the line just in front, the flanking force had taken a position where they could sweep our whole brigade line. We had already been moved several rods beyond our Corps line by the drunken Colonel commanding and it became apparent that we were in a critical and very dangerous situation. Not receiving orders to fall back we laid down and receive the concentrated fire on three sides. After a few moments of dreadful slaughter the panic stricken men of the 48th Penn. fled pell mell to the rear which feeling infected those of our regiment less resolute till at last in spite of threats and remonstrances from the officers, the whole regiment was flying like frightened sheep over the field, many dropping down in their tracks. For a few moments a small band of us remained around Col. Hawkes, then at last he gave the order to retreat and jumped up and fled. I immediately followed but owing to the fact that I was afflicted with two large boils very painful which make locomotion very difficult, I had only gone a half dozen rods when I fell down into a little pit which had been used by pickets. This was nearly full of water but so long as I hugged the ground I was in comparative safety. When I began to realize my situation, I found I was right halfway between the two opposing lines. Such a pandemonium I can never believe can be surpassed in this world. The artillery playing upon all the heights around seemed directed to the very spot where I laid. Shell after shell in rapid succession exploded over and around me, tearing up the ground and covering me with dirt. Once I raised my head to find out the situation when "thud" came two bullets within a foot of my

12. Captured at Cold Harbor

resting place striking in the ground. As it began to grow dusk and I was wondering if our lines were not preparing to charge, for the musketry firing had diminished. I heard the murmur of voices and knew that an advance was in progress though from which side I was unable to distinguish. The sounds grew more distinct and I could distinguish the orders from various commanders preparing their men to charge. As soon as they had advanced within a dozen rods I raised my head and found to my horror the long lines stretched across the plain of graybacks sweeping up over my living grave. As there seemed but one way for me now I at once arose and received the order from the nearest rebel officer to "Surrender," which I did, by pointing down to my gun which laid half buried in the mud and water. Thus I became a prisoner of war.

The officer who ordered me to surrender I learned was a colonel of a North Carolina Regiment belonging to Ramseur's Brigade and the line was composed of Rodes' Division of Ewell's Corps. A man was taken from the ranks and instantly divested me of my equipments and hurried me to the rear, over the ground we had just passed in our advance and retreat. Here I saw rebels busy in disrobing our dead and wounded. This was not a time to remonstrate or express any indignation for the advancing lines were just uttering their yell and as they charged against our lines they met a terrible storm of minies which rattled about us very fast. We hurried back through the woods while the darkness and a drizzling rain set in. The rebel forces appeared to be massed in these woods from which they were hurled against our lines as the incessant rattle and thunder indicated. The narrow road was crowded with batteries hurrying up to the front or to new positions, ammunition trains and ambulances all drawn by mules. There was an opposite stream of ambulances pressing to the rear loaded with wounded men, and crowds of skedaddlers and prisoners.

As we went back over the breastworks I had help build, I began to comprehend the situation somewhat and wonder if I was in a fair way to know by experience all the horrors which rumor had made familiar to me. After a tramp of a mile I was delivered into the charge of a provost guard which had already received under guard about a hundred prisoners, most of our own Brigade. A rebel officer came and took away my rubber blanket and as we pushed forward through the mud, hardly a word passed between fellow prisoners, each one too fully occupied with the gloomy thoughts of our present uncomfortable situation and of our very dark future prospect. We dragged along three miles and were "turned out" into an open field where we laid down in the wet ground and passed the night.

[*On June 2, 1864, the Union Second Brigade in the First Division of the IX Corps lost 137 men: 80 casualties in the 100th Pennsylvania Regiment, 46 casualties in the 21st Massachusetts Regiment and 10 casualties in the 3d Maryland Regiment.*]

June 3—Looking about me at daylight. I discovered eleven of our boys [*Prentice J. Banks, Daniel E. Barker, James Cane, Thomas B. Dyer, George O. Emerson, Alvin S. Graton, German Lagara, Martin D. Leach, Thomas Marshall and William L. Orcutt*] of our regiment. Among the number was Jim Miller, as sorry comfort to me, and yet a comfort. We started out early, a long string of fresh "fish" we were, nearly half a mile in length. Taking a northwesterly direction we passed through Mechanicsville directly by Gen. R.E. Lee's headquarter tents. The roar of artillery and rattle of musketry opened at daylight [*Battle of Cold Harbor*] and became unremitting as the day advanced although we were constantly moving away from the sound it grew more distinct, indicating that the rebels were being closely pressed in different parts of the line. We struck the Fredericksburg and Richmond R.R. and following along its track crossed the Chickahominy Swamp; passed the remaining earthworks of McClellan of the Peninsula Campaign and after a round about march of ten miles reached the outside fortification of Richmond, four miles <u>west</u> of the city. Here we were searched by a pretended provost guard and after four hours went on. We passed through the suburbs of the city which nature had endowed with surpassing beauty but stern war, who is no respecter of romance or beauty, has made a large portion of the surrounding country a desolate waste. We come in sight of the city two miles away and have to pass over a cleared level plain a mile across which is unobstructed by even a fence or bush, beyond which, extending as far as the eye can reach are the formidable fortifications partially hiding the city beyond. Passing by these we see the almost insurmountable obstructions which have been prepared to receive the Yankee Army. We enter the city, passing by the large State Almshouse and around the rebel capitol building with its rebel rag floating over it; then down through the principal business streets where we see the frequent signs "Fresh Arrival of Blockade Goods" at business houses. The streets were lined with the accursed rebel population which delighted in heaping on a worn-out, hungry, dusty band of defenseless prisoners, all manner of insults, hooting and groaning. At the opposite end of the city from which we entered we reached the large Pemberton Tobacco Warehouse directly opposite "Libby" on Cary Street and overlooking the James River. Here were six hundred of us stored away in three large, low, damp, dirty rooms—the privies at the end of each room open and emitting an abominable stench almost suffocating. we were notified that orders to shoot any person looking out of the windows, wither sitting in the window or leaning against it, would be strictly carried out. One young Kentuckian was shot about twenty four hours before while standing near a window, the ball striking him in the shoulder making a painful wound. This was a warning to us, which we were careful to heed. Here we again underwent a rigid examination, where we were relieved of money, extra clothing, knapsacks, haversacks and canteens, which work was not completed till after midnight.

13

Prisoner of War

"Brisk trading all day between the guards and prisoners."
—Hitchcock, June 12, 1864

While George Hitchcock was headed toward Richmond as a prisoner of war during the predawn on June 3, 1864, Union troops began a full-scale frontal assault against the strongly entrenched Confederate lines at Cold Harbor. The attack was disastrous almost as quickly as it began—Union casualties were appalling. More than 5,000 men were killed and wounded in less than thirty minutes, and another 2,000 more would be listed under one of those categories before the dreadful day ended. Once again, the Union army failed to capture the embattled Confederate capital, which was nearly encircled by fortifications. Extending for more than 65 miles, the outer ring of defenses was five to ten miles from Richmond. There was an intermediate line of fortifications four miles from the city, and then, on the perimeter of the city limits, a series of star forts provided an inner defense.

The battles Lee and Grant waged across the Virginia countryside generated thousands of prisoners of war. From late July 1862 to November 1863, captured Union and Confederate soldiers were either exchanged or paroled on their oath of honor not to bear arms against their captives. Irresolvable disagreement over the exchange system led in late October 1863 to the cessation of prisoner exchanges. In December 1863, there were more than 13,000 Union prisoners in Richmond: 6,300 confined on Belle Island, a small island in the James River, and the others imprisoned in converted tobacco warehouses known as Libby, Crew's, Pemberton's, Smith's and Scott's prisons. Brigadier General John H. Winder, who had graduated from the United States Military Academy at West Point in 1820, was responsible for the supervision of the prisons in Richmond.

Since there was a limited number of prison guards, the people of Richmond were constantly apprehensive about an uprising by Union captives. General Lee realized in late October 1863 that the prisoners in Richmond posed a problem to the Confederacy. They added to the acute shortage of food and clothing, increased the cost of food for civilians, overburdened the limited transportation system and endangered the city from attacks by Union raiders. As a result, Lee recommended that prisoners be sent to "some point or points in the deep south" where there was little chance of attack and where wood was cheap and provisions abundant. In late December, Andersonville, Georgia, was selected as the best, available site for a stockade to accommodate 10,000 prisoners.

Two events hastened the removal of prisoners from Richmond to Andersonville. On February 9, 1864, 109 officers escaped from Libby Prison by digging a 57-foot tunnel to a shed near the prison. The escape was remarkably successful for only forty-eight of the escapees were recaptured. The mass breakout was followed on February 28 to March 3 by a Union raid on the capital by Brig. Gen. H. Judson Kilpatrick and Col. Ulric Dahlgren. The two Union officers each led a column of horsemen toward Richmond with the avowed objective of liberating prisoners, setting fire to the city, and assassinating President Jefferson Davis and members of his cabinet. The attack was not successful—Dahlgren was killed outside the city and the failure of the two columns to unite doomed the expedition to failure.

On February 17, The Richmond Dispatch pleaded for the removal of prisoners. The first prisoners sent south, 200 men in four boxcars, left Richmond on February 18 and arrived at Andersonville on February 24. Four hundred prisoners a day were sent to Georgia for the next few months. Between May 5 and June 4, more than 8,000 Union prisoners of war, captured in the Wilderness, at Spotsylvania, North Anna, Totopotomoy Creek, Bethesda Church and Cold Harbor, passed through Richmond en route to Georgia. By the end of June, there were 26,367 prisoners at Andersonville, including George Hitchcock, in a stockade designed to hold only 10,000 men.

* * * *

June 4, 1864—We were divided into messes of twenty men each and drew rations. Some of our number had been without food for three long days. I had eaten nothing for twenty four hours. A piece of corn bread three inches square, bacon an inch square, and a gill [*quarter of a pint*] of muddy looking water with two beans and a dozen bugs floating in it went by the fictitious name of Bean Soup.

June 5—We were joyfully surprised with the information that we could send letters home, and in a couple of hours we had the appearance of a crowded writing school. I wrote to Col. Hawkes and home. Drew rations the same as yesterday. I begin to feel the want of outdoor air.

June 6—The green fields stretching away on the south side of the James River appear very inviting and tantalizing to us. The occupation through our crowded room has principally been "Skirmishing" for lice, reading Testaments and sleeping, but the hours are tedious and long. Our letters were sent down the river in a flag of truce boat.

June 7—The rebel Lieut. in command called the roll at half past seven. I read my Testament and a sketch of Col. James Gardner which both served as help to keep my courage up. A lot of wounded rebels from opposite Butler's Army passed by the prison. At night each man was called out by name and marched across the street to Libby where we spent the night.

[*James Gardiner, 1688–1745, British Colonel of a regiment of light dragoons, was slain in a battle at Prestonpans on September 21, 1745, immediately after saying, "Fire on, my lads, and fear nothing." According to Gardiner, he was reading Thomas Watson's* The Christian Soldier, *when he saw a vision of Jesus Christ upon the cross and was immediately converted.* The Life of Colonel James Gardiner: The Christian Warrior *by Philip Doddridge, dated 1745, was one of the most frequently printed books; the 1854 and 1856 editions were printed in New York.*]

June 8—A large crowd of prisoners was sent away to Georgia from our Pemberton quarters and we were returned to them again. I am on the fourth floor this time, which is a lighter room. I tried to wash my clothes today. Feel very hungry.

June 9—Was roused at three in the morning and took one days rations of corn bread and bacon, marched across the James on a passenger bridge to Manchester where we were packed away in rickety box cars, fifty in a car, very hot and close. Started away on the Richmond and Danville R.R., but as the guard filled up the only opening of the car, I was unable to get much of an idea of the country through which we passed. Passed through Burkeville, the junction with the Lynchburg and Petersburg R.R. where we saw large stores and munitions awaiting transportation to Richmond. Reached and crossed the Roanoke at dark.

June 10—Spent a sleepless night in the stifled car. Reached Danville at eleven A.M. where we disembarked and marched a short distance to the military prison, a more comfortable place than that at Richmond. Here we drew rations. We are one hundred and fifty miles from Richmond southwest. Just before dark we were again put into cars, smaller than those of yesterday but fifty in a car as before. The road for quite a distance is new, having been just built and we proceed very slowly all night.

[*In November 1861, President Jefferson Davis requested that the railroad ending at Danville, Virginia, be connected with Greensboro, North Carolina. Construction was delayed for more two years pending completion of satisfactory surveys, examination of rival routes and arrangements for procuring labor and supplies. The connection was completed in May 1864.*]

June 11—A short time before light, my car, being very dilapidated, caved in owing to the heavy weight of the guards on the top. This produced great consternation among those inside as the framework swayed from side to side threatening to crush us all. We were saved from accident, however, by our own efforts, the prisoners inside holding up the roof by man force, for several miles until we reached Greensboro, N.C., a beautiful town almost entirely hid under immense shade trees. Here we change cars for better ones. Passed through Salisbury at noon when it began to rain. Rode very slowly all the afternoon and arrived at Charlotte at five at night. Here we disembark and bivouac in the wet field. Drew rations and lie down feeling very hungry and tired. We are one hundred and twenty miles from Danville.

June 12—An East storm set in and we were wet to the skin, cold and uncomfortable. A cargo of prisoners was brought in and another sent off during the day. Brisk trading all day between the guards and prisoners. The guard selling bread at the rate of ten dollars per loaf, biscuits three dollars per dozen, onions at fifty cents apiece. We hogs had rooted up the ground until it had become very muddy and we were moved to a drier spot to pass the night.

June 13—Cold and stormy. Got on the cars at daylight and left Charlotte for Columbia, S.C. Crossed Cape Fear River into South Carolina, also the Catawba, a wide, deep river. Passed through Winnsboro in the afternoon and reached Columbia at dark one hundred and ten miles from Charlotte. Were "switched off" two miles below the city where we drew, each, four sea biscuits and pork. Pass the night in the cars.

June 14—Cold and Rain. Started at four in the morning on the Branchville R.R., [*South Carolina Railroad from Columbia to Branchville and then to Augusta*]. A very rough hard riding. Rode nearly all day through swampy land, one hundred and forty miles across the Savannah River.

June 15—Very warm and bright. Laid in the cars at Augusta under strict guard until one P.M. when we got out and drew rations. Embarked on another train on the Georgia Central R.R. This is the smoothest road I have been over, passing through a very level swampy country.

June 16—Thursday. Cloudy. Slept soundly through the night and at four in the morning crossed the Ocmulgee, a branch of the Altamaha River and arrived at Macon, a thriving city one hundred and sixty miles from Augusta. Our route during the forenoon laid through immense swamps where trestle-work several miles in length was required for the railroad. The heavy thick foliage, the towering pines adorned with pendant mosses and clinging parasites gave the appearance of the different climate we have already reached. At noon we drew near our destination at Andersonville, Sumter County, Georgia, sixty miles south of Macon, in the midst of a level wilderness of pines.

13. Prisoner of War

The main gate at Andersonville, drawn by George A. Hitchcock for his 1890 diary from a sketch he made in 1864.

14

Andersonville, Georgia

"It is very hard to sit day after day with nothing to occupy my thoughts, but the harrowing question constantly: Must we die here?"
—Hitchcock, October 4, 1864

Andersonville was the largest military prison, North or South, established during the Civil War. It was officially called Camp Sumter. Located adjacent to the Southwestern Railroad—ten miles northeast of Americus and more than fifty miles southwest of Macon. Andersonville was populated by about twenty people when it was selected as a site for a prison. The hamlet included a railroad depot, church, store, cotton warehouse and a dozen dilapidated houses. The United States Post Office Department changed the name of the railroad depot from Anderson to Andersonville in 1856 to avoid confusion with Anderson, South Carolina.

The prison stockade was still not completed when the first prisoners arrived in February 1864, and thus two pieces of artillery were deployed to guard the one open side. The stockade was completed by the third week of March. It covered more than 16 acres with a log palisade 17 feet high in the shape of a parallelogram—780 feet by 1,010 feet. The ground sloped toward the center of the compound where a shallow creek ran from west to east. Sentry boxes, called "pigeon-roosts," were located on platforms on the outer side of the stockade. In late March, a three-foot-high railing was constructed about 19 feet from the palisade. This warning was designated the "deadline," marked the point beyond which no prisoner was allowed to cross upon threat of death. Despite the abundance of timber in the vicinity of the camp, there were no buildings inside the prison pen. A bakery was completed in May and was located outside the stockade on the bank of the stream running through the prison. There were two entrances on the west side of the stockade—the North Gate and the South Gate. Earthen forts were constructed around the exterior to quell any prison riots and to defend against any Union attacks.

For administrative reasons the prisoners were divided into detachments for

14. Andersonville, Georgia

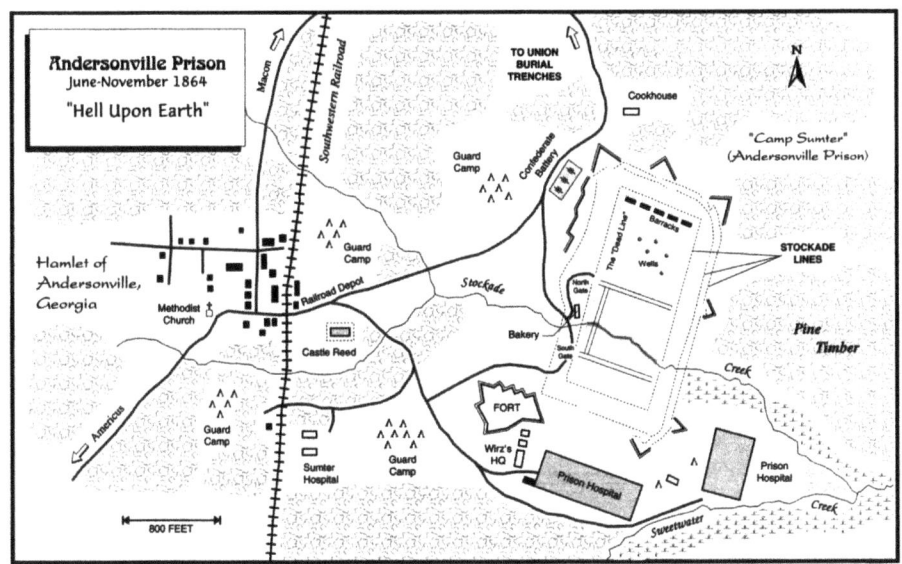

Andersonville Prison, June to November 1864 (© Mark A. Moore).

issuing rations and maintaining discipline. Each detachment had 270 men, which was divided into three squads with a Union sergeant assigned to each squad. When rations were issued once a day, the sergeant distributed the ration to the three messes of his squad, and a sergeant of each mess distributed the rations to 30 men.

When the prison opened in February and until May 17, 1864, prison guards were assigned from regular Confederate units: 55th, 56th and 57th Georgia regiments, Leon Florida Artillery and the 26th Alabama Regiment. The prisoners were cognizant of this and the relationship between captor and captive was largely based on mutual respect. In May, however, the relationship between guards and prisoners changed drastically when the guards were replaced by the newly formed 1st, 2d, 3d and 4th Georgia Reserves. The Georgia reserves, composed of young boys and older men, were rarely drilled, very disorganized and inexperienced.

While the changing of the guard created some problems, the prisoners faced a more direct threat to their health from lack of fresh water and the buildup of sewage. Although the creek originally provided clean drinking water, the prisoners had no choice but to use it for bathing as well as a latrine (called sinks by the soldiers). The slow moving stream also carried the waste from the Confederate camps outside the stockade as well as the bakery. East of the stockade the creek drained into a swamp caused by blockage from fallen timber, which generated a horrible odor and provided a breeding ground for mosquitoes and other vermin.

According to Confederate records, 45,613 Union soldiers were confined at Andersonville, and on August 8, 1864, there were 33,114 prisoners in the stockade—the largest number on any one day. Between February and May 1865, 12,912 prisoners died from disease, poor sanitation, malnutrition, overcrowding and exposure to the weather. During the course of just one day, August 23, 1864, 127 prisoners died—the largest number of deaths on any day. Diarrhea and dysentery accounted for 59 percent of the deaths at Andersonville, while scurvy was the other major medical problem.

From May 22 through November 1864, a general hospital was located on three acres near the southeast corner of the stockade. There were tents but no beds to accommodate 2,000 patients in an area that the prisoners regarded as simply a stopping point between the stockade and the burying ground. Seventy-six percent of the hospital patients died. On June 30, thirteen doctors cared for 26,000 prisoners and by August, with more than 30,000 prisoners behind Andersonville's walls, only four doctors were on duty. The other doctors and half of the 24 hospital staff were on sick leave or "leave of indulgence." The tremendous increase of prisoners compelled the Confederates to enlarge the prison, and on July 1, the captives were redistributed into an enlarged stockade with more than 26 acres—the length of the fence was expanded to 1,620 feet.

The Confederate guards also suffered ill effects from being stationed at Andersonville. In July and August, inspection reports noted that 66.4% of the Southern soldiers reported sick with a mortality rate of 2.3%. In late July, a Confederate inspector general noted that of an aggregate force of 3,600 men: 647 were on sick report, 452 were without arms, 227 were on leave, 385 were absent without leave, 297 were on detached service and 48 were in the guardhouse. The remaining 1,544 officers and men were divided into three shifts to guard 30,000 prisoners.

Although there was gross mismanagement at Andersonville, the problems were almost unmanageable; the Confederate leaders were unable to relieve the situation. They lived with the fear of small groups of prisoners escaping, fear of a general prison uprising, fear of escaping prisoners burning the neighboring towns and fear of Union raiders from Sherman's army. With the limited manpower available, the Confederates concentrated on reinforcing their defensive barriers rather than improving the sanitation facilities. In August they constructed a second barrier 90 to 150 feet beyond the main stockade to prevent prisoners from escaping and to provide resistance against attacks. The earthen forts surrounding the stockade were reinforced and a third stockade line, which was designed to provide a covered way for marching troops between fortifications, was started but never completed. Most of the prisoners were transferred to other locations by October and at the end of November there were only 1,359 prisoners remaining.

George Glover, a former prison guard when he was 15 years old, wrote in

14. Andersonville, Georgia

1908: *"The people of Americus, ten miles away, were in constant dread—a terror which only the people who lived during those days of weeks and months can fully realize. They believed that should the prisoners make a dash and escape the stockade, Americus would be their first point of attack and the town would be burned."* On August 13, 1864, Brig. Gen. John Winder reported on the status of the camp: *"We have now here 33,000 prisoners of war, and more arriving almost daily. We are crowded to excess, and the mortality is very great—amounting to 633 in seven days. I think no more prisoners should be sent here if it can be avoided. I do beg that you press everything for the prison at Millen so that we may relieve this prison."*

The causes for suffering and death at Andersonville were many: Lack of shelter, overcrowding, insufficient food, extremely poor sanitary conditions including the accumulation of human excrement that polluted the water facilities, extreme weather conditions, inadequate hospital facilities and medical supplies, shortage of qualified medical personnel and prison guards and generally a lack of Southern resources. The only prisoners who were able to escape some sickness were those who were paroled to work in connection with routine affairs of the prison. General Winder rejected overcrowding as a major cause of the high death rate. He acknowledged that hospital conditions were poor but nothing could be done to rectify the situation and blamed commissary officials for the food shortages. Winder emphasized that congestion could not be prevented without additional troops—the shortage of guards required his men to remain on duty for over 48 hours without relief.

Lieutenant Colonel Alexander W. Persons of the 55th Georgia Regiment served as first post commander. He was replaced by Brig. Gen. John Henry Winder on June 17, 1864. On July 26, General Winder was appointed commander of all prisons in Georgia and Alabama, and he was named commissary general of all prisons east of the Mississippi River on November 21. During the first week in October 1864, Col. George Gibbs assumed command of Andersonville until May, 1865, when General Winder moved his headquarters from Andersonville to Camp Lawton (Millen, Georgia) and then to Augusta and finally to Columbia. He died suddenly of a heart attack on February 6, 1865, a day after his arrival to inspect Florence Stockade, South Carolina. Although General Winder was criticized as a tyrant in the Southern press and vilified as the "inhuman fiend of Andersonville prison" in the North, he performed an impossible task with limited supplies and manpower. Undoubtedly, if he had survived, General Winder would have been charged with war crimes for his treatment of Union prisoners, and probably executed with Henry Wirz.

Captain Hartmann Heinrich "Henry" Wirz, who was born in Zurich, Switzerland, commanded the interior of the prison from March 27, 1864, to May 7, 1865, except for a convalescent furlough during August. The man most closely associated with Andersonville's horrors, Wirz, "the demon of Andersonville," was executed on November 10, 1865, for war crimes. When prejudices flourished from a long war and were greatly aggravated by the assassination of President Lincoln, his death was encouraged by "vindictive politicians, an unbridled press and a nation seeking revenge"—the only Confederate official executed.

William Best Hesseltine's succinct comment is worth noting: "The complete inadequacy of the Confederacy's material resources and the failure of its transportation system was fully illustrated in the prisons"… "the Union soldiers became the wards of an impoverished government."

Hitchcock said in 1890: *"At first but little could be seen which indicated any presence of the great body of men known to be here: a few rough-board sheds for railroad purposes and a few scattering camps of rebel soldiers. Soon, however, we were made conscious of the presence of the ruling genius of the place. As the weary, cramped and homesick prisoners tumbled out of the cars, they were met by Captain Wirz, a grizzly, dirty looking Dutchman whose head was adorned with a snarly mass of long, unkempt, wiry, gray hair surmounted by a shapeless, gray, military cap—much too small for his head. His face, what could be seen above a thick and tangled beard, was drawn out of human shape or appearance by scowls and wrinkles, presenting generally a very wolfish appearance. As he rode up and down the line on his white horse cursing the 'damned Yankees,' occasionally striking a prisoner with the slave driver whip in his hand, he appeared the incarnation of evil, the devil in human form."*

Confederate Captain Hartmann Heinrich (Henry) Wirz, who was born in Zurich, Switzerland, in 1823,

Captain Henry Wirz, in a photograph purportedly taken during his 1863 journey to Europe. He commanded the interior of the Andersonville Prison from March 27, 1864, to May 7, 1865 (Library of Congress).

14. Andersonville, Georgia

immigrated to Kentucky in 1849 and then moved to Milliken's Bend, Louisiana, where he functioned as a homeopathic physician. He commanded the interior of the prison at Andersonville, officially known as Camp Sumter, from March 29, 1864, to May 7, 1865 (absent on sick leave during August 1864).

* * * *

June 16, 1864 [*continued*]—Reached the gates of the Andersonville Stockade soon after noon where we were taken in charge by Capt. Wirz, a grizzly, dirty looking Dutchman, whose head was adorned with a snarly mass of long, unkempt, wiry, gray hair surmounted by a shapeless gray military cap much too small for this head. His face, what could be seen above a thick and tangled beard, was drawn out of all human shape and appearance by scowls and wrinkles, presenting on the whole a very wolfish appearance, and as he rode from one part of the line to another on his white horse cursing continually, occasionally striking a prisoner. Under the present surroundings he appeared the incarnation of evil, the impersonation of the devil in human form.

As we stand outside the stockade, waiting for our names to be enrolled, our eyes take in a view of the inside, a dense black mass of seething, moving humanity not unlike the appearance of a mammoth ant-hill just broken open. Over the whole hung a cloud of smoke from the thousands of little fires where rations were being cooked. After which we pass through the heavy timbered double gate which shut us in from the world and for the first time made painfully aware of the horrors of the place. As we pass along through the packed crowd of our fellow prisoners who are looking for old familiar faces, we see squalor and filth everywhere. The pitch pine smoke has given the clearest complexion, an African hue which we are assured will be our fate in a week or two. As we move along, we find the crowd does not decrease and anxious to secure a good clear spot where I can sit down, I break away from the rest of our crowd but do not find my desired haven. I am told that I had better sit down where I find my first chance for if I wait till dark I may not find even room to stretch out. I accept the advice and "squat" while Jim goes to hunt up the boys of the 21st who were lost at Spotsylvania.

We found Bailey of Company I. He was seen by us (Dec. 23d) while advancing on the skirmish line in the Clinch Mts, East Tennessee. He tells us a story of hardship which makes the heart ache. Being swooped up by two Tennessee guerrillas while passing through a dense thicket, he was hurried forward on a lonely path over the mountains and out of the way of our outposts, made to march ninety miles to Bristol, from thence to Richmond, to Belle Isle, and early in the spring brought down here. He is troubled with scurvy and complains of the cold nights for he has worn out all his clothing, a worn out pair of cotton drawers make up his only covering. His face black as a negro by smoke, he is hardly recognizable. He directed us to the spot where we found

Osgood, Potter and ten others of the 21st. And what a sorry looking set of fellows, so poor and emaciated, though prisoners but one month. The day was passed in hearing their stories of the horrors which seem to be our inevitable lot. We went back to our "spot" at dark, sadly out of spirits. Jim says, "I wish I was dead" and I—well I am glad my friends don't know how I am situated. As we lie down in our bed of sand we are cautioned to "freeze" to our ration bags so we fasten them to our blouses and try to sleep. Jim wakes me at ten o'clock and find it raining so sleep is banished for the night and morning finds us drenched to the skin.

June 17—We found three men of Sherman's Army who have just come in and one has a woolen blanket. We have gone in together and after looking several hours secure sticks and are able to make a shelter in shape of two woolens sewed together. Five of us get under but find we can only lie on our sides for the limited room will not allow any to lie on the back. There are now over twenty thousand prisoners here and the stench which pervades every part of Camp is well nigh unendurable. We are assured however, that we shall get accustomed to that after a few days. Great numbers are dying every day, many from scurvy. At night drew rations of rice and sow belly. The rice is half cooked and only half a pint of it at that.

[*There was an average of 22,291 prisoners at Andersonville during June 1864; the prison population was 26,367 on June 30, 1864.*]

June 18—Our squad was called to the gate and divided. As several of our number could not readily be found, the Dutchman informs us that we will not have any rations till all are found. This would seem a difficult task, like "hunting for a needle in a hay mow," but our stomachs crave, and each man makes a personal effort to find them until all are found. We are formed into the 83rd detachment (of 270 men each). The only regulation in camp is that each Detachment has a man appointed who draws rations for them and each man is supposed to know who this man is from whom he is to receive his rations. These are brought into camp in the latter part of the afternoon. The view of the country outside is a dreary monotony of pine forest circling around us a half mile away.

The center of the camp is an impassable swamp where all the refuse matter of the thousands settles. Each morning, this is found on close examination a living mass of corruption and worms "born and bred" in a night. This alone would be reason enough for the dreadful mortality which increases every day. Several prisoners from Sigel's West Virginia Army came in today, many of them wounded whose wounds have not been dressed. Thirty six prisoners, while out under guard after wood, escaped by overpowering the guard and driving them along with them. Our rations today: corn bread two inches square and sow belly.

June 19—Very hot. Heavy shower in the afternoon. A lot of prisoners from Sherman's and Butler's armies came in. Miller and Dyer sick with diar-

14. Andersonville, Georgia

Andersonville Prison, drawn by George A. Hitchcock in June 1864 and then redrawn for his 1890 diary.

rhea. Found Walter Lamb, who was taken prisoner June 1st At Drury's Bluff. Two men were shot by the sentry who fired at another prisoner who had got over the "Dead Line," a little rail running around the entire stockade inside about twenty feet from it over which, if a man reaches or passes, becomes the mark of the two or three sentries nearest him. This rule is over diligently carried out and it not only becomes a "dead line" but also a very dangerous one to approach. A man was killed about two rods from us last night falling into a well. It is rumored that Grant has got into Petersburg.

June 20—Very hot till afternoon when rain began and continued incessantly several hours. Dyer is better and I am troubled with the same disorder which he has had. My mental vision begins to take in the different phases of prison life and I am prepared to see almost any form of suffering now. I wonder if I shall ever see home again.

June 21—Warm as ever with the usual shower in the afternoon. Another man was shot on the dead line. Over one hundred men died today but their places were made good by a larger number from Sherman's army.

June 22—Very hot. Rations of a pint of meal and a small piece of sow belly. Hear the tantalizing report of an exchange of prisoners to begin July 1st

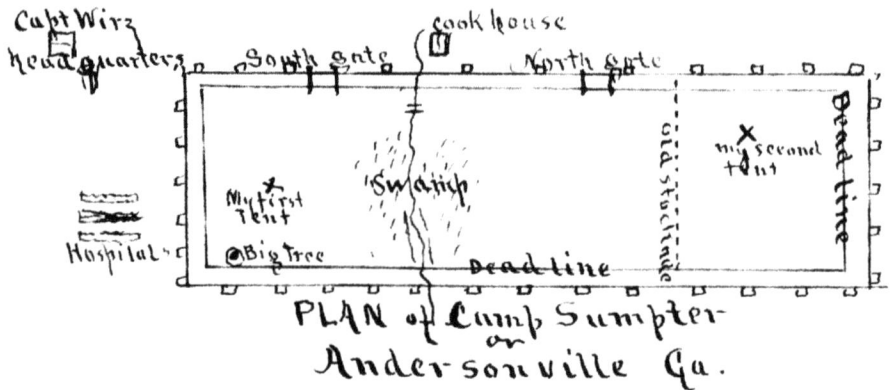

Location of George A. Hitchcock's tents at Andersonville, drawn by Hitchcock in his 1890 diary.

transports already en route for Savannah to receive us. This is official because the *New York Herald* says so.

[*The* New York Herald *was respected by Hitchcock. From the beginning of the war the New York newspapers surpassed the journals of other cities in acquiring news of the Union armies in the field by maintaining large number of field reporters, spending vast sums of money, developing better organizations, and procuring special concessions. The* New York Herald *spent more than half a million dollars on war reporting—maintained thirty to forty writers in the field with five reporters at one time in prison in the South; one special correspondent was killed and three perished from illness in the line of duty.*]

June 23—Very hot. A lot of prisoners from Grant's army came in taken at Petersburg. A great display of eggs, cucumbers, biscuits, squashes, potatoes, beans and parsnips is seen, torturing the poor fellows who are dying by scores each day for want of these same luxuries. They are brought in by rebel guard. There was the usual number of free fights in camp where clubs, razors and fists freely used.

June 24—Very warm, drew ration of mush and sow belly yesterday, and raw meal and salt today. We do not venture from under our shelter during the middle of the day when the torrid rays melt us quickly.

June 25—Very hot. Rations of raw meal and meat but no wood to cook them with so we eat our meat raw. Never supposed I should be expected to eat and live like a dog. I had a good wash at the creek today though without soap. Rows are increasing and camp presents a scene very like a second Babel. [*In 1890 Hitchcock added:* "First, a few loud words; then a rush of several men at each other and a sound of murderous whacks; when the crowd dissolves, bloody faces or blackened eyes show us how companions in misery can treat each other."]

June 26—Prisoners from Gen. Steele's army came in. I washed my pants

14. Andersonville, Georgia

in the creek. Am feeling quite week from diarrhea which causes me to feel desponding. It is the Sabbath, but how unlike our quiet peaceful New England Sabbaths. Poor starved men of almost every nationality, men without a spark of principle, bounty-jumpers, New York "Dead Rabbits," Baltimore "Plug Uglies," the sick and dying all around make this a scene of horror which will ever be vivid in my memory, if I can trust a good God has us under his keeping.

June 27—There are rumors of heavy fighting, Sherman's army. Prisoners from Grant's army came in. Two prisoners were brought in who tunneled out ten days ago and traveled over a hundred miles living on sweet potatoes from plantations along their route. The blood-hounds overtook them near the Florida line so they have returned to prison life refreshed with pure air. Several shots were fired at men on the dead line.

[*The first pack of dogs kept at Andersonville to pursue escaping prisoners consisted of eight hounds and a "catch dog"—a bull terrier. The hounds were white, yellow, and spotted "plantation dogs." In May, Sergeant Edward C. Turner, 1st Georgia Reserves, reported to Andersonville and brought two packs of hounds, numbering about 15, which he used to capture escaping prisoners.*]

June 28—Hot. Heavy shower in the evening. Six hundred prisoners from Grant's army taken near Petersburg came in. Among them we found the familiar faces of Winn, Stevens and Tyler from the 21st. Thirty Indian Sharpshooters from Northern Michigan also. My poor Company A came out of the fight with only two men who were not killed or wounded. I learn that Brother Henry has joined the regiment and is acting adjutant.

[*Thomas Winn, Thomas Stephens and William Tyler were captured on June 17—Federal troops of the Ninth Corps (including 21st Massachusetts) made a surprise attack at the Shand House on the Petersburg lines but with only limited results.*]

June 29—A soldier from Ohio who laid sick with fever within arms length of me died in the night. He was a large powerful framed man full of health and vigor but Death would not pass by him for all that. Showers in the afternoon. Rations tonight two quarts of meal. Can it be that we are to be fatted to stock the pork market or for the rebel army. It has been found that the outlaws in camp have formed a league styling themselves the "Raiders" and for the past two days matters have come to a terrible state. Two men murdered, one thrown into a deep well and many knocked on the head and plundered, nearly all of whom were known to have money, watches or other valuables, having just arrived. The rebel authorities have authorized the prisoners to form police organizations of several hundred who are armed with "Shillelaghs" and hunting up the desperadoes. The afternoon has been one of great excitement as twenty or thirty of the Raiders have already been secured and sent out.

June 30—Passed a sleepless night, for the Police and Raiders have kept up a continual fighting. This morning the camp is in the wildest excitement. The ring leader had not been found, but several were found buried under blankets with valuables to escape detection. At three in the afternoon the ring leader was found under a pile of blankets and pine boughs. The excitement was so great that it was difficult to get him outside the stockade unharmed. The rebel authorities sent him immediately back to the tender mercies of his fellow prisoners. Hardly had he come inside again before he was taken and beaten to death in fifteen minutes. His carcass was then carried out. We feel that the ring is effectually broken though we are told that the rest are to be pardoned, but if they are to be returned, there'll be no pardon for them.

July 1, 1864—At noon an opening was made from the stockade leading into the new addition. And during the afternoon, fifty detachments or over thirteen thousand men moved into it, ours among the number. We have now twenty five acres enclosed but the camp appears just as crowded as ever. Jim Miller and I found a 34th fellow, Levi Shepard, who had a rubber blanket so we three go in together. My woolen now serves for a shelter from the sun and rain, Shep's rubber for the ground, so we are in more tolerable comfort. There was some order planned in the arrangement of detachments into streets but our allotted ground was much too small so we are in as great a jumble as ever.

July 2—Very hot. Found an old tent mate of the 36th Mass. who was taken near White House Landing when on his way to his regiment on the 30th of May. Water is very difficult to get and of poor and filthy quality. We drew two rations owing to a misunderstanding on the part of the rebels. Owing to the poor state of our morals we did not return the extra ration.

July 3—Very hot. Roll was called throughout camp. Our detachment lost their rations on account of the absence of half a dozen men. So our extra rations of yesterday were very opportune.

July 4—Very hot. The "Glorious Fourth" dawns upon this free and enlightened community finding us in captivity. Feasting is the order of the day. Of our pint of meal we had burnt meal for breakfast, mush for dinner and raw pork for supper. The detachments were reorganized and ours is now the 63d. In place of the usual fireworks in the evening, our thirty thousand filled the night air with songs of "John Brown's Body," "Star Spangled Banner," "Down with the Traitors." Cheers for Vicksburg and Gettysburg of a year ago and groans for Hog Winder and the Dutch Captain. All of which were given with an unction which did not fail to reach the ears of those for whom they were intended. [*In 1890 Hitchcock added: "The joyous notes of the inspiring songs died out in a wail of despair—most realistic and seeming to rise from the blackness of the world of woe. How many lives were going out and rebel hate becomes powerless to hurt."*]

July 5—Very hot but a fine breeze blows up from the swamp. A death from cholera last night is reported, but that does not create undue excitement for Death does seem to have all he can attend to at present. Rumors of the fall of Richmond on the 2nd.

[*The Confederate government did not evacuate Richmond until Sunday, April 2, 1865—Union troops occupied Richmond and Petersburg, Virginia, on April 3, 1865.*]

July 6—Very hot. More prisoners came in today. The camp is full of rumors of an exchange to begin tomorrow. Succeeded in getting an axe for a few moments and cut up some wood.

[*By July exchange rumors abound at Andersonville almost every day with promises of release within a week. Some rumors of exchange and parole originated from northern newspapers while others were only wishful thinking. Nevertheless, there was a persistent rumor that an exchange would begin by July 7, but after the day passed universal gloom was present throughout the stockade.*]

July 7—Very hot. The day passed off without any paroling or exchange. Several "Wood Riots" and knockdowns occurred for the amusements of prisoners. The quartermaster has issued axes to each detachment thereby stopping the letting of axes at fifty and seventy five cents an hour which the bloodsuckers have been practicing.

July 8—Very warm. Several hundred prisoners from Grant's army and James Island came in which made unusual commotion outside. One poor fellow of our squad died during the night (diarrhea). He had no friends with him to care for him when he died. The cause of his dropping away so suddenly was owing to the great change of temperature from the hot day to the cold night. A large prayer meeting was held near us to which many a poor fellow delighted to crawl. Every moment of the time was taken up in prayers which went up from earnest hearts.[In 1890 Hitchcock added: Men, who never had framed words into prayer, felt that a higher than human helper must be appealed to.]

[*There were no chaplains at Andersonville; however, prisoners held religious services—small groups organized prayer meetings in the spring of 1864. These meetings, which had no fixed location, attracted large groups of prisoners by July—a song leader would go to a location and sing a familiar hymn and prisoners interested in spiritual inspiration would assemble.*]

July 9—Very hot with shower in the afternoon. Another man of our squad died today. A large number of prisoners from Hunter's West Virginia Army came in. They report a large number of prisoners from the 2nd Corps on their way to this place, which appears to be the general prison for all that the rebels get hold of. Washed shirt in creek.

July 10—Very hot with showers around us at night. More prisoners came in. The monotony of camp was broken by the parade of several camp-police, with two or three prisoners with their heads and faces shaved on one side and a card attached to their backs bearing the word "Thief." They were greeted with brick bats and cudgels as they passed along through the noisy unsympathetic crowd.

July 11—Another day of excitement. Seven hundred prisoners from Grant's army came in. Afternoon a scaffold was brought into camp and erected near the South Gate. At three the rebel camps were in commotion, the entire guard came out under arms and were placed in line of battle in different points around camp and the batteries were all manned. At four o'clock six of the condemned raiders were brought in under a strong guard of Union prisoners for the rebels were too shrewd to allow the Government to make stock of it by laying "blood on their hands." After they had ascended the scaffold, a catholic priest attended their spiritual wants individually. Meal bags were tied over their heads and the ropes adjusted, when every living soul inside and outside which was able was looking on in silence, more than forty thousand in all. At a given signal, the six dropped off. Five went struggling into eternity, while the rope of the sixth broke, and falling to the ground he gave a bound and was away like a frightened deer over tents and smashing in shanties in his race of despair. He reached the swamp and after floundering about a few moments was retaken. After begging most piteously for his life, he was taken up to the scaffold and the second time launched off, this time into eternity. One man was from Rhode Island, one from New York, one from New Jersey, one from Pennsylvania, and two were Marines. There is now a feeling of greater security than there has been for a long time, but may I never witness another scene like that.

[*These villains were called Mosby's Raiders, Mosby's Gang or more frequently "Raiders." The six Raiders, who were hanged at Andersonville on July 11, 1864, are listed on their grave markers as: Jno Sarsfield—144 NY; Wm Collins, 88 Pa, Co D; Chas Curtis, 5 RI Artillery, Co A; Pat Delaney, 83 Pa, Co E; A. Mun, U.S. Navy; and W. R. Rickson, U.S. Navy. Official military records indicate that the men were: William Collins, alias "Mosby," Company K and then Company D, 88th Pennsylvania Regiment, who straggled during the retreat from the Rapidan and was captured on October 12, 1863, confined at Belle Isle and arrived at Andersonville on March 4, 1864; John Sullivan, Company F, 76th New York Regiment, straggled during the retreat from the Rapidan and was captured near Stevensburg, Virginia, on October 10, 1863, and confined at Belle Isle and arrived at Andersonville on March 4, 1864; James Sarsfield, Company C, 140th New York Regiment, who deserted and surrendered at the Wilderness on May 5, 1864; Charles F. Curtis, Company C, 5th Rhode Island Heavy Artillery, who deserted and surrendered while confined at the hospital in Morehead City, North Carolina, in April 1864; Patrick Delaney, Company E,*

83d Pennsylvania Regiment, who deserted and surrendered on October 14, 1863, at Bristoe Station, Virginia; and Andrew Muir, seaman on the Federal steamer U.S.S. Water Witch, who was captured on June 2, 1864, near Ossabaw Island, south of Savannah, Georgia.]

July 12—Showers around us have cooled the air and it is quite comfortable. Six hundred prisoners from Grant's army came, among them Allen from Baldwinville of the 36th Mass. I bathed in the muddy creek in the evening. Prayer meetings every pleasant evening and very largely attended. The poor fellows now feel the need of a Higher Power than any earthly to save and protect us and this is the means of bringing many to put their trust in a Saviour.

[During the Spotsylvania campaign on May 12, 1864, Courtland A. Allen, Sergeant in Company D, 36th Massachusetts Regiment, was wounded in the hand and captured going to the rear. He was imprisoned at Andersonville. While being removed from Andersonville, he and five others jumped from the railroad train and escaped into the swamps. They remained for several weeks, subsisting on roots and berries, found a dug-out and made their way down the Altamaha River to the blockading Union squadron—six weeks after their escape.]

July 13—Very warm but cloudy. An extra ration of rice was dealt out to all in camp. Two men were shot on the dead line and a third was fired at. There are now one hundred and ten full detachments of two hundred and seventy men each in camp besides the crowded hospitals of several thousand troops more outside. These hospitals are nothing more than rough covered sheds—no bunks or beds or comforts of any kind.

July 14—Warm in the forenoon but cloudy in the afternoon. Several were shot on the dead line during the day. The sergeants were ordered to appear at the gate where they were told the pleasing information that grape and canister would be fired into camp without further notice, if large crowds should collect or any unusual commotion occur. There was a general review of the camp guard outside and a salute of two guns fired, all showing how the authorities fear an uprising in camp. "A guilty conscience needs no accuser."

July 15—A few cripples and bummers from Sherman's army were sent in. The authorities have suspicions that a tunnel of large dimensions has been in progress near the dead line, through which a large body of men might escape and overpower the guard, so they have been hunting for it. A petition has been made up, to send to our Government praying for a speedy release of all here. Death is doing his share of the work, faithfully.

July 16—Two tunnels have been discovered, one of them running fifty yards outside the stockade and would have probably been a great success had the place not been betrayed by a fellow of the 7th Maine who, for the extra "mess of pottage" "sold his brethren." Jim Miller has gone in with Osgood so Shep and I have the tent to ourselves.

July 17—Very chilly last night, but warm today. The 7th Maine fellow was hunted down by the police and put to torture after which his head was shaved and with "traitor" on his back was most unmercifully beaten by the justly indignant prisoners. Rations of molasses in place of meat.

July 18—We slept with our tent folded about us. A man was shot near the dead line by the <u>accidental</u> discharge of the sentry's gun and killed. Prisoners who came in today report Montgomery, Alabama, burnt by a Federal raiding party.

[*On July 10, 1864, Major General Lovell Harrison Rousseau, Union cavalry commander, led 2,500 men from Decatur, Alabama, to operate against the railroad lines between Columbus, Georgia, and Montgomery, Alabama. However, Union cavalry did not reach Montgomery until April 12, 1865.*]

July 19—Very hot. Hog Winder has allowed six men to go to Washington to present the petition. The men were appointed by a committee of twenty men inside the stockade. The Federal raiding party is said to be steering for this place.

[*The petition, written and supported by prisoners who held similar views, was directed to northern people, state governors and President Lincoln, advising them of the conditions at Andersonville and requesting immediate action for an exchange. The petition was signed by sergeants of 107 detachments, and General Winder permitted six sergeants to take the document to Washington. President Lincoln ignored the petition and nothing happened. The petition was printed on the back page of the* New York Times *on August 30, 1864. The names of the six sergeants printed in the newspaper were: "Edward Bates, 42 New York; H. C. Higginson, Co K, 19 Illinois; S. Noirot; William N. Johnson; F. Garland; Prescott Tracy, Co G, 82 New York." Many of the prisoners did not approve of the petition.*]

July 20—The rebels have become thoroughly alarmed. Negroes have been impressed who are throwing fortifications all around camp. Raw militia is being hurried in on the cars. Two prisoners were discovered escaping from the outside end of a tunnel and fired at. Several others had already escaped.

July 21—Sergeant Webster was put out of his place, Mumford succeeding him in charge of the detachment. The Johnnies are very active outside. Trains have been running all day and night. A few prisoners taken near Atlanta came in. Another ration of molasses instead of meat, a very poor substitute for those troubled with diarrhea.

July 22—Three hundred prisoners from Grant came in who were captured on the 29th of June. Work on the fortifications continues, but the influx of troops is not so great as yesterday. Several tunnels partly dug were found. Sentry fired at a man near the dead line but missed.

July 23—Cloudy and comfortable. Rations of corn bread, sow belly and salt. "Raiding" has been going on and several fights but the police are on the alert.

July 24—Last night was very cold and today very hot which increases the mortality. Rations of rice and sow belly. Today is Sabbath.

July 25—Last night was the coldest of the season. I could not sleep much but laid awake listening to the coughs and groans from all directions. I have a canker in my throat which is painful. More tunnels were found. Rations of rice but no salt to go with it.

July 26—Watermelons, apples, eggs, doughnuts, berry pies, biscuits for sale in camp but no one has any money. Cloudy and rain. I have taken cold and throat is quite sore. Rations of raw meal and sow belly.

July 27—I have been a soldier two years. Four hundred men from Grant and Sherman came in today. Several were one hundred day men whose time was nearly out and one was shot soon after coming in, while reaching under the dead line for clear water, not knowing the rules. His brains were blown into the water. I traded my ration of pork for cayenne pepper and treated for my throat which is filling up with cankers and very painful.

July 28—Hot. Shower in afternoon. I have great difficulty to talk and eat from the filling up in my throat. Seventeen hundred prisoners from Sherman came in during which the rebs fired a solid shot a few feet over our heads which struck in the marsh outside. It caused a big scare and dispersed the crowd in quick time. The fort around headquarters is nearly completed.

July 29—Very hot. The usual shower in the afternoon. A line of white flags have been stationed through camp marking the limit beyond which no crowd must collect. The rebs hardly dare put their threat into execution without modifying it. Three hundred prisoners from Grant and Sherman came in. Webster and Laid went outside to work on their parole of honor. Two men of the 11th Mass died near me. I have been digging roots for fuel.

July 30—Very hot. Our rebel sergeant has been calling for shoe makers and Shep has sent in his name. Macon is reported captured by a raiding party. The coarse uncooked corn meal has brought on diarrhea again.

July 31—Very hot. The rebs have been felling trees all about camp to serve as blockade against charge of cavalry. More rumors of exchange and parole. I have been suffering from a severe headache and fever.

August 1, 1864—Very hot. Rain last night. I was sick all night but feel better this morning. A preacher from outside held services in camp and read the exchange report in a newspaper. Ambulances have been taking out sick all the afternoon.

August 2—Very hot. Heavy thunder shower in the afternoon which flooded us all, soaking everything. I am quite sick, very weak from cough and diarrhea. A lot of prisoners came in who report that they were taken at Macon while en route for this place to relieve us. Gen. Stoneman and staff were also captured. The sick have been going out all day.

[*Major General George Stoneman, who graduated from the USMA in 1846, commanded a cavalry division in Sherman's army. He planned to raid Macon and liberate the Union prisoners at Andersonville. However, unable to cross the Ocmulgee River at Macon, he headed north—a few miles beyond Clinton at Sunshine Church, he was cut off and surrounded by three brigades of Wheeler's cavalry. General Stoneman and 700 men were captured.*]

August 3—Very hot. The moving of the sick to the outside has been going on all day, causing much talk and rumor as to the "why and wherefore." The remainder of the prisoners captured at Macon came in making a total of about seven hundred.

August 4—Very hot. No sick were taken out. Neither roll-call nor sick-call took place. Prisoners from Sherman came in. One of our squad died near me this noon. Prayer meeting was held near me in the evening.

August 5—Very hot. All the sick of the first eight detachments were taken out. Prisoners from Sherman came in. I was taken with a severe headache at night. We are continually tormented and tantalized with the sight of peaches, apples, chicken and soda water offered for sale at fabulous prices.

August 6—Very warm. The dread monotony of our miserable life is broken only by the hundreds of rumors of exchange which serves to aggravate the believing. A man was killed on the dead line and another shot at in the evening.

August 7—Very warm. Several convalescents came in from the hospitals and report an awful condition of affairs there. Prisoners from Sherman came in. Reports of exchange are on the wane. I am feeling better, excepting an irritating cough.

August 8—A row of sheds inside camp at the west end are being built for the sick. Rain all the afternoon.

[*On August 8, 1864, 33,114 Union prisoners were confined at Andersonville—the largest number on any one day.*]

August 9—Very warm. The heaviest thunder shower of the season occurred in the afternoon which flooded camp and undermined the stockade in several places so that it fell over, causing wild excitement among the authorities outside. All the guard were called by the long roll, the batteries all manned and turned on us poor fellows who were greatly amused by their alarm. Four hundred prisoners from Sherman came in. Poor old Boyer [*Buchele*], a German from Ohio, died near me. He has been lying for several days almost within arms length of me perfectly helpless, exposed to the pelting rain all day yesterday and last night, he laid moaning and crying for water, while every draught seemed to throw him into spasms and when he rolled over his eyes became fixed with the glassy stare of death. We all felt relieved to know that rebel hate could do no more for him. In the evening I went over and had a good talk of old times with Walter Lamb [*school friend from Templeton, Mass*].

August 10—Heavy shower in the afternoon. The rebels worked all day very lively on the stockade. Drew half rations of bread, raw beans and fresh meat but no wood to cook. I feel well today but mighty hungry. The wet weather caused rapidly increasing mortality.

August 11—Very warm, rain in the afternoon. The rancid bacon, flinty corn bread and beans "that are not all beans" make us dainty. The beans come to us cooked up with all sorts of chaff, dirt and bean-bugs. But it all fills up and we ought to be grateful. Prisoners came in from Sherman. The old stockade is all up and the negros are at work erecting another one twenty rods outside, so that tunneling will have to be dispensed.

August 12—Rations of bread (half cooked), rice (quarter cooked), meat (slightly warmed). More prisoners from Sherman today. Report of an exchange of officers who are confined at Macon.

[*The only duly mustered officers at Andersonville were a few colored troops—Confederates refused to recognize colored officers.*]

August 13—Very hot and clear. Beautiful moonlight evening. We have two new neighbors from Iowa who have stretched their blankets with ours. They were taken in the rear of Johnson's army, while raiding. They were robbed of a large amount of money, watches and clothing. The bank of the creek has been boarded up so that we are able to dip for water without making it muddy. Shower in the evening. Our rations better tonight.

August 14—Prisoners from Sherman today report Atlanta taken by our forces.

[*The Confederate Army evacuated Atlanta at five in the afternoon on September 1, 1864, and Union troops took possession the next morning. General Sherman wired Washington: "Atlanta is ours, and fairly won."*]

August 15—Very hot. Cloudy in the afternoon. Headache at night. Rations smaller than ever.

August 16—Very hot with shower in the evening. Two years ago today, I sold myself to Uncle Sam to help "put down the rebellion." This day finds the tables turned and the accursed rebellion trying to put me down. It remains to be seen whether all this wholesale persecution of the helpless will avail in establishing a new and honored government in the South.

August 17—Very hot, which makes my head ache constantly. I found a book on temperance which I have been reading. The first I have seen except my little testament since my capture.

[*George A. Hitchcock refers to his copy of* The New Testament, *published by the American Bible Society in New York, 1853 (Pocket-size army testament that included the Psalms). This army testament was his daily companion in prison, and his copy was marked with his favorite verses: Romans 12; Psalms 37, 51, 90 and 91; John 14, 15, 16 and 17; Hebrews 11 and 12. He carried this army testament from August 7, 1862, to January 1865. It is presently located at the Fitchburg Historical Society.]*

August 18—Very hot. A new rebel sergeant called our roll, who finds it difficult to read writing and in his haste does not get answers to nearly all the names whose rations are consequently cut off. I am "down sick" with diarrhea and headache. More prisoners from Sherman came in.

August 22—Tonight finds me better able to write. I feel that I have passed through one of the severest experiences of my life and have been very near death's door. The weather has continued hot as ever and my diarrhea which took the form of dysentery make me nearly helpless. Then my head ached till I thought I should become crazy. I thought of the regiment as the nineteenth of August came around when I suppose they were to be mustered out. My spirits went down to zero as I thought of the prospect of my old comrades compared with my own. Oh that the Old Pale Horse would not stare me in the face so hard and so constantly. Yesterday I felt that my pluck had nearly vanished, and it seemed as if the only hold on life which I had was in the comfort

A.J. Riddle's photograph of Andersonville Prison, taken August 16, 1864, showing sinks (open latrines) and the unchanneled end of the small creek (Library of Congress).

derived from the precious words which I read "My son, despise not thou the chastening of the Lord, nor faint when thou art rebuked of him, for whom the Lord loveth, he chasteneth and scourgeth every son whom he receiveth." "If ye endure chastening. God dealeth with you as with sons." [*Hebrews: Chapter 12, Verses 5, 6 and 7—King James Version of the Bible*] My constant prayer was for submission and in the mental agony of my heart, I prayed that God would give me life till I could die with some friend near. Shep has been very kind and I feel thankful that my prayers have been answered and I am really better. The mortality on these cold, wet nights is terrible. A large prayer meeting was held on the flat in the evening. Rations of cornbread, beans and molasses.

August 23—Very hot all day and night. Mosquitoes very troublesome. Baker of the 34th Mass. of our mess and another member of the 34th [*Robert Wilson*] died tonight nearby. Prisoners from Kilpatrick came in.

[*On August 23, 1864, 127 prisoners died at Andersonville—the largest number of deaths on any day.*]

August 24—Very hot. I am feeling much stronger. Shep went outside to the dead house with a dead body. When he returned after a stay of some ten minutes, he seemed greatly refreshed. Another man close by us died tonight. Some commissioned officers disguised as privates were taken out and sent away. [*In 1890 Hitchcock added: "Men, who never had framed words into prayer, felt that a higher than human helper must be appealed to."*]

August 25—Very hot. Rations of raw beans and beef. A few prisoners came in.

August 26—This roasting hot weather does much toward driving men to idiocy. Many a poor fellow has been "sun struck and gone up." Yes, this is what drives the humanity out of us. Rations of bread (one morsel), sow belly (one bit), molasses (plenty), salt (one globule). Funeral services were held over a dead comrade near my tent which seemed civilized. .[In 1890 Hitchcock added: It is rarely the case that anything follows the death of one but to immediately hustle the body up to the main gate; guards are always in attendance to watch the bearers until the sad task is performed of laying it alongside the last one in the long trenches and the living corpses are safely returned to camp.]

August 27—Very warm but a good breeze which keeps the dust stirring. Rebs report heavy fighting at Petersburg on the 19th when Grant was <u>defeated</u>. Camp is full of rumors of an exchange. "Wish is father of the thought." Showers in the night.

[*August 19, 1864: Battle of the Weldon Railroad—A. P. Hill's Confederate corps assaulted Warren's Federal infantry in the dense woods south of Petersburg with 382 Union casualties and 2518 soldiers captured.*]

August 28—Macon Telegraph gives notice of a General Exchange but, thanks that I am beyond believing anything now till the stars and stripes are between me and hell on earth. Prisoners from Sherman came in.

August 29—More prisoners from Sherman today.

August 30—Warm and clear. Last night was cold and uncomfortable. Providence opened a new spring during the heavy shower of a day or two since washing away a large bank of dirt near the dead line. There has ever since been a large stream of pure cold water flowing out which supplies a large part of camp. The man's a fool who doubts a kind and benevolent Providence after such a manifestation.

[*Providence Spring: Residents of the area had known about this spring for more than thirty years. When the prison stockade was erected in February 1864, the workmen filled up the spring while excavating the trench for the pine fence posts so that the water oozed through the sand to the creek without rising to the surface. The flood, which swept the stockade walls away during the severe August storm, washed the earth from over the spring, and it burst out clear and as strong as ever.*]

August 31—Very warm and cloudy. A third stockade is being erected outside the others for the <u>more sure</u> protection of the prisoners.

September 1, 1864—Last night was uncomfortably cold. Drew rations of beef, bread, ham, beans and salt. Some detachments had rice in place of bread. We find it necessary to use microscopes in eating—that is when we can get any.

September 2—Another cold night. I have been a prisoner three months. I find time to count the days and weeks and months. How dreary the prospect ahead.

[*In 1890 Hitchcock added: "I realize that I have been a prisoner three months. What an age it seems, since I saw the good old flag and heard from home."*]

September 3—Cloudy with north east wind. A crowd of convalescents came in from the outside and a lot of sick went out. In the afternoon an unusual stir announced the arrival of a mail from the north. Lagara, the Frenchman of Company K, received a letter from his wife and the generous soul has been reading it to us greedy ones who receive none. Sherman is reported having got into the rear of Hood.

September 4—Mild. I read a letter written from Templeton, Mass. to Wilbur Potter in which I learn that Col. Hawkes has resigned and gone home; also that Geo. Potter had become a Christian. This was all, but no one but those in our situation can understand or analyze the pleasure of hearing even this and seeing a letter from home. Clark of our squad died tonight and Dwinnell of Company G went out to the hospital and I presume we shall never see him again as his strength is all gone and he is very badly emaciated.

14. Andersonville, Georgia

September 5—Very hot. Drew rations of rice and molasses, bread and pork which we found to be a mistake as Squad 3 lost theirs so most of our boys gave up their extra.

September 6—The whole camp is wild with excitement over the prospect of an exchange for the first eighteen detachments are now under marching orders. Nobody understands it, but there is a universal uplifting of heads by those who had already shut out hope.

September 7—[*On September 7, the first prisoners left Andersonville by train—7,000 reached Charleston by September 12 with plans to send them to Florence, South Carolina, where a new stockade was under construction. Since the new stockade was not completed, prisoners were sent to another new stockade at Millen, Georgia—designated Camp Lawton. By the end of September, most of the prisoners and the Confederate guards had left Andersonville.*]—Very hot. Ten detachments were taken out but part were sent back for want of transportation. All went in the afternoon and ten more ordered to be in readiness at night. Many are the surmises as to their destination. Drew a pint of meal and pork. Holshoult of the 34th Mass, a noisy uncomfortable fellow of our squad, died tonight a terrible death in a terrible place and no hope for anything better in another world. [*Buried in unmarked grave—not listed among Massachusetts soldiers and not listed in Atwater List of prisoners who died at Andersonville.*]

September 8—Cloudy. Mosquitoes troublesome. Several detachments left during the night and a large number went out tonight. Our turn will not come till the last end. Rations of raw meal and beans.

September 9—All the sick have been moved into the sheds at west end. Prisoners from Sherman came in and many went away at night. Rations of bread and beans but no salt.

September 10—Rourke of our squad died tonight [*unmarked grave—not on Atwater List*] and I was detailed to carry him out to the dead house. This is the first time I have been outside those horrid gates since I came in three months ago and though outside less than three minutes, I caught a breath of fresh air which gave me a new lease of life. Rations of rice, meal and molasses and no salt. Several detachments went out at night and in the morning. Forty detachments have now gone and camp looks quite deserted though there are yet over twenty thousand here.

September 11—There's a beautiful harvest moon shining down upon us. Wonder if the dear friends at home are looking at the same object and thinking of me. Ten detachments left tonight. Nearly all the 21st boys have left, Miller among the number. How home-sick it makes a fellow feel to see all his friends leaving him in such a place as this.

September 12—Graton and Shepard stopped with us last night. Eighteen detachments go today.

September 13—A large number of "flankers" from our squad got out last night with those who went away so that our rations are larger in consequence. Go it boys while you can. Tonight we receive orders to be in readiness to start in the morning.

September 14—Very hot. The train which left last night collided with a freight train six miles away. For me, it was another manifestation of the protecting care of a heavenly Father who would not permit me to go on that train. The rebs did not take much notice, so trifling an affair, only to send all the uninjured back to camp and we do not leave today. [*In 1890 Hitchcock added: "The train which left last night collided with a freight train six miles north. The result was that eight cars were thrown from the track and smashed—killing and wounding about sixty Northern 'mudsills.'"*]

[*This train accident was not a "trifling affair." According to the* Macon Telegraph, *dated September 5, 1864, this "railroad catastrophe" occurred on Friday, September 2, about half past one in the afternoon near Fort Valley (26 miles north of Andersonville). "The two trains approached each other round a curve and were within two or three hundred yards when the alarm was given. The down train was moving at a speed of twenty-five miles an hour, and the up train about eighteen. The speed of neither was perceptually affected by the breaks before they struck. Five of the cars were utterly demolished. The tender of one engine was driven bodily through a grain car behind it, compressing the grain into a solid mass. The other tender was turned up on end and driven through the car behind it. Many soldiers who sat upon the tops of the cars and suspended their legs between, lost them. Twenty-nine were reported dead on Friday night and, about fifty wounded (Confederate soldiers). Some thirty-five Yankee prisoners on the rear car of the down train, rendered the most efficient service in extricating the unfortunate victims" (there is no record of Union prisoner fatalities). On September 23, 1864, the* Macon Telegraph *listed the names and regiments of 41 Confederate soldiers and two civilians who were killed in the accident. The Union soldiers were buried in an unmarked grave that has never been located.*]

September 15—Days hot and nights cold. Eleven hundred sick went away today. Two thousand men of Sherman's command are ordered to be ready to leave on a special exchange, for which reason we do not get our rations till late in the night. A heavy shower in the afternoon.

September 16—Hot. A large number of sick been going out all day. Six hundred of yesterday's batch returned to camp for want of transportation.

September 17—Cloudy. Much rain during the night. Seven hundred men of Sherman's exchange left. Several of them from our detachment. It is very lonely and seems dreary to see the thousands of deserted burrows and dens.

[*On September 17, 1864, General Winder, post commander at Andersonville, issued a pass into the stockade for Dr. Joseph Jones, a respected Confederate physician and medical researcher, who was investigating the reasons for the very high mortality rate at Andersonville. Dr. Jones spent three weeks at Andersonville and he has provided historians with the most complete account of the hell that was Andersonville. With the aid of his secretary, Louis Manigault, Dr. Jones prepared reports on the abysmal facilities, rampant diseases and the medical condition of the prisoners; these reports are the most detailed and accurate descriptions available. Dr. Jones reported that "the manner of disposing of the dead was also calculated to depress the already desponding spirits of these men"—"whose strength had been wasted by bad air, bad food, and neglect of personal cleanliness." He stressed "the dead house is merely a frame covered with an old tent cloth and a few bushes, situated in the southwest corner of the hospital grounds. When a patient dies, he is simply laid in the narrow street in front of his tent, until he is removed by the Federal Negroes detailed to carry off the dead." Dr. Jones further stated that "in the dead house the corpses lie upon the bare ground, and are in most cases covered with filth and vermin." His investigations showed that diarrhea, dysentery, scurvy, and hospital gangrene were chiefly responsible for Andersonville's extraordinary mortality. Manigault described the prison as a "Hades on Earth."]*

Dr. Joseph Jones, a well-trained and respected young Southern doctor and medical researcher, spent three weeks at Andersonville Prison in September 1864. Captain Henry Wirz, the commandant, refused him admission to the stockade but General John Winder, commander of Andersonville Post, intervened, and Wirz backed down. Jones provided detailed accounts of the terrible facilities and diseases and the very poor condition of the prisoners (courtesy of Joseph Jones Papers, Louisiana Research Collection, Tulane University).

September 18—Stormy. This will pass for the Equinoctial storm. No prisoners went out and no more signs of any going at present. Consequently there are many long faces. Shep is sick with diarrhea.

September 19—Cloudy, rain all night. Webster and Laird were sent into camp because two or three of their comrades ran away. They say that it is expected that the prisoners have only been transferred to other prisons in Charleston and Savannah. Eleven hundred more of Sherman's exchange went out, each man's name called to prevent "flankers."

September 20—Cloudy, rain in the night. Signs of scurvy have appeared in my mouth around the gums of my diseased teeth. The gums swell up and turn to a dark purple. Where others have it and do not recover, this swelling spreads in a few days until the face and neck turn black as if the blood settled all over it; then the teeth drop out—the jaws become set and a general rotting process is the last stage. With others the disease shows itself first in the limbs, rendering them stiff and helpless. My general feeling is one of complete lassitude and low spirits. Am feeling very poorly. Drew no bread today.

September 21—Cloudy and rain, very chilly and damp nights. Great numbers sick with colds. Drew a ration of <u>hardtack</u> (would it were hardtack), molasses and beans. The hardtack is a lot of condemned sea biscuit which the soldiers outside would not eat as it was so moldy. Nevertheless, the little handful was a desirable change from the "grits."

September 22—Sun came out scorching hot at noon and shower in the afternoon. The camp has been reorganized into new detachments of two hundred and forty men, each containing four squads of sixty men. They number from 45 to 73, ours is the 72nd so that makes our present number of prisoners at 6,720.

September 23—Shower in the afternoon. A lively trade between the guard and prisoners. The prisoners articles of traffic are military buttons and the rebs—sweet potatoes. Some rebel officers visiting here rode around the dead line to view the human menagerie.

[*Dr. Joseph Jones left Andersonville at the end of September to resume a study that he started the previous summer by visiting the Gangrene Hospital at Macon, Georgia—he was primarily interested in the effect of gangrene on the Confederate Army of Tennessee.*]

September 24—Several showers during the day. Washed in the creek. Ration of raw meat. The Dutch Captain has been inspecting the ration wagons and tells us we are entitled to more rations than we get! O Well! Don't we know it?

September 25—Clear and mild. It was so cold we could not sleep last night. We are beginning to close our eyes to the stubborn fact that we must remain here through the winter. Will hope keep us up much longer is the question we are constantly asking ourselves.

September 26—Roll call and all men not found in line were deprived of their rations. Prisoners who came in from Sherman say that the special exchange is true but no general exchange. We don't like to believe that however. The chief quartermaster has been inspecting us. Wonder how he likes the looks. [*In 1890 Hitchcock added: "Perhaps the rebs have begun to wake up to the fact that the civilized nations of the earth have something to say and that it is wise to be heeded."*]

September 27—Roll was called and men put into our detachment to fill up the places of the flankers. Our ration of beans very, <u>very</u> small and the most filthy we have ever had: dirt, bugs, worms, chaff and pods being the principal ingredients. The shout was raised, "Fall in" and several more detachments were went away, but ours will be the last so our cause is well nigh hopeless. More prisoners from Sherman came in.

September 28—Warm, comfortable last night. Drew rations of meal, beef, beans, wood, pork, salt and molasses, which was dealt out to the men in crumbs, drops, splinters and teaspoonfuls. Three and a half detachments went out today.

September 29—I found a "History of the World" by Peter Barley which has been a rare treat to me for the hour or more which was allowed me to keep it. Drew very small rations of meal, beans and beef. Five more detachments prepared to leave but the train did not come for them.

[*This book by Peter Parley, which was published in Boston in 1849, stressed the world and its inhabitants. Samuel Griswold Goodrich, who was a very prolific writer during the 19th century, was better known under the pseudonym of Peter Parley. He embraced geography, biography, history, and science as well as juvenile literature and books of fables.*]

September 30—Very warm and sultry. At roll call all detachments were filled up. Drew molasses in place of meat, a very poor substitute for these hungry starving skeletons. Tasted a sweet potato which was a great luxury. Presto! A ration of a teaspoonful of soft soap was distributed throughout camp and nobody knows what to do with it.

October 1, 1864—Washed in the creek, just to use up the soap <u>that was all</u>. I found several <u>suspicious white</u> places on my body and am convinced that I should have found more if my soap had held out. Rations of bread and beans. A train load of prisoners went away.

October 2—Four months a prisoner, and O how long ones. A few Sherman prisoners captured near Atlanta came in. Drew a splendid ration of <u>beans</u>—we know <u>beans</u>. We find it difficult to remember the Sabbath as it comes around but conclude that this is one, up in God's country if we haven't lost our reckoning.

October 3—Heavy showers. Several men went to work on their parole of honor as teamsters and choppers.

October 4—It is very hard to sit day after day with nothing to occupy my thoughts, but the harrowing question constantly: "Must we die here?" Time can only ease my woe. Another load of prisoners went away this evening among who were Graton and Barker of the 21st. Two shots were fired on the dead line.

October 5—I was detailed to "pack" the sick and dead to and from the sheds for this I drew an extra ration of bread, rice and molasses. My teeth and jaws are quite sore.

October 6—Cloudy and rain. My sleep was broken by teeth ache. I trade away my ration of meal for beans which I eat as dry as possible to check the progress of scurvy. Rations today of bread, beans, bacon, beef and molasses just enough to keep life in the lice and fleas which companions in misery "stick closer than brothers."

October 7—Cloudy and damp. Had a suffering night from my teeth and gums. Shep is sick as also many others with chills and ague. Sherman is reported fighting again and his rear cut off.

October 8—Clear and cold—sudden change in the weather during the night. Lost another nights sleep from teeth ache. How fast the poor fellows sink down from exposure to this hard weather, many going to their death each day from this cause.

October 9—Clear and cold, very chilly last night. We are all moved over to the south end of this great deserted camp and are formed into detachments of five hundred men in each. We are in the "fourth." Shepard and I dug a hole in the ground, over which we spread our blanket for another cold night is expected and we must work to keep from getting a "death chill" on us if it is the Sabbath.

October 10—Spent a night of suffering and sleeplessness. Coldest night of the season. The guards were very noisy all night long who from their elevated posts found a freezing wind and were impatient to get off. There are now about twenty five hundred men in camp. Shep and I mess with Sergeant Phelps of Vermont and twenty others. Teeth ache all day very severe. Part of the time it was the "jumping ache." Ten Dutchmen went out on their parole of honor for special service for the Dutch Captain. O, that I were a Dutchman.

October 11—Mild. Spent a more comfortable night. The sick at the sheds get hardtack. Three hundred prisoners from Sherman came in, captured between Atlanta and Marietta. They report Sherman fighting.

October 12—My jaws are very sore. I lose much sleep for want of covering and shelter. The entire camp was kept in line all the morning while the sergeants arranged the rolls and the quartermaster arranged the camp into streets. A new dead line was put up.

October 13—More rearranging and moving about. We now lie very compact, occupying about three acres of ground, about a thousand men to the acre or allow two thirds of this space for streets, it could be a thousand men covering solid a third acre. I have been peddling coffee at the hospital sheds made from burnt meal.

October 14—Cloudy and cool. Spent another night of suffering. Men are at work fixing up their tents for winter. Quite a large number are admitted to the sheds of those who were sick. Street sutlers are plenty and sweet potatoes and biscuit in abundance.

October 15—Shep and I have been digging our <u>grave</u> deeper over which we spread our blanket. Teeth ache all day and another sleepless night.

October 16—I was detailed to "pack" dead out to the dead house from the sheds. I carried two men belonging to the 19th Mass., one of whom had died in great agony whose body had stiffened in the position he was in when he died, which was bent out of all shape and whose head was drawn back and eyes rolled up giving an appearance which would never be effaced from my memory. We lie down to our bed of a rubber blanket to wear the long, long nights away which are very cold and frosty, and no wood to keep warm with.

October 17—Large details have been made to go out for wood. Rations of beans and raw molasses, but no bread. Made candy of my molasses. Rain in the evening.

October 18—Cloudy but cleared up in the afternoon. I went outside the stockade for wood, the first time for four months and O how like a new life it seemed. Saw green grass and leaves and fresh air, sights and smells which no one can ever appreciate as fully as those who live as we do. It gives me a new longing to live, consequently a new torture, in the doubt and hopeless look of the future. Shep and I have been writing letters home sending for boxes. Several convalescents tried to escape from the hospitals but the hounds caught them.

October 19—Shep sick with diarrhea. Rations of rice and molasses.

October 20—Warmer last night. Went out for wood again so we have fire to sit by this evening. Beans and beef for todays rations.

October 21—Pleasant day but cold night. Several went to the hospital from our mess—Webster among the number. Rations of rice and molasses in place of beans and beef.

October 22—Shep and I have fixed up blankets with Laird of Pennsylvania, by which means we get an extra blanket for nights.

October 23—Very cold and heavy frost last night for which could not sleep much. Went out again for wood.

October 24—Had a comfortable nights rest for a rarity. We think we have our tent made very comfortable. The sutler was cleaned out by the Dutch Captain for selling liquor and his goods confiscated for the benefit of the sick about camp.

October 25—Camp rumors of an exchange of ten thousand Potomac men. The wood detail has been stopped because some of the men have escaped. Salt is very scarce,

October 26—An order for confiscating all salt offered for sale in camp has been issued by the Dutchman. Teeth ache very severe this evening.

October 27—Stormy. Our tent was flooded. I am hoarse and used up generally because of want of sleep. Rations of bread and rice, very small barely enough to sustain life.

October 28—Hard toothache and poor nights rest last night. Washed in the creek and mended shirt. Traded my ration of beans for an excellent ration of rice. A mud shanty fell in breaking one man's back and badly crippling two others.

October 29—Very cold and heavy frost last night. Toothache very severe. Fixed up our tent so that it is weather proof. Six prisoners came in.

October 30—Had about an hour sleep last night. Shepard applied for admission to the hospital but was refused admission. The whole camp has received orders to be ready to march.

October 31—Warm and lowering. The 1st, 2nd and part of the 3rd went away in the morning, but no enthusiasm can be raised for we believe it is only a change of prisons, the report of exchange being only a dodge of the rebels to keep us from any attempt to escape during transportation. The rebel sergeants have been taking out carpenters to work on their parole of honor. Rations of bread and rice cooked without a particle of salt.

November 1, 1864—The sheds are being cleared of all sick who are either taken outside or returned to camp.

November 2—Storm commenced before midnight and rained hard about twelve hours. Fortunately for us our tent was kept quite dry while most of the others were flooded.

Brigadier General John Henry Winder, C.S.A., was appointed Andersonville Post commander on June 17, 1864, and commander of all prisons in Georgia and Alabama on July 26, 1864, and later, commissary-general of all prisoners east of the Mississippi River. He died February 7, 1865, from disease contracted while visiting prisons. He had an impossible task due to the inadequacy of the numbers of men and supplies of food, clothing, and medicines (Library of Congress).

14. Andersonville, Georgia

Well, this is about the last of Andersonville for us and it is a general abandoning of this horrid place for orders came for us all to be ready to start at eleven in the forenoon, but as means of transportation did not arrive, we did not start until ten at night when we were roused out of a sound sleep. And went out through the gates in perfect darkness and in a pitting rain, a most fitting and appropriate time and aspect for us to pass out of a place that, if we are allowed to live long, will always combine more of the realities which we expect will be found in that dark and terrible region of despair of a future world known as "hell" than any other can to us. Thankful for past favors (we cannot feel too thankful that we have been allowed to remain to see almost the termination of the glorious reign of the Dutch Captain), we cast one (not long lingering) look back into the darkness and pack into old freight cars, eighty three in a car and move out on the northward track toward Macon.

[*In 1890 Hitchcock added: "We now feel assured that this prison pen is about to be abandoned and whatever the future may have in store for us, we are devoutly thankful to look back into the blackness, lighted from the outside of the stockade by a few dim fires of the rebel guard, and feel that we are permitted to get out of it alive while so many thousands of our comrades are now under the sod all around us."*]

15

Camp Lawton—Millen, Georgia

"When at last more dead than alive and chilled to the heart, we get on the cars at four in the morning sixty in a car."
—Hitchcock, November 22, 1864

Camp Lawton was located five miles north of Millen, Georgia, at Magnolia Springs, near the Augusta Railroad. The site provided a good water supply, an abundance of timber to construct the stockade and was surrounded by hills for artillery positions. It was constructed during the late summer of 1864 to accommodate 40,000 prisoners. Lack of funds and the failure to impress labor delayed the occupation of the prison until early October. After being shuttled from Andersonville, the prisoners at Savannah were sent to Millen on October 10, 1864—10,299 prisoners were transferred from Andersonville by November 8. All the prisoners at Andersonville able to make the move were shipped to Millen along with their guards. Seven hundred sick prisoners were included in the relocation.

The stockade, one of the largest prisons in the world, measured 1,398 feet by 1,329 feet and enclosed forty-two acres—the design of the stockade was modeled after Andersonville. The stream running through the prison was large and there was no swamp as there had been at Andersonville. The ground was divided into thirty-two sections by streams sixteen feet wide; each area was designed for a thousand prisoners and then separated into ten subdivisions. The prisoners constructed huts from tree branches that were left within the stockade. The prisoners were only allowed to use the upper half of the creek for drinking and bathing while the lower half was used for latrine purposes. Water flowed beneath the sinks, insuring adequate removal of excrement.

However, the cooking facilities were not completed, and the hospital and health supplies were only slightly improved from Andersonville. On November 8, 1864, Capt. D. W. Vowles, commander of the prison, reported 486 deaths among the 10,299 prisoners. He also stated that 285 prisoners were detailed to work at the post and 349 prisoners were enlisted in Confederate service. The popular term for these men was "Galvanized Yankees," although to be fair, some prisoners used enlistment as a means for escape.

The departure of William T. Sherman's army from Atlanta on November 16 and its rapid advance east across the state forced the abandonment of Camp Lawton. On November 22, General Winder reported that all the prisoners had been sent to Savannah including George Hitchcock. Although some prisoners were sent by rail to Blackshear and Thomasville in south Georgia, the majority of the Camp Lawton prisoners, including George Hitchcock, was transferred to Florence, South Carolina.

Sherman's March was wreaking havoc on a system that was already collapsing. There was a constant reshuffling of prisoners to avoid their release by Union troops.

* * * *

November 3, 1864—Of course, being packed as we were, it would not admit of a change of position, and I sit all night long as the rain pelted against the sides of the car, finding hardly any sleep. Passed through Macon at light where we turn onto the Charleston R.R. and ride all day in the same sitting position till late in the night when we arrive at the Millen Station, two hundred miles and find relief in getting out and stretching. Several men escaped from the train on the route and one man of my mess died in the car before we

The stockade at Camp Lawton in Millen, Georgia (*Harper's Weekly*, January 7, 1865).

reached here. He had been sick but his death was brought on by being crowded. Marched a half a mile and found another stockade [*Camp Lawton*], camped down outside for the night.

November 4—Clear but very cold wind. Suffered for want of shelter and clothing, have taken cold. We were formed into detachments as before and marched inside where we drew rations of rice, meal, beef beans and salt. Camped by the side of the creek. Find this place a nice, clean and roomy place although about ten thousand of our old prisoners are here.

November 5—Drew two days rations better in quantity and quality than at Andersonville, and if we could have more comfortable shelter, I think we should think the change a better one. Those who came in first have made comfortable winter quarters of logs. Several hundred in despair of getting away this winter have taken the oath and gone into the rebel army. [*In 1890 Hitchcock added: "Poor soldiers they will make for a falling cause."*]

November 6—Chilly. Did not sleep much on account of the cold. Laird and I went out after wood.

November 7—Warm night. Found Lamb and Graton. Our 9th Division move across the creek on the slope nearer the rest of the prisoners where we make a temporary shelter. A Savannah newspaper has notice of an exchange of ten thousand to begin next week. The man who hung the raiders last summer was chased out of camp by a party of the old ring, but he escaped unharmed.

November 8—Light rain. Had a comfortable nights sleep. This is supposed to be Presidential Election day. And a great deal of excitement and sport was made in voting for the two candidates—Little Mac and Old Abe. My vote proved to have been cast for the triumphant candidate in camp. Abraham received a majority of 975 in a total casting of over 9000.

[*Official 1864 presidential election results: Abraham Lincoln 2,218,388 (55.02 percent) and 212 electoral votes; George B. McClellan 1,812,807 (44.96 percent) and 21 electoral votes*]

[*In 1890 Hitchcock added: "This is the Presidential election day in the North, and as the rebel authorities appear to have great interest in it, the prisoners propose to show them what we can do. They evidently think they have reduced our spirits by starvation to that state whereby we will all be anxious to have peace declared by recognizing the Southern Confederacy, and this they expect to be accomplished if McClellan is elected. Early in the day many stump speeches were made and vigorous campaigning done in behalf of both candidates. Considerable blatant talk was indulged in by the hoodlum class who always vote the democratic ticket. Betting away rations but as usual those who talk least can do more; when we organized a polling booth, great efforts were made to overawe the doubtful voters. At night the result showed that out of a vote of over 9000, Honest Old*

15. Camp Lawton—Millen, Georgia

Abe received a majority of 975. Many of the old Potomac boys vote for McClellan because they still remain loyal to him, yet believe in seeing the war pushed until the rebellion is overthrown. Others in their weakness and misery are made to believe that our Government has heartlessly abandoned us. Therefore, I am highly satisfied with the result, and much chaffing of the rebel guard is indulged in over their disappointment."]

November 9—I went out for wood twice today. Saw Gen. Cottrell [*Gartrell*] the commander of the rebel forces in this vicinity. There was great cheering outside among the rebs which the guard told us was caused by the news of a general exchange. If we could believe it we would do the cheering for both sides.

November 10—Rain in the morning but cold and cloudy at night. An inspecting officer has been taking the names of those most ragged in camp for clothing.

November 11—Clear and cold. A recruiting officer has been in camp enticing prisoners to enlist into the rebel army. Several went from our division. The clothing inspector examined us in the afternoon. Roast chicken, boiled sweet potatoes and eggs, biscuit and butter, pumpkin and potato pies, rice and bean soups, soda cakes and molasses for sale in abundance, but the Ancient Mariner's experience is our own. "Water, water everywhere, but not a drop to drink." There was a jollification at the police quarters in the evening.

November 12—Very chilly wind all day. Our two days rations did not come till late at night because a number of the enlisted recruits could not be found and the authorities feared they had been murdered by our boys who are very indignant at their action. A man near me perished with the cold. He was nearly naked. All the remaining prisoners came in tonight from Sumter.

November 13—Chilly wind and frosty night. Names of sick, seventy five from each division, were taken to the surgeons who examined and passed them out to be sent to Savannah for exchange. Shepard and Graton were examined and passed and expect to go out tomorrow. Savannah papers [*Republican and Daily News and Herald*] have accounts of the meeting of commissioners and the agreement of exchange. What an inducement to be sick!

November 14—Coldest night of the fall. The camp was agreeably surprised to receive a ration of sweet potatoes in place of meal and of hard soap. I wrote a letter home to send by Shepard.

November 15—Milder, though very frosty and cold last night. Shep and his crowd left us. It did me good to see him go although my selfish longings made my heart sink to feel that I must be always left behind. The sutlers and those having money bought the positions of nurses to attend the sick on their homeward trip. A few prisoners from Sherman came in.

November 16—Very pleasant weather. Sweet potatoes were issued again.

The sick did not leave today on account of our transports at Savannah harbor having run aground so they all returned inside the stockade. A train load of rebel exchanged passed through to Augusta and another train of sick arrived from Andersonville.

November 17—Had a good nights rest last night. Drew rotten sweet potatoes and a small piece of meat. Wood is very scarce in camp for no squads are allowed to go out.

November 18—Warm with rain last night. A new sergeant who could not read very well called our roll and did not get through so that we could not draw our rations till after dark. So we starve on three spoons full of rice all day. Laird and I drew rations in another mess. Shep's lot of sick went away this time and the surgeons are examining in camp for another load.

November 19—Storm came on at night. Another change of sergeants which caused another day's starvation on a mouthful of beef for today. Another train load of sick went away at dark.

November 20—More sick were examined and passed out. All the Chickamauga and Belle Isle prisoners were taken out to exchange. At midnight the cry went around. "Fall in all the First and Second Divisions." They packed up and went away.

November 21—Storm all day. Arose at one in the night and took possession of a fine shanty abandoned by the 2nd Division fellows, which we occupied and enjoyed until night when lo, our turn arrived and we were ordered to pack up and start off in the rain in great wonderment what means all this haste, Though rumors are rife among the prisoners that Sherman has something to do with it, our suspicions are confirmed when we reach the depot and see train after train pass headed for Savannah loaded with every description of household goods, furniture, countrymen and their families, negroes of all ages. Numberless trains of all descriptions arrive and deposit their freight along the side of the railroad. We meanwhile have to stand waiting in a terrible freezing, biting wind for hours waiting for transportations.

[*On November 15, 1864, General Sherman had started his "March to the Sea" and reached Savannah, Georgia (285 miles from Atlanta) on December 10, 1864.*]

November 22—When at last more dead than alive and chilled to the heart, we get on the cars at four in the morning, sixty in a car, and glide away on one of the smoothest railroads I ever passed over. The country through which we passed was dead level almost entirely covered with pine forests. Arrived at Savannah at sunset, passed through the beautiful suburbs of the city and right through the heart of this handsome Southern city to the opposite side of the city where we disembark at dark finding the weather biting cold. There are no quarters provided, neither fuel, and as we have had no rations

15. Camp Lawton—Millen, Georgia

for two days, we are most of us too weak to move about and keep our blood moving. So a remaining spark of Yankee ingenuity gives a novel mode of keeping warm, which was generally adopted and at daylight we presented, if it had not been for our distressed and awful situation, a ludicrous sight. Two or three men would sit down on the ground locking and interlacing each other in their arms and legs while others would pack on and against them until there would be a solid stack of humanity of twenty, more or less, to keep life in each other.

November 23—But when at light we unpacked and found several of our number frozen stiff and ice a quarter inch thick, and all this within stones throw of a large lumber yard, with all facilities for being made comfortable, we heartily curse our captors. During the day a little wood is brought in and we hug the smoking fires. We drew two days rations of hardtack and a little thick syrup.

November 24—Milder than yesterday. Beef and salt was given out. Citizens have been bringing food and clothing all day but I am not smart enough to get any. Several trains arrived from the upper country bringing in rebel troops, negroes and household goods to escape from Sherman, who we learn is pushing into the heart of Georgia. A lot of prisoners were taken away going south on the Florida road. The sick were also taken away and the rest of us were allowed to get wood from the lumber yard with which we keep more comfortable at night.

[*Savannah had a long history of generosity and residents of Savannah believed in "with charity for all" (philosophy of Lincoln's famous Second Inaugural Address). Knowing the destitute conditions of the Union prisoners, they adopted*

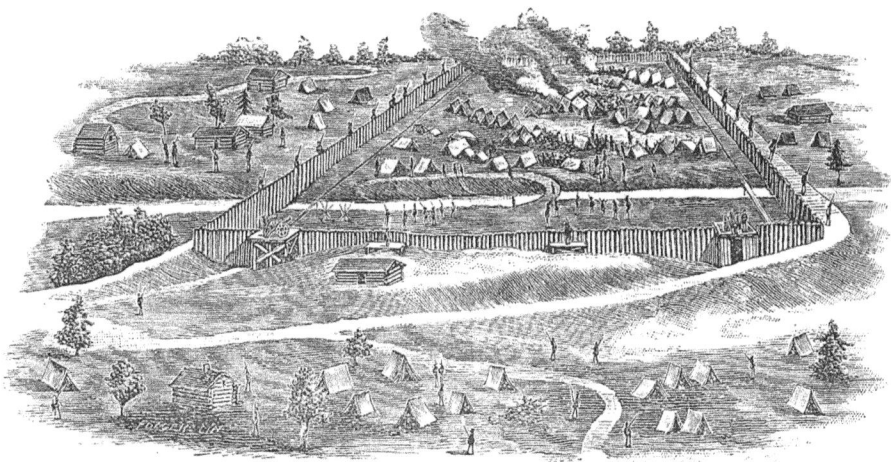

The only known rendition of the Confederate prison at Florence, South Carolina (*Prisoners of Military Prisons, 1890*).

measures to relieve their sufferings by offering food and clothing—only hospitality exhibited toward prisoners in the South. One prisoner, Daniel Kelly, who transferred from Andersonville in late September, recalled the "numbers of women, both white and colored, who brought us water to drink, wheat bread, and such other things as they could provide" even when they were discouraged by Confederate guards.]

November 25—Clear. Could hear the distant rumbling of heavy guns in the direction of Charleston, which had a more welcome sound than any noise I have heard for a long time. The kind hearted people of Savannah continued to bring in food and clothing all day. I found some rice which kept me until the rations came at dark, which was hardtack and molasses. A train came at nine in the evening when we were suddenly hurried on board them. A rebel officer whom we asked whither we were bound (for we had half begun to believe that we were really to be exchanged) told us we were going to Charleston to be exchanged. We rode all night through the wilderness of rice flats and savannahs of Georgia and South Carolina which lie back of Beaufort along the line of the Charleston and Savannah Railroad.

November 26—At sunrise we find we are approaching the noted hotbed of the Palmetto rattlesnake, Charleston. We cross the broad Cooper and Ashley Rivers and reach the city. Our cars stand in the streets all the forenoon while many spectators come to see the Andersonville pack. Afternoon we move out of the city and when about five miles from the city change cars and find our exchange is "of cars only" for we turn Northward again up through the same low level monotonous pine region of central South Carolina, ride till ten o'clock at night when we find ourselves in Florence, a junction with the Columbia and Wilmington R.R., one hundred miles from Charleston.

16

Florence, South Carolina

> "I feel that the change of air and scenes had stimulated us somewhat, and do not feel ready to say 'die' yet."
> —Hitchcock, November 27, 1864

The Confederate military prison two miles from Florence, South Carolina (a village of 200 residents that was located where three railroads crossed), was under constructed in September 1864 to provide facilities for prisoners sent to Charleston and Savannah from Andersonville and Camp Lawton. The first prisoners arrived in Florence on September 15, 1864. While the stockade was being erected, the prisoners were restrained in an open field. Twenty-three acres were enclosed by a palisade which measured 1,400 feet long and 725 feet wide and was surrounded by a ditch five feet deep and seven feet wide that discouraged tunneling. Dirt was piled against the stockade to form a guard walk about three feet from the top of the wall. A stream flowed through the prison, but the Andersonville swamp was duplicated (six acres were swampy). The dead-line was ten to twelve feet from the stockade and was marked by a small ditch and in some places by a pole-fence. On each corner of the stockade a platform was erected for a piece of artillery. Six hundred blacks were utilized to construct the facilities, and they were still working on November 5.

There were 12,362 prisoners at Florence on October 12 while 860 were hospitalized and 20 were paroled. Most of the prisoners were emaciated and covered with vermin. They had no blankets and very little clothing. A Confederate inspection report, dated November 5, 1864, reported 11,424 prisoners: 599 were hospitalized and 90 were paroled. The paroled prisoners were limited to within a half mile of the stockade, except the prisoners working at trades such as blacksmiths who worked in the town of Florence. The prisoners were divided into detachments of 1,000 men with companies of 100 men. Colonel George P. Harrison, Jr., was the commander of headquarters post at Florence. Lieutenant Colonel John F. Iverson, 5th Georgia Regiment, was commandant of the prison and in charge of the guards.

The hospital, which was located within the stockade and was built with branches from trees which afforded protection from the direct sun but not the rain. There was only one medical officer assigned on October 12. In November, although a rough frame-work was partially completed for a proposed 100-patient hospital, the sick prisoners were separated by a pole-fence within the stockade.

When Hitchcock entered the prison on November 27, Confederate Ration Records indicated 8,904 prisoners in the stockade with 1,134 in the hospital, 173 paroled, 553 on extra rations with a total of 10,894 prisoners on rations. The prisoners received very little meat and subsisted primarily on sorghum syrup and meal.

Since the Union soldiers at Florence had been imprisoned for some time, the mortality rate was high: Twenty to fifty died each day usually from diarrhea, scurvy or malnutrition. A total of 18,000 prisoners were confined at Florence with 2,802 deaths—all unidentified since most of the prison records from Florence were lost or destroyed after the post was abandoned in March 1865.

* * * *

November 27, 1864—Bivouac by the side of the railroad till morning when our names are taken and we are sent inside another stockade, which we find crowded with old prisoners from Andersonville. Laird and I spread our blankets together and at night draw a ration of meal and flour which with a few chips we make a supper. Lie down at night on the cold damp ground and although our hopes had been checked by this termination of "the exchange," still I feel that the change of air and scenes had stimulated us somewhat, and do not feel ready to say "die" yet.

November 28—After a cheerless, sleepless night I get a breakfast of flour paste. Found all the old comrades of the 21st, Miller, Middy and all well. This camp is crowded fully as bad as that at Andersonville and the location damp and swampy and the rations poorer and smaller than ever. The sick from each thousand are being paroled each day. [*The ability of the Confederate supply system to provide rations for the prisoners was a concern from the beginning. On September 14, Confederate officials expressed concern over their ability to collect enough rations "in time to prevent privation" for the Union prisoners. On September 17, there was "a sufficiency of meat" to supply the prisoners, but molasses was in short supply—recommended reducing the syrup ration to a quarter pint until the supply improved.*]

November 29—Milder night. I bought some straw with a borrowed five dollar confederate scrip. Mended clothes which are in a miserable condition The sleeves of my blouse and shirt almost entirely gone showing some skeleton arms; the backs of both garments are as thin as gauze while my pants are worn entirely away from the knees down. My cap is two simple pieces of cloth sewed together. Was detailed to go out for wood. Ration of a pint and a half of flour and a splinter of green-gum-wood. More prisoners from Millen came.

November 30—Had the chills last night so lost my sleep. Jim Miller was admitted to the hospital. Bathed in the creek. Rations of a pint and a half of meal with beans and salt. The sick have been stopped going out for the road is occupied in rushing troops down to intercept Sherman who we imagine is up to some unusual game.

December 1, 1864—Winter has arrived and we still live. All the portion of camp on one side of the creek was moved to the other and the entire camp made to move back to the other again being counted as they passed across the little bridge. A lot of "Galvanized Yanks"—the turncoats were sent back into camp by the rebs for fear they would escape to our army.

December 2—I am six months a prisoner. Light rain in the night. I traded away a dollar and a half "Confed" for a meal of sweet potatoes. The railroad this side of Savannah is reported cut off by General Foster—only a few days too late.

December 3—Roll call and wood rations were omitted on account of a large number of the paroled sick returning though we do not see the connecting cause. I traded a map of the seat of war for a mess of sweet potatoes. Rations of a pint of meal and half a pint of "grits."

December 4—The prisoners were again transferred back and forth in order to get a "correct count"—so much for the education and mathematics of our chivalrous southerners. I copied a map of the States of North and South Carolina, which for unexplained reasons has become a favorite occupation among certain prisoners. Rations of a pint of rice. A sick man was shot dead on the dead line.

December 5—Frosty night but beautiful today. The sick have been passed out today. I drew a ration of a pint and a half of meal but no wood to cook it with.

December 6—Foggy in the morning but clear and cold at night. I hear preaching from a clergyman from Florence. Went out for wood. Rations of meal and grit and half a dozen spoonfuls of molasses which last revives trade around camp.

December 7—Chilly wind and some rain. All the sick from four thousand were taken out. Two hundred prisoners from Sherman's raiding party came in, who were captured at Milledgeville. This is the first authentic news we have yet had concerning Sherman's great movement toward the sea coast and was hailed with great interest.

17

Release

> "But one object alone united our gaze, and that was the Grand Old Stars and Stripes."
> —Hitchcock, December 10, 1864

Since November 25, 1864, Sherman's March had prevented the Confederacy from delivering prisoners to Savannah for the purpose of exchange. By late in 1864, the logistical infrastructure of the Confederacy had been devastated. Many transportation lines were cut or just worn out, and much of the space on those railroads still in operation was preempted by the Confederate military authorities for movement of men and supplies. When Confederate authorities were compelled to abandon the further exchange of all Union prisoners at the Savannah River, Lt. Col. John E. Mulford, United States Agent for Exchange of Prisoners, suggested the continuance of the exchange at Charleston Harbor. Lieutenant General William J. Hardee, Confederate commander at Charleston, consented to the change and Union authorities, Maj. Gen. John G. Foster and Rear Adm. John A. Dahlgren, agreed upon a truce for the exchange.

On December 4, Mulford arranged for a suspension of hostilities. Firing on the city and works in and about the harbor was suspended for the transferring of prisoners to Union ships. The agreement provided that no labor be performed by either party on works, forts, batteries or military defenses during this period. The truce did not affect the blockade of the port of Charleston by Union ships, and Union military and naval forces were not restricted from attacking, capturing or destroying any Confederate ships entering or leaving Charleston. Mulford stated on December 7 that 1,000 Union prisoners had already been received under this new arrangement, and he expected to finish the exchange in a week if the weather permitted. On December 16, Mulford notified his superiors that the truce arranged with Confederate authorities at Charleston Harbor for the exchange of prisoners would terminate at ten in the morning the following day, and that the status existing previous to this truce would be resumed by the respective bel-

ligerents. George Hitchcock was exchanged at Charleston Harbor on December 10, 1864.

* * * *

December 8—Very chilly and cloudy. I am not prepared to understand my situation yet, so unexpected has it come upon me, but in the morning the remaining four thousand of camp were called out into the "dead line" and examined. Laird and I were near the last end of one of the lines. As the rebel surgeon came along glancing at one and another speaking to perhaps one out of a dozen, he passed by me, an incident that did not attract my attention much, as I had no idea I was worth noticing anyhow. But what—He turns and looks back at me and then steps back, asks my condition, examines me more closely, thumps me (and my heart thumps back), asks the name of my regiment, state, time of expiration of term of service, asks if I want to reenlist and fight again, and then turning away says abruptly—"You may go." No words will ever strike me as did those coming as unexpectedly as they did. Asking him to repeat them, not fully understanding. I bounded out of the stockade as if I had been shot out. Hardly was I out and looking about me, when I saw Laird following me. Too overjoyed to think of anything else we clasped each others hands and cried like babies. Found and signed our parole papers after which we were sent out on a large level field where we went with a large number of others without much guard all day and night. Rations of meal and sweet potatoes.

December 9—Opened cloudy and cold. Suffered severely as the small fires could not afford us—bloodless creatures—much warmth. Then the smoke filled our eyes until many of us were made nearly blind. After our names were called at night and each of us had drawn a <u>loaf</u> of <u>wheat</u> <u>bread</u> the sound of a whistle from the north started every man to his feet and away we all rushed for the cars. Men who would have been helpless at any other time found legs to walk with and before dark we were all on board a long train of rickety broken cars. My condition at this time, could I have stopped to realize it, was decidedly unpleasant. Pain in all my joints, cold and shaking, blind almost as a bat in the daylight, after being pulled into a car I laid down to wonder if death were not then really creeping over me.

December 10—Cold and cloudy. Rode all night and found some sleep. At eight in the morning reached Charleston and disembarked in the lower part of the city near the mouth of the Ashley River [*Cooper River*]. Passed through three or four streets which laid in that part of the city which had received the fire of our troops, a disfigured, blackened mass of ruins. Large store houses with ragged holes in them, while the deserted streets showed tufts of grass growing among the pavements. Waited nearly all day on a wharf for the dense mist to clear up. By the middle of the afternoon it rose enough for

The *City of New York*, built in 1861, was the "flag of truce boat" stationed at Charleston Harbor from which prisoners from both sides were exchanged. George A. Hitchcock was exchanged at Charleston Harbor on December 10, 1864 (National Archives).

us to see down the Harbor and take in a view of places made memorable in our country's history. Our greatest object of interest was a little rusty looking steamer which rounded the wharves and came toward us. With bursting hearts we packed on board, a thousand in all, beginning to realize an end of our present sufferings. Steamed down the harbor through the keen December air hugging our blankets and watching the various places of interest, Castle Pinckney, Fort Moultrie, and Sullivan's Island. We peered through the mist looking for Fort Sumter, at last it was described, the ragged pile of ruins rising out of the sea. So closely were we watching it that we hardly noticed the stopping of the paddlewheels. The vessel began swinging around when suddenly the sight loomed up before which fairly made us hold our breaths for a moment. There a few rods off lay at anchor the majestic steamer "New York" whose decks were covered with the stores of hard tack and pork, but one object alone united our gaze, and that was the Grand Old Stars and Stripes which floated at the top. The scene which followed cannot be fully described. Men shouted, cheered, laughed like idiots and cried like babies. Men looked up at the sight as if in dreams. Others danced, hugged each other and the whole was one scene of perfectly wild enthusiasm. For the next few minutes, while the boats were being locked together our decks rung with all the patriotic songs and cries that delighted hearts could think of. The "City of New York" was our Flag of Truce boat and receiving vessel. Before dark we were all counted off on to our vessel and were at last breathing the blessed air of liberty though at present it as a very chilly, biting air. The first thing was to draw—each man—a new suit entire of clothing and blankets which we put on and then pass on to another boat "Star of the South" where we drew rations of hard tack, boiled pork and hot coffee and O how good. At ten I crawl off into a quiet corner on the upper deck, wrap my new warm woolen around me and drop to sleep.

December 11—The air is keen and cold. Had a late breakfast. Onions were issued. We learn we are in the care of the Sanitary Commission and fine care it is too. A beautiful view of the harbor opens. A boat load of our boys came down from the city and were exchanged onto our flag-of-truce boat, a boat load of Yankee officers lays nearby awaiting exchange. At night we all get on board the steam transport "United States" where Laird and I found quarters down in the hold near the prow in a warm nook.

[*On June 13, 1861, the United States Sanitary Commission was formed by northern physicians and women to supplement the inadequate and outdated facilities of the Army Medical Bureau. Their goal was to do for soldiers what government did not do, including raising the hygienic standards of the camps and army hospitals. Sanitary Commission nurses helped staff hospital and exchange vessels.*]

December 12—Beautiful day finds us out on the broad ocean having left the harbor at about light. The air is very wintry. Passed by our gunboat fleet which is blockading the harbor. All the sickest were attended by surgeons and nurses. The sea rolled considerably toward night and there was considerable sea sickness among the men. Beautiful evening with full moon, but cold.

December 13—Cloudy and chilly wind from the northeast so the sails were taken in during the night. Vinegar, soap, pickles, towels and underclothing were distributed by the Captain's wife. Rounded Cape Hatteras at three in the afternoon. Saw the light house and our blockading fleet off the inlet. The clouds were heavy and considerable swell at dark but no "Hatteras Gales" yet.

December 14—Cloudy and light rain. Reach Hampton Roads at light and touched at Fortress Monroe for mails. A large fleet of vessels of all sizes lay at anchor here. After an hours stop we proceed up the Chesapeake. Passed Point Lookout at three p.m. The boys became quite jovial as we near our destination.

December 15—Laid down at night and secured a good nap but at midnight we are aroused and transferred to the steamer *Olas* and landed at the Naval School Buildings, Annapolis, Md. where the ground is covered with snow and ice. The keen wintry air takes hold of our weak frames and almost overcomes me. I learn that thirty three men died during our three days voyage. We find quarters in the College Green Barracks. At daylight I find Capt. Davis of the 21st is in charge of the barracks so hunt him up. He takes charge of me, takes me to his house where I stop for dinner and learn the news which I have been deprived of over six months. At these barracks we are again stripped of all our clothing and furnished (after thorough baths) with entire new clothing again so that we may be entirely free of all vermin. I wrote home.

December 16—A cold day. We were mustered in for pay and at night were marched through the city out to Camp Parole two and a half miles where each State's troops are put into barracks by themselves so that I am at last separated from my good friend Laird who goes into the Pennsylvania Barracks.

December 17—Bunk with Church of the 2nd Rhode Island. Draw three meals a day, soup for dinner and sauerkraut for supper which is very acceptable to us scurvy eating fellows.

December 18—Reported to the surgeon's call for medicine for cold. Feel very rusty and mean.

December 19—Cold north east storm all day. Heard from home, through Orville Booth, for the first time.

December 20—Very cold. Found Isaac March who is doing duty here. He and Booth belong to the 26th Mass. Saw Gethings who says Potter and Osgood are on their way here.

December 21—Storm. Snow and Rain. Signed muster and payrolls. My cough is very hard and I feel almost sick.

[*In 1890 Hitchcock commented: "My greatest flight of fancy could hardly reach the stupendous change in my condition which took place before I again took up the record. Three days later, under the dear old stars and stripes with a restful comfort that I had never known before, I recall the events: December 22—Fair but very cold; freezing all day. More paroled prisoners came up from town. I have a very sore throat. We seem to be undergoing a system of general building up while awaiting the various red tape requirements after which furloughs will be furnished. December 23—Clear and cold. Went over to headquarters the forenoon where my descriptive list was made out for my furlough."*]

December 24—Received furlough and pay of thirty days, bought ticket to New York. Walked down to Annapolis and took steamer for Baltimore where we arrive at eleven at night.

[*In 1890 Hitchcock added: "When the train for Baltimore arrived, there were not half cars enough to accommodate our number. In their intense desire to get started for home, the crowding and jam was fearful. I became frightened, expecting to be crushed to death but managed to get free and saw the train move off with men hanging on to every inch of available space. Was thankful to get out unharmed but disappointed to again be left behind as is my usual lot. I found, however, that I could take the night boat from Annapolis, so I walked down to the city and boarded the steamer,* Star *for Baltimore, where I found comfortable quarters and a quiet ride—arriving at Baltimore at eleven in the evening."*]

December 25—After a long delay at the B.&O. Depot, found we could not go on till morning so the policemen who were very kind to us found us all lodgings. I, with several others, laid down on the floor of a kitchen of a lager beer saloon, where there was a warm fire all night. Caught an hour's nap and at light got a nice breakfast, the saloon keeper very kindly furnishing all the egg-nog we could drink free of charge. At ten o'clock left Baltimore, went on to Philadelphia where we arrive at four p.m. Walk across the city to the Union Refreshment Saloon, where we had a fine supper and the kindest of attention. At dark, cross the ferry and took cars for New York. The train being late, we made the fastest speed I ever knew in my travels, reaching New York at ten at night. Were taken in charge by Col. Howe, the New England agent, and found nice quarters on Broadway at the New England Rooms, where I slept between sheets for the first time for almost eight months.

December 26—After looking about the city in my one room, partook of a grand Christmas dinner at the rooms prepared by New York friends. After which, listened to toasts and speeches by Col. Howe and E.C. Bailey of the Boston Herald and others, also fine music. At dark left these good quarters and embarked on the Sound Steamer, *New York*, for Allyn's Point reaching there at midnight.

December 27—Reached Worcester at four where I found Banks of Company K who had been one train ahead of me from Annapolis. He was in a shocking condition having been crushed in by the crowd at Camp Parole depot when he got on board the cars at that place. I presume there can be no chance for him to get up again. Arrived at Fitchburg at night and found friends who gladly welcome me. Was entertained until next night.

[*In 1890 Hitchcock added: "Banks had been cared for and helped along so far and was now about to take the last stage to his home in Westminster. I learned after reaching home that he died soon after he had been carried into his own home in the presence of his mother and sisters, but he was unable to tell them anything. I was, therefore, able to give them the particulars of the sad case."*]

December 28—Father came down from Ashby and received his "prodigal son who was lost and is found, who was dead and is alive again." Reached my dear old home which never before had such a charm about it to me as after the past few months severe experience. I learned that I had been heard from but once and that from Richmond just after I was captured and that all my friends had given me up as dead, except my mother. The severe experiences I had passed through left me completely exhausted for several days.

[*Hitchcock commented in 1890: "All my friends had long given me up and mourned for me as dead. The last news of or from me was the letter I had written in Richmond just after my capture. No others which I had written were ever received until I arrived at Annapolis. The newspaper had reported me as "wounded and captured" after the Battle of Cold Harbor. Then the terrible reports of the mortality in Andersonville had confirmed the feeling that I should never again be heard from. The excitement over all I had passed through during the journey home left me prostrate, and I was kept quiet for a few days but gradually recovered and soon felt that I was nearly as good as new."]*

December 31, 1864, and January 1, 1865—The closing day of the year found the whole family together once more, Henry and wife having come over from Templeton. And when the beautiful New Years day dawned upon us, which was the Sabbath, we all united in the heartiest most truly Thanksgivings I had ever seen. Not on my account alone but for all and especially for Henry, who had been laid near death's door for a long time from the effect of a bullet which was shot through his right side at the Mine Explosion at Petersburg, and he has now recovered.

Last entry in Hitchcock's 1865 Diary—My closing career in Uncle Sam's service was in Boston where at the expiration of my furlough I received all my back pay and commutation pay up to that time, January 26, 1865, and my discharge papers.

[*In 1890 Hitchcock added: "The brightening skies in our country's storm removed all thought of any need for any future services so that when the thirty-day furlough had expired, I received my discharge from Uncle Sam's service on the 26th day of January 1865 together with back pay and commutation pay in Boston. Truly such a generous and paternal Government deserved all the best services which her loyal subjects could give to her. The 21st Massachusetts Regiment was mustered out of service on August 30, 1864, when discharge papers were made out for every member present or absent. I was absent and the discharge I found awaiting me. If I was technically out of the service, I was not so considered either by John Reb or Uncle Sam; so when the date of my furlough expired on January 26, 1865, another discharge paper was furnished me on which was indorsed the payment of bounty, back pay, commutation, subsistence furnished and transportation."*]

[*The 21st Regiment of Massachusetts Volunteers, which was mustered into U.S. service for three years at Worcester from July 23, 1861, was reduced to a battalion of three companies on August 18, 1864, and was consolidated with the 36th Massachusetts Regiment on October 21, 1864. The total enrollment in ten companies was 1,178, of whom 159 were killed or died of wound, 91 died of disease, accidents or in prison and 39 deserted. Hitchcock's Company A had a total enlistment of 119, of whom 14 were lost and 7 died in of disease, accidents or in prison. Six soldiers in the 21st Massachusetts Regiment died in Confederate prisons.*]

18

Hitchcock's Commentary in 1890 on Union Prisoners of War

"Fear may and does have a place in every man's breast."
—Hitchcock, *The Army Experiences of George A. Hitchcock,* 1890

During the Civil War, the United States housed approximately 220,000 prisoners and the Confederacy about 200,000 prisoners. Adjutant General Fred C. Ainsworth, Chief of the Records and Pension Office, reported in 1903 that "according to the best information now obtainable, from both Union and Confederate records, it appears that 211,411 Union soldiers were captured during the Civil War, of which number 16,668 were paroled on the field and 30,218 died while in captivity; and that 462,634 Confederate soldiers were captured during the war, of which number 247,769 were paroled on the field and 25,976 died while in captivity." This resulted in a mortality rate of 12 percent in the North and 15.5 percent in the South. Historians agree that these figures are based on incomplete records and that the numbers for Union prisoners are undoubtedly too low. Several hundred Union prisoners died shortly after being exchanged, but their deaths were not included in the mortality figures. In 1890 Hitchcock's resentment is reflected from his suffering as a prisoner.

A popular misconception exists concerning the Union prisoners of war: First, as to their value in determining the result of the war, and second, as to their ability to avoid capture. Public sympathy for these unfortunate men has always been heartfelt and widespread, but just as in the John Brown episode before the war, many believed its importance was magnified beyond all reason and overlooked its real significance and far reaching influence; so in this, the treatment of the prisoners of 1864 by the Confederate government was a potent force in the overthrow of slavery.

First: In its direct effect, as in a game of checkers where one side is able to pen and hold enough of its opponents "hors de combat" [*out of the fight*], its victory is assured; so in the spring of 1864 while the South was drained completely of fighting material, the North with its unlimited supply was abundantly able to hold back its great army of captured rebels. Without any intention or desire on the part of the Union government, all exchange of prisoners was withheld many mouths and this kept a hundred thousand men of the best fighting material on both sides out of the arena of war.

How little the North ever felt the burden of caring for her captives—not so with the South. Every one of her men was needed, and her only claim of excuse for starving the Union prisoners—her total inability to procure food—would seem to testify to the great straits in which she was placed. Looking at it from this standpoint, our government could well afford to await the pleasure of the Confederates. This view was often discussed by the Union prisoners in Andersonville with great satisfaction. If we were not fighting in the ranks, we were holding back each his man from the other side.

But a wider and yet more far-reaching influence upon humanity was felt as the actual cause of the delay in exchange of prisoners became known. General Butler could hardly have realized how great was the question which he was attempting to decide in the world's history when he insisted that, in the exchange of man for man, the negro must be considered an equal in the sight of law by the rebel government, as well as by the United States. Thus the grand struggle for human freedom went on, in which the Union prisoner was a factor, until the attention of the whole civilized world was drawn to the spectacle and "Andersonville" became the synonym—not alone of "fratricidal animosity" but was understood to be the result of the barbarism of slavery. Intelligent and humane persons, the world over and notably of the South, were educated to know the devilishness of human bondage. The forty thousand maltreated captives in Andersonville were, in this view of the case, accomplishing more in the grand results of Appomattox than perhaps they could have done by laying down their lives on the bloody battlefields all over the South.

Second: From various sources, both friendly and unfriendly, I have seen statements so misleading in regard to the way our prisoners were captured that to the dispassionate and unbiased mind there must often come the conviction that the prisoners as a class were not the bravest of the brave. For example: In the consideration of the pension bill for prisoners of war by the House of Representatives in Congress on April 21, 1890, Tarsney of Missouri is quoted as saying: "Many—a large proportion—were put in prison while evading their duty." The Honorable Mr. Cummings of New York also said: "many a man became a prisoner to escape fight, because he felt safer in prison than alongside his comrade in arms." These may be said to be "unfriendly" criticisms, which are despicable because they were given—not because they believe them—but for an ulterior purpose; namely, to please their constituency. With Tarsney, these utterances were doubly damning because he enforced his words with the assurance that he had been a Union soldier and a prisoner and knew where of the affirmed. It is true that every community has its blacklegs and every army its cowards and traitors, but if ever there was a self confessed Judas, this Tarsney surely is one. Their words are unworthy of notice only for the fact that they were uttered in the halls of Congress and as such have become a part of the history of the nation.

A more worthy critic is found in the historian of the 21st Massachusetts Regiment, General Walcott of Cambridge. In commenting on this subject on the closing page of his book [*History of the Twenty-First Regiment Massachusetts Volunteers, published in 1882*], he used these words: "It is a good thing for an army when men dread to be taken prisoners more than to face the horrors of such battlefields as the summer of 1864 furnished so lavishly in Virginia. It is often so much safer to cling to cover, and surrender, than to run out from an untenable position under fire, that it is well to have the temptation lessened by a lively dread of the consequences of capture. I have heard more than one of the very best and bravest of our comrades say that fear of being sent to Andersonville had a very bracing influence on keeping them up to their work in those dreadful, never-ending days of bloody attrition against earth-works, when it seemed so often as if every real fighting man (and the army was by no means wholly composed of such men) must die before the end was reached."

Now General Walcott was not only a brave soldier but an astute lawyer. He was one whom I delighted to honor and for whom I had high admiration. These are reasons why his words will carry conviction to many minds which have no personal knowledge of the facts but does grave injustice to thousands who were so unfortunate as to fall into the hands of the enemy. Let us examine his statements: "It is a good thing when men prefer to face the horrors of the battlefields of 1864, than to be taken prisoners." Face what horrors? Why, the horrors of standing right up to the work of loading and firing into the enemy as fast as you can when they are making a fierce charge upon you—the moment which tries men's souls and the very moment when cowards and skulkers take to their heels for the rear out of harms way. The horrors of charging on a protected enemy when you see your comrades falling all about you, while you must push forward to secure the coveted position—how, in the name of common sense, can the enemy capture you unless you go where he is?

General Walcott stated that "it is often so much safer to cling to cover and surrender than run from an untenable position under fire." Is this the advice of a brave officer to his men to run from an untenable position for fear of capture? Who is to decide whether it be untenable, you or the enemy? If the commanding officer sees the wisdom of retreat and so orders it, I allow that the act of retreat under fire is as brave as in going forward. But the suggestion is absurd that when a body of soldiers is ordered to yield a position, a part of them deliberately disobey the order and lie, and they watch their retreating comrades, while they willingly welcome the advancing enemy and a "furlough in the South." The opposite is always true; cowards are the ones who will make the quickest time out of harms way. Military discipline had become so perfected in the summer of 1864 that men had learned to become almost automatous—to move as the rest did if they knew it was in obedience to orders. It was only in the earlier years of the war that men took the law into their own hands. Men had no clear knowledge of the movements or intentions of the enemy, and they understood only that the way of safety was with the rest of the command. I speak from the standpoint of a private in the ranks, not as the officer whose duty gives him the opportunity to know more of the situation.

General Walcott stated that "I have heard more than one of the best and bravest of our comrades say that fear of being sent to Andersonville kept them up to their work.." Kept them up to what work? Running away from the enemy for fear of being sent to Andersonville? Or daring the risk of capture to hold a seemingly untenable position. Why did not General Corse, when ordered to "Hold the fort," become "brave" by yielding the untenable position through fear of Andersonville. General Walcott was a good officer, but he could not have been a good private and followed these suggestions.

Or if your take the General's words as a whole you become decidedly mixed in your understanding: "keeping up to the works," "running away from untenable positions," "bloody attrition," "clinging to cover"—I claim that these expressions as they are used, give one the impression that the "bloody attrition" of "keeping up to the work" was the best safeguard from capture, while the very opposite was true. The very large proportion of prisoners captured on the battlefield were those who "clung" not "to cover," but to a coveted position. Men, who having become separated from their commands because their commands had melted away in disorder, are forced to act for the moment on their own responsibility; they believed the wisest and bravest way was to "stick" to their position until the smoke of battle cleared or until it was clearly ascertained where they were to go.

The great routs of the First Bull Run and the 11th Corps at Chancellorsville were well nigh impossible in 1864, because the soldier had got over the foolish though natural habit of "dreading." And this is the one thing I desire to affirm, not for myself alone, but for the forty thousand or more like me, who, possibly not on account of undiluted bravery, but through recklessness it may be or momentary confusion, lost the opportunity to escape; and not one in a hundred found the element of fear the cause of capture. Large numbers were captured in whole commands by the act of surrender on the part of a superior officer.

General Walcott may have in mind some of the soldiers around Petersburg who were sent out—not led out—on some difficult task, and because they failed to execute the task, they were not ordered to retreat—their cowardly brigade commander dared not go to them but "clung to cover." I refer to a well known Pennsylvania officer of the 9th Corps.

Of the number who were captured while straying away from commands on foraging expeditions with or without leave, I can have no idea, but I believe the number to be comparatively small and even these cannot be claimed to have been captured through fear; it was rather through the lack of fear that they permitted themselves to go beyond our lines to secure some coveted plunder.

I trust my friends may take especial pains to understand what I have tried to show: that although fear may and does have a place in every man's breast, it did not control the actions of the prisoners of war—only in very rare instances.

Major General Benjamin Franklin Butler, who the Confederates referred to as "Beast Butler," was appointed a special agent for exchange of prisoners of war on December 17, 1863. His detailed letter on August 27, 1864, to Robert Ould, Commissioner for Exchange, stressing the willingness to renew exchanges whenever the Confederacy was ready to exchange all classes of prisoners, was published widely in newspapers and was printed as a leaflet by the government for general circulation. However, General Grant opposed any exchange: "It is hard on our men held in Southern prisons not to exchange them, but it is humanity to those left in the ranks to fight our battles. Every man we had, when released on parole or otherwise, becomes an active soldier against us at once either directly or indirectly. If we commence a system of exchange which liberates all prisoners taken, we will have to fight on until the whole South is exterminated. If we hold those caught, they amount to no more than dead men. At this particular time to release all rebel prisoners North would ensure Sherman's defeat and would compromise our safety here (Richmond campaign)."

John Charles Tarsney entered military service from Hillsdale, Michigan, on August 26, 1862, and served in Company E, 4th Michigan Regiment. He was taken prisoner at the Battle of Gettysburg on July 2, 1863, and was exchanged. He was taken prisoner at the Battle of the Wilderness on May 5, 1864, and imprisoned at Belle Isle, Andersonville, Millen and Savannah. He returned to his regiment at Petersburg on January 10, 1865. He was discharged on June 5, 1865. As a Missouri Democrat, he was elected to the House of Representatives in 1889 and served for four terms.

Amos Jay Cummings served as a sergeant in Company E, 26th New Jersey

Regiment from September 1, 1862, to June 27, 1863. He was promoted to sergeant major on March 6, 1863. As a New York Democrat, he was elected to the House of Representatives in 1887 and served until his death in 1902.

As reported in the New York Times *on April 22, 1890, Mr. Tarsney objected to the bill "as indiscriminate, as proposing to reward indifferently the men who had struggled with captivity or chosen to be prisoners rather than serve in the field. It offered a premium to all soldiers of the Union hereafter to surrender." Mr. Cummings stated that "while he would favor the pensioning of worthy prisoner's of war, he could not support so carelessly prepared a bill as that before the House." Many representatives objected to the proposition to pay $2 per diem to each of the surviving prisoners of war, because it seemed to be an injustice to other veterans of the war. The opponents of the bill were of the opinion that "no legislation should be enacted that would give one class of soldiers any advantage over another, and certainly none that ranks the soldiers who suffered in actual service below the ones that fell into the hands of the enemy." The commissioner of pensions estimated that 30,000 ex-prisoners have survived. The House bill "For pensioning prisoners of war" was defeated.*

Major General John Murry Corse, who commanded the Fourth Division of the XIV Corps, was surrounded by French's Division at Allatoona, Georgia, on October 5, 1864. He was ordered to surrender by Major General Samuel Gibbs French. However, General Corse received two messages by signal: "Sherman is coming. Hold out!" and then later, "General Sherman says hold fast. We are coming." On October 6, the Confederates broke off the engagement and withdrew. This engagement inspired P.P. Bliss, who wrote the hymn "Hold the Fort, For We Are Coming."

Colonel Joseph M. Sudsburg commanded the Second Brigade on June 2, 1864, when George Hitchcock was captured. Colonel Daniel Leasure, who organized and commanded the 100th Pennsylvania Volunteer Infantry Regiment, The Roundhead Regiment, was the "well known Pennsylvania officer."

The First Division of the IX Corps had a leadership problem after May 10, 1864, when Brigadier General Thomas Greeley Stevenson was killed in front of the Spotsylvania Court House, and was not corrected until after the Battle of Cold Harbor. Colonel Leasure assumed command of the First Division on May 10. In a letter to home on May 11, 1864, Charles J. Mills, assistant adjutant general of the First Division, wrote: "The division falls to the command of Colonel Leasure, who was in command of the Second Brigade. He did so well at the Wilderness that I had a favorable opinion of him, but I can't say that I retain it. If he is to have command of the division permanently, I shall not stay as A.A.G. that is sure, but my plans are very unsettled at present." Major General Thomas Leonidas Crittenden replaced Colonel Leasure on May 12, and he was replaced on June 9. On May 12, Colonel Leasure returned to command the Second Brigade;

however, he was "disabled by sickness on May 14" and was never active in field command again.

The Second Brigade of the First Division changed commands frequently during three critical weeks and appeared leaderless during the Battle of Cold Harbor. The brigade was commanded:

Until May 10 by Colonel Daniel Leasure,
May 10—12 by Lieutenant Colonel Gilbert Robinson,
May 12—14 by Colonel Daniel Leasure,
May 14—31 by Lieutenant Colonel Gilbert Robinson,
May 31—June 4 by Colonel Joseph M. Sudsburg.

Colonel Leasure's son, Lieutenant S. George Leasure (Adjutant), wrote to his father that on June 2 "the only General I saw in the front was General Griffin, 5th Corps, who gave some orders which I obeyed, or I suppose the [Second] Brigade would never have received any orders." He wrote on June 4: "I asked to be relieved and sent to my Regiment, as I had become disgusted with Brigade affairs." Lieutenant Leasure was killed on July 30, 1864.

19

Hitchcock After the War

"Another War Veteran Gone."
—*Fitchburg Daily Sentinel*, November 4, 1915

A memorandum from prisoner of war records at the National Archives noted that George A. Hitchcock, Company A, 21st Massachusetts Regiment, was captured at Cold Harbor on June 2, 1864; sent to Andersonville, Georgia, on June 8, 1864; and paroled at Charleston, South Carolina, on December 10, 1864. On December 22, 1864, he was furloughed for 30 days. The muster-out roll, dated December 15, 1864, New York, New York, stated that Hitchcock was a "prisoner of war since June 2, 1864; enrolled for unexpired time of regiment and entitled to be mustered out when inside our lines." Hitchcock's individual muster-out roll, dated January 23, 1865, Boston, Massachusetts, stated that he was mustered-out on January 23, 1865. In the roster of the 21st Massachusetts Regiment, History of the Twenty-First Regiment by Charles F. Walcott, Hitchcock was listed as discharged on January 26, 1865.

The life of this literary-minded and intelligent young man was impacted by the ravages of war. He was not able to continue his education and all future employment was hampered by his debilitative health. Henry Hitchcock, George's brother, stated that "at the time of his release from imprisonment and discharge, George was a broken down man with a complication of ailments all of which were due to the exposure of army life and the confinement and privation and starvation while in prison." Francis Wright, a resident of Ashby, noted that when he returned from military prisons, George "came to his father's at Ashby; he was then much emaciated and very feeble—he was a frightful sight."

Although his health prevented him from seeking any strenuous work, he was employed as a clerk at Baldwin's grocery store on Main Street in Fitchburg during April 1865. James Baldwin indicated that "when he came to work for me, he plainly showed the effects of his long imprisonment at Andersonville. He lacked vigor and endurance and was generally debilitated in health, had a cough whenever he caught cold and seemed liable to go into a decline from consumption."

After being employed at Baldwin's for less than two years, Hitchcock traveled to Cincinnati, Ohio, from 1867 to 1869, where he boarded with Charles Hayward, his old school companion. He served as a clerk in the book publishing business, and taught a large class of negro boys, most of whom were former slaves, at the Fowell Buxton Mission in Cincinnati. A fellow Sunday school teacher, Levi Goodale, mentioned that Hitchcock "was not in good health, although he was desirous of having his condition unnoticed." According to Charles Hayward, Hitchcock's hardships as a prisoner of war "had so completely undermined his constitution that any continued close confinement would result in his breaking down completely. He was finally obliged to leave the city on account of his health." When he returned to Fitchburg, Hitchcock was rehired at Baldwin's grocery store and remained until April 1872. James Baldwin noted that "he was not so well and thought the work was too hard for him."

On October 6, 1868, George Hitchcock married Elisabeth Phelps Lowe in Fitchburg. They had two children: George Preston Hitchcock, who was born on June 30, 1870, and Annie Louise Hitchcock, who was born on October 15, 1873. In the early 1870's, George and Elisabeth lived with a friend, S. Austin Childs, and remained there most of the time for three years. Childs was very concerned with Hitchcock's health and "thought he would not live many years—that he would die of consumption. Hitchcock's health, however, continued to slowly improve and by 1875, Hitchcock was employed as a clerk by the United States & Canada Express Company at the railroad station in Fitchburg. He served for 30 years as a messenger for the United States & Canada Express Company and the New York & Boston Dispatch Express Company. During his career, he traveled more than a million miles on trains between Fitchburg and Boston. James Baldwin stated that he "often met him after his return from Boston on a trip as messenger, when he appeared to be all 'used up.'" Baldwin also noted that

Carrie Black Hitchcock, wife of George Preston Hitchcock, George A. Hitchcock's only son (courtesy of Martha Hitchcock Price).

"he had always been a man of exemplary habits, strictly temperate, honest and industrious."

Hitchcock was actively involved with the Calvinistic Congregational Church in Fitchburg most of his life: Teacher and superintendent of the Sunday school, and treasurer, clerk and deacon of the church. He wrote the centennial history of the church, *A History of the Calvinistic Congregational Church and Society, Fitchburg, Massachusetts,* published in 1902.

He was an active member of the Grand Army of the Republic—serving as historian for the Edwin V. Sumner Post 19 and compiling hundreds of sketches of the war records of Fitchburg veterans. On September 15, 1876, during the tenth reunion of the 21st Massachusetts Regimental Association at Fitchburg, Hitchcock presented a paper on the prison life of the regimental members at Andersonville which included several extracts from his diary. Charles F. Walcott, a former captain in the regiment, reviewed the "almost perfect daily diary " of Hitchcock's prison life at Andersonville and included an edited version in History of the Twenty-First Massachusetts Volunteers, published in 1882. According to Walcott, Hitchcock "inserted a few general descriptions, but the record of his daily experiences is exactly as he made it from day to day." Hitchcock's literary tendencies and patriotic fervor stimulated a deep commitment to the Fitchburg Historical Society after his election as a member on March 19, 1900. He served as vice president from 1907 until his death in 1915. While Hitchcock was a member of the society, he wrote and presented many papers at society meetings: 1901—"First half-century of the Calvinistic Congregational Church"; 1904—"From Ashby to Andersonville, a historical reminiscence"; 1906—"A colonial patriot [Robert Kinsman], ancestor of an old Fitchburg family"; 1907—"Early Fitchburg homes" (presented the society with a bound volume of photographs of early homes in Fitchburg); 1911—"From hamlet to city"; and 1913—"Dr. Alfred Hitchcock."

Spending many years seeking an invalid pension from 1873 to 1912 without success, Hitchcock was consumed with federal bureaucracy. The lack of medical information—all his doctors were dead or had no record of his examinations—was fatal to his application. In reply to the commissioner of pensions in Washington D.C., on August 29, 1881, George noted that "the only medical examination I received at the date of my discharge was by a surgeon of the rebel army in the Florence stockade (South Carolina) on December 8, 1864, regarding the exchange of all sick prisoners of war." Unfortunately, Hitchcock did not return to the military after his final furlough and was discharged without any examination. After more than four decades of fighting the government, his application for an invalid pension under the act of May 11, 1912, was approved—one year before his death. This time consuming frustration resulted in his bitterness toward Congressmen John C. Tarsney and Amos Cummings in 1890 as noted in his "Commentary on the Union Prisoners of War."

George Hitchcock refused to succumb to his frail health—he was a survivor, outliving his brother who died in 1897, and his wife who died on February 6, 1905. In remembrance to Elizabeth, George wrote that "her domestic traits, her love of simplicity and her quiet life, all combined to endear her to the many friends she made all her life by her thoughtfulness and gentleness, and by all will she be remembered most tenderly.

The Hitchcock's children followed widely divergent paths in life. George Preston Hitchcock, graduated from Amherst College in 1892, and served as: English and science teacher at Ansonia, Connecticut, High School from 1892 to 1893; chemistry teacher at Fitchburg High School from 1893 to 1896 and principal from 1896 to 1903; director of the high school department at Pratt Institute in Brooklyn, New York, from 1903 to 1905; and headmaster at Brookline, Massachusetts, High School from 1905 to 1913. He earned a law degree in 1910, became vice chairman of the faculty at Pratt Institute from 1913 to 1918, and was employed by Nichols Copper Company in New York City from 1918 to 1936.

George A. Hitchcock at 60, then a resident of Fitchburg, Massachusetts (courtesy of Martha Hitchcock Price).

Annie Louise Hitchcock never married, and spent her life living and working in Fitchburg as a bank clerk. George Hitchcock lived with his daughter for the last three years of his life.

Time was catching up to the Civil War's veterans. By the beginning of World War 1 newspapers around the country were mourning their passing. On November 4, 1915, the Fitchburg Daily Sentinel announced in a headline: "Another War Veteran Gone—Death of George A. Hitchcock, Soldier in Civil War and Respected Citizen." The lengthy obituary began with: "George Alfred Hitchcock, a resident of Fitchburg for over 40 years, a deacon of the C. C. Church and a veteran of the Civil War, died Wednesday evening [November 3, 1915] at his home at 46 Arlington street, aged 71 years, 9 months and 19 days."

Editor's Reflections

The Civil War initiated a new era of a modern United States. According to Mark Twain, this disastrous conflict "uprooted institutions that were centuries old [and] transformed the social life of half the country, and wrought so profoundly upon the entire national character that the influence cannot be measured short of two or three generations." However, five generations have passed, and the influence of the Civil War has not vanished.

The Civil War casualty toll has been listed for almost one hundred and fifty years as 618,222 deaths—360,222 from the North and 258,000 from the South. Now, in 2012, David Hacker, a demographic historian, who is a specialist in 19th Century demographics from Binghamton University in New York, has recalculated the death toll and determined that 750,000 died, based on newly digitized census data. This war resulted in a tremendous and horrific loss of life but as stated by Oliver Wendell Holmes, it resulted in "One flag, one land, one heart, one hand, one Nation evermore."

Bibliography

Addison, Henry. *A Complaint ... upon the Subject of the Potomac Bridge* [Long Bridge], *as an Obstruction to the Commerce of Georgetown*. Washington, D.C.: H. Polkinhorn, printer, 1856.

Alderman, Edwin Anderson, ed. *Library of Southern Literature*, Vol. IV. Atlanta: Martin & Hoyt, 1907.

Andrews, John L., ed. *Friends of the Florence Stockade Newsletter, Winter 2009: History of the Use of the Florence Stockade*. Hartsville, SC, 2009.

Atwater, Dorence. *The Atwater Report: List of Prisoners Who Died in 1864–5 at Andersonville Prison*, Andersonville, GA: National Society of Andersonville, 1981.

Bates, Samuel P. *History of Pennsylvania Volunteers, 1861–5*. 5 vols. Harrisburg, PA: B. Singerly, State Printer, 1869–71.

_____. *Martial Deeds of Pennsylvania*. Philadelphia: T.H. Davis, 1875.

Bearss, Edwin C. *Andersonville National Historic Site: Historic Resource Study and Historical Base Map*. Washington, D.C.: National Park Service, 1970.

Beaver, Patrick. *The Big Ship: Brunel's Great Eastern, A Pictorial History*. London: Hugh Evelyn, 1969.

Black, Robert C., III. *The Railroads of the Confederacy*. Chapel Hill: University of North Carolina Press, 1952.

Boatner, Mark M., III. *The Civil War Dictionary*. New York: David McKay, 1959.

Breeden, James O. *Joseph Jones, M.D., Scientist of the Old South*. Lexington: University Press of Kentucky, 1975.

Bryan, T. Conn. *Confederate Georgia*. Athens: University of Georgia Press, 1953.

Clark, Walter, ed. *Histories of the Several Regiments and Battalions from North Carolina in the Great War 1861–65*. 5 vols. Goldsboro: Nash Brothers, 1901.

Cogswell, Leander W. *A History of the Eleventh New Hampshire Regiment, Volunteer Infantry, in the Rebellion War*. Concord, NH: Republican Press Association, 1891.

Committee of Publication. *A Memorial of The Great Rebellion: History of the Fourteenth Regiment New Hampshire Volunteers, 1862–1865*. Boston: Franklin Press, 1882.

Committee of the Order. *An Authentic Exposition of the Knights of the Golden Circle or A History of Secession From 1834 to 1861*. Chicago: Clarke & Company, 1861.

Committee of the Regiment. *History of the Thirty-Sixth Regiment, Massachusetts Volunteers, 1862–1865*. Boston: Rockwell & Churchill, 1884.

Committee of the Regimental Association. *History of the Thirty-Fifth Regiment, Massachusetts Volunteers, 1862–1865*. Boston: Mills, Knight and Company, 1884.

Coulter, E. Merton. *The Civil War and Readjustment in Kentucky*. Chapel Hill: University of North Carolina Press, 1926.

_____. *The Confederate States, 1861–1865*. Baton Rouge: Louisiana State University Press, 1950.

Current, Richard N., ed. *Encyclopedia of the Confederacy*. New York: Simon & Schuster, 1993.

Daniel, John M. *The Richmond Examiner During the War*. New York: Arno Press, 1970.

Doddridge, Philip. *The Life of Colonel James Gardiner*. New York: Carlton & Phillips, 1854.

Eggleston, George Cary. *A Rebel's Recollections*. Bloomington: Indiana University Press, 1959.

Emerson, William A. *Fitchburg, Massachusetts—Past and Present*. Fitchburg, MA: Blanchard & Brown, 1887.

Emmerson, George S. *The Greatest Iron Ship: S.S. Great Eastern*. North Pomfret, VT: David & Charles, 1980.

Fermer, Douglas. *James Gordon Bennett and the New York Herald: A Study of Editorial Opinion in the Civil War Era 1854–1867*. New York: St Martin's Press.

Fox, William F. *Regimental Losses in The American Civil War, 1861–1865*. Dayton, OH: Morningside, 1985.

Freeman, Douglas S. *R.E. Lee: A Biography*, 3 vols. New York: Charles Scribner's Sons, 1934–35.

Futch, Ovid L. *History of Andersonville Prison*. Gainesville: University of Florida Press, 1968.

Gavin, William G. *Campaigning with the Roundheads: History of the Hundredth Pennsylvania Veteran Volunteer Infantry Regiment in the American Civil War, 1861–1865*. Dayton, OH: Morningside, 1989.

Grant, Ulysses S. *Personal Memoirs and Selected Letters, 1839–1865*. New York: The Library of America, 1990.

Griffin, James David. *Savannah, Georgia, During the Civil War*. Athens: Dissertation for Ph.D. in History, University of Georgia, 1963.

Hawkes, George P. *Diary*. Carlisle Barracks, PA: U.S. Army Military History Institute.

Hesseltine, William Best. *Civil War Prisons: A Study in War Psychology*. Columbus: Ohio State University Press, 1930.

Hesseltine, William Best, and David L. Smiley. *The South in American History*. Englewood Cliffs, NJ: Prentice Hall, 1960.

History and Roster of Maryland Volunteers, War of 1861–65. Baltimore: General Assembly of Maryland, 1898.

Hitchcock, George A. *The Army Diary of George A. Hitchcock—Extending from August 1862 to January 1865, Including Service in the Southern States of Maryland, Virginia, Kentucky, Tennessee, North Carolina, South Carolina, and Georgia*. "Transferred from the pocket diaries which were carried during the War of the Rebellion"—dated 1890. Manuscript located at Fitchburg Historical Society, Fitchburg, Massachusetts.

Hitchcock, George A. *The Army Experiences of George A. Hitchcock—A Private of Company A, 21st Massachusetts Regiment of Volunteers, 9th Army Corps—Beginning August 7th, 1862; Ending January 26th, 1865*. Manuscript copied in 1865 from the original diaries carried throughout the war and now in the possession of Hitchcock's great-great granddaughter, Martha Hitchcock Price.

Hitchcock, George A. *Memoirs of Ashby in 1850*. Manuscript at Ashby, MA, Public Library.

Jackman, Lyman. *History of the Sixth New Hampshire Regiment in the War for the Union*. Concord, NH: Republican Press Association, 1891.

Johnson, Allen, and Dumas Malone, eds. *Dictionary of American Biography, Vol. III*. New York: Charles Scribner's Sons, 1958.

Jones, Jacqueline. *Saving Savannah—The City and the Civil War*. New York: Alfred A. Knopf, 2008.

Keegan, John. *The American Civil War*. New York: Vintage Books, 2009.

Kelly, Daniel G. *What I saw and Suffered in Rebel Prison*. Buffalo, NY: Thomas, Howard and Johnson, 1868.

Lexington Cemetery and Henry Clay Monument. A National Register of Historic Places. Lexington, KY: National Park Service, 2011.

Lincoln, Abraham. *Speeches and Writings 1859–1865*, vol. 2. New York: The Library of America; distributed by Viking Press (Fifth Printing), 1989.

Long, E.B., and Barbara Long. *The Civil

War Day by Day: An Almanac 1861–1865. New York: Da Capo Press, 1971.

McGee, Benjamin F. *History of the 72d Indiana Volunteer Infantry of the Mounted Lightning Brigade*. Indianapolis: S. Vater & Company, 1882.

McPherson, James M. *Battle Cry of Freedom*. New York: Oxford University Press, 1988.

McPherson, James M. *Out of War a New Nation*. Prologue ("Quarterly of the National Archives"), Spring 2010, Vol. 42 No.1

Marvel, William. *Andersonville: The Last Depot*. Chapel Hill: University of North Carolina Press, 1994.

_____. *Burnside*. Chapel Hill: University of North Carolina Press, 1991.

Massachusetts Soldiers, Sailors and Marines in Civil War. 8 vols. Brookline: published by adjutant general at Riverdale Press, 1935.

Mills, Charles J. Letters. Carlisle Barracks, PA: U.S. Army Military History Institute.

Moore, Frank. *Civil War in Song and Story, 1860–1865*. New York: P.F. Collier, 1892.

Morrison, James L., Jr., ed. *The Memoirs of Henry Heth*. Westport, CT: Greenwood Press, 1974.

National Cyclopaedia of American Biography, Vol. 1. New York: James T. White & Company, 1892.

New York Times, April 3, 2012, Page D1: "New Estimate Raises Civil War Death Toll."

New York Times Almanac—2011. New York: Penguin, 2011.

Ohio Roster Commission. *Ohio: Official Roster of the Soldiers of the State of Ohio in War of the Rebellion, 1861–1866*. 12 vols. Cincinnati, OH: Werner; Wilstach Baldwin; Ohio Valley; and Laning, 1886–1895.

Peck, Theodore, S., comp. *Revised Roster of Vermont Volunteers, 1861–66*. Montpelier, VT: Watchman, 1892.

Pingrey, Jennette D., ed. *Birth, Marriage and Death Records of the Town of Ashby, Massachusetts from 1754 to 1890*. American Data Services, 1989.

Priest, John M. *Antietam: The Soldiers' Battle*. Shippensburg, PA: White Mane, 1989.

_____. *Before Antietam: The Battle for South Mountain*. Shippensburg, PA: White Mane, 1992.

Quint, Alonzo H. *The Record of the Second Massachusetts Infantry, 1861–1865*. Boston: James P. Walker, 1867.

Record of Massachusetts Volunteers in the Civil War, 1861–1865, 2 vols. Boston: Wright & Potter, 1870.

Record of Officers and Men of New Jersey in the Civil War, 1861–1866, Vol. I. Trenton, NJ: John L. Murphy, Steam Book and Job Printer, 1876.

Record of Service of Michigan Volunteers in the Civil War, 1861–1865, Vol. 4. Kalamazoo, MI: Ihling Brothers & Everard, 1915.

Report of the Adjutant General of the State of Illinois, Containing Reports of the Years 1861–66, Vol. III (Roster of Officers and Enlisted Men from 36th to 55th Regiments). Springfield, IL: Phillips Brothers, State Printers, 1901.

Rhea, Gordon C. *The Battle of the Wilderness: May 5–6, 1864*. Baton Rouge: Louisiana State University Press, 1994.

Rogers, George A., and R. Frank Saunders, Jr. "Camp Lawton Stockade, Millen, Georgia, C.S.A." *The Atlanta Historical Journal*, Vol. XXV, No. 4, Winter, 1981.

Sandburg, Carl. *The American Songbag*. New York: Ticknor & Fields, 1988.

Sears, Stephen W. *Landscape Turned Red*. New York: Ticknor & Fields, 1983.

Shorter Oxford English Dictionary, Fifth Edition. New York: Oxford University Press, 2002.

Sifakis, Stewart. *Who Was Who in the Civil War*. New York: Facts on File, 1986.

Stone, James Madison. *Personal Recollections of the Civil War: By One Who Took Part In It as a Private Soldier in the 21st Volunteer Regiment of Infantry from Massachusetts*. Boston: published by the author, 1918.

Swinton, William. *Campaigns of the Army of the Potomac: A Critical History of Operations in Virginia, Maryland and Pennsylvania from the Commencement to the Close of the War, 1861–1865*. New York: Charles Scribner's Sons, 1882.

Sword, Wiley. *Sharpshooter: Hiram Berdan, his Famous Sharpshooters and their Sharps*

Rifles. Lincoln, RI: Andrew Mowbray, 1988.

Thorn, John. "Debate over Baseball's Origins Spills into Another Century," *New York Times*, March 13, 2011.

Townsend, Billy. *Camp Lawton (Millen, Georgia).* Atlanta: Parks and Historic Sites Division, Georgia Department of Natural Resources, 1975.

Trudeau, Noah Andre, *Bloody Roads South: The Wilderness to Cold Harbor, May–June 1864.* Boston: Little, Brown and Company, 1989.

Underwood, Adin B. *The Three Years' Service of the Thirty-Third Massachusetts Infantry Regiment.* A. Williams, 1881.

United States War Department. *The War of the Rebellion: A Compilation of the Official Records of the Union and Confederate Armies*, 128 vols. Washington, D.C.: Government Printing Office, 1880–1901.

Vandiver, Frank E., ed. *War Memoirs of Jubal Anderson Early, Lieutenant General, C.S.A.* Bloomington: Indiana University Press, 1960.

Walcott, Charles F. *History of the Twenty-First Regiment Massachusetts Volunteers in the War for the Preservation of the Union, 1861–1865.* Boston: Houghton, Mifflin & Company, 1882.

Welcher, Frank J. *The Union Army, 1861–1865: Organization and Operations, Vol. I.* Bloomington: Indiana University Press, 1989.

Wert, Jeffry D. *General James Longstreet: The Confederacy's Most Controversial Soldier: A Biography.* New York: Simon & Schuster, 1993.

Wheeler, Kenneth W., ed. *For the Union—Ohio Leaders in the Civil War.* Columbus: Ohio State Press, 1968.

Wilkinson, Warren. *Mother, May You Never See the Sights I Have Seen—The Fifty Seventh Massachusetts Veteran Volunteers in the Army of the Potomac, 1864–1865.* New York: Harper & Row, 1990.

Williams' Cincinnati Directory. Cincinnati, OH: Williams & Company, June 1865, 1867 and 1868.

Willis, Henry A. *The Fifty-Third Regiment Massachusetts Volunteers.* Fitchburg: Blanchard & Brown, 1889.

_____. *Fitchburg in the War of the Rebellion.* Fitchburg, MA: Stephen Shepley, 1866.

Woodbury, Augustus. *Major General Ambrose E. Burnside and the Ninth Army Corps.* Providence, RI: Sidney S. Rider & Brother, 1867.

Woodbury, Augustus. *The Second Rhode Island Regiment: A Narrative of Military Operations in which the Regiment was Engaged from the Beginning to the End of the War for the Union.* Providence, RI: Valpey, Angell & Company, 1875.

Index

Adams, Pvt. Sam 104, 121, 122, 128, 129
Ainsworth, Adj. Gen. Fred C. 225
Alabama Regiment: 26th 179
Aldrich, Capt. Harrison 68, 86
Allen, Sgt. Courtland 105, 191
Anderson, Maj. Gen. Robert 23
Andersonville National Historic Site 3
Andersonville Prison 3, 27, 174–207, 228
Andersonville prisoners, from: Butler's troops 184; Grant's army 187, 189–193; Hunter's West Virginians 188; Kilpatrick's troops 197; Sherman's army 184–186, 191–196, 198, 200–204; Steele's troops 186
Andrew, Gov. John 45, 139, 146, 150
Annapolis, Maryland 57, 74, 151, 221, 222
Antietam-Sharpsburg, Maryland 5, 23, 24, 28–31
Army balloon 58
Army of Northern Virginia 23, 39, 41, 56, 88, 148
Army of the Potomac 2, 5, 13, 18, 36, 39, 54, 55, 65, 66, 73, 148, 155, 156, 158
Ashby, Massachusetts 7–9, 13, 15, 17, 48, 148, 154, 223

Bailey, Pvt. Ransom 138, 183
Baker, Pvt. Erastus 197
Baldwin, James 232, 233
Ball, Chaplain George 30, 32, 33
Baltimore Clipper 46
Banks, Pvt. Prentice 172, 223
Barker, Cpl. Daniel E. 102, 103, 117, 120, 172, 203
Barksdale, Brig. Gen. William 37, 38
baseball 90, 92
battles: *see* Antietam; Bull Run, 2nd battle of; Chancellorsville; Chantilly; Cold Harbor; Fredericksburg; Knoxville campaign; New Bern; Roanoke Island; South Mountain; Spotsylvania; Wilderness

Belle Plain, Virginia 160
Benjamin, Capt. Samuel N. 29, 118, 132, 136
Berdan, Col. Hiram 21
Bethesda Church, Virginia 3
Bible 175, 195–197
Biddle, Col. James 110
Blackmer, Pvt. Charles 121, 124, 138
Blackshear Prison, Georgia 209
Boone Cave 100, 101, 107
bounty 121
Boyle, Gen. Jeramiah T. 100
Bragg, Maj. Gen. Braxton 108–111, 118, 121, 123, 133
Brooks, Gen. W.T.H. 56
Brooks, Sgt. Joel J. 64
Brownlow, Parson 134
Bryan, Brig. Gen. Goode 111
Buchele, Pvt. John J. 194
Buckner, Maj. Gen. Simon Bolivar 109
Bull Run, 2nd battle of 10, 22
Burnside, Maj. Gen. Ambrose Everett 2, 13, 23–25, 28–31, 34, 36–39, 42, 44, 53–56, 60–63, 66, 69–73, 80, 81, 85, 87, 90, 98–106, 151, 166, 168; East Tennessee campaign 108–137
Burpee, Pvt. Frank 150, 151
Butler, Maj. Gen. Benjamin 70, 226, 229

Camp Chase 97
Camp Convalescent 159
Camp Dick Robinson 102, 112, 143
Camp Distribution 159
Camp Lawton 3–5, 208–214
Camp Nelson 5, 98–107, 101, 112, 137, 139
Camp Parole 4, 34, 46, 222–223
Camp Pitman 142
Camp Staunton 16
Cane, Pvt. James A. 172
Carruth, Pvt. James A. 89, 116
Chamberlin, Cpl. Moses A. 98

Index

Chancellorsville 25, 88, 140, 156, 228
Chantilly 22, 31, 57
Charleston, South Carolina 214, 215, 218, 219
Charleston Harbor 218, 219
Chattanooga, Tennessee 111, 120, 132, 136, 140
Christian Commission 97, 102
Church, Pvt. Benjamin J. 222
Churchill, Cpl. Eliab R. 58
Cincinnati, Ohio 72, 73, 80, 86, 90, 91, 97, 98, 144, 145, 232
Clapp, Pvt. Joseph W. 34
Clark, Pvt. Elon 197
Clark, Pvt. J. Warren 150, 167
Clark, Pvt. Samuel (George) 198
Clark, Capt. William H. 116, 139
Clark, Col. William S. 21, 27–30, 45–46, 52, 58, 67–68, 75, 82, 86, 116, 139
Cluke, Col. R.S. 72, 73, 83
Cobly, Pvt. Henry 31, 102
Cold Harbor 5, 157, 168–173
Cole, Pvt. Freeman 67, 92, 94, 96, 100, 143, 146, 150, 151
Collins, Sgt. Joseph 50,
Collins, William 190
Columbus, Ohio 73, 76–80, 86
USS *Congress* 66
Copperheads 73, 152
Corcoran, Brig. Gen. Michael 56, 65, 69
Corps, Federal: I 23, 36; II 23, 37, 189; III 22, 36; IV 23, 136; V 3, 36, 47, 169; VI 23, 36, 56; IX 2–4, 15, 22–23, 26, 30, 32, 37, 45, 53, 58, 60, 64–65, 68, 70, 72–73, 108–136, 151–152; × 37; XII 23, 37; XVIII 168; XXIII 85, 108, 110, 134
Corse, Brig. Gen. Montgomery 228, 230
Couch, Brig. Gen. Darius 41, 44, 63
Cox, Maj. Gen. Jacob 85
Crampton's Gap, Maryland 23
Crittenden, Maj. Gen. Thomas L. 166, 168, 230
Cullen, Brig. Gen. George 37
Culpeper, Virginia 41–42, 148
USS *Cumberland* 66
Cumberland Gap 3, 5, 99, 105, 107, 109, 112–113, 135, 139
Cummings, Amos J. 226, 229–230
Cummings, Sgt. Israel 89
Curtis, Charles F. 190
Curtis, Sgt. Christopher A. 87, 90
Cushman, Pauline 164
Cutter, Calvin 138, 142–143, 145

Dahlgren, Col. Ulric 174
Dahlgren, Rear Adm. John A. 218
Dailey, Pvt. Dan 29

Daniel Boone Cave 100–101, 107
Davis, Capt. Albert H. 35, 43, 46, 57
Davis, Garret 82
Davis, President Jefferson 70, 111, 133, 174–175
Davis, 1st Lt. Jonas 99, 121
DeCourcy, Col. John F. 96, 99
Delaney, Patrick 190
Department of Ohio 2, 70, 72–80
Dillenback, Lt. Henry G. 124
Dix, Maj. Gen. John Adams 68, 88
draft riots in N.Y. City 96–97
Dwinnell, Pvt. Waldo 198
Dyer, Pvt. Thomas B. 88, 172, 184–185

Early, Lt. Gen. Jubal A. 169
East Tennessee Campaign 108–136
election, presidential 210
Emancipation Proclamation 24, 30, 70, 81
Emerson, Sgt. George O. 172
Emerson, James 154

Falmouth, Virginia 44, 48, 51, 93, 163; 1862–63 winter 55–64
Ferrero, Brig. Gen. Edward 33, 35, 37, 42, 46–47, 51, 56–58, 62, 67–68, 75, 4–85, 102, 110, 118, 166
Fitchburg, Massachusetts 7, 30, 154, 159, 223, 232–234, 235
Fitchburg Daily Sentinel 232, 235
Fitchburg Historical Society 6, 234
Florence, South Carolina 4–5, 199, 209, 214, 215–217
Florida artillery (Leon) 179
Fort Clay 97, 145, 152
Fort Elsworth 21
Fort McHenry 74
Fort Washington 21
Fortress Monroe, Virginia 66, 68–71, 221
Foster, Maj. Gen. John G. 217–218
Foster, Maj. John W. 33–34, 40, 45, 58, 60, 109, 111, 135
Fox's Gap, Maryland 23, 27
Franklin, Maj. Gen. William B. 23, 36, 39, 56, 163
Frazer, Capt. John D. 31
Frazer, Brig. Gen. John W. 109
Fredericksburg, Virginia 2, 15, 36–54
Fredericksburg Campaign 36–54, 56, 58–59, 161
Fredrick, Maryland 22–23, 26
Fry, Gen. Speed Smith 100, 102, 104–106
Fuller, First Lt. Benjamin F. 88, 90

Gaffney, Pvt. James 193
Gardiner, Col. James 175
Gartrell, Brig. Gen. Lucius J. 211

Index

Georgia Regiments: 5th 181, 215; 20th 23; 55th 109, 179; 56th 178; 57th 179; Reserves 1, 2, 3, 4 179
Gethings, Sgt P. Francis 86, 222
Getty, Brig. Gen. George 65
Gettysburg 54, 73, 89, 98
Gibbons, Brig. Gen. John 38
Gibbs, Brig. Gen. George 181
Gilson, Pvt. Marlin 84
Glover, George 180
Goodrich, Lt. Ira B. 89
Gordon, Brig. Gen. John B. 169
Goss, Sgt. Charles 89
Gould, Pvt. Marcus (Jule) 121, 131, 150
Gould, Sam 139–140, 151–152
Granger, Brig. Gen. Gordon 136
Grant, Maj. Gen. Ulysses S. 3, 53–54, 90, 108–109, 111, 127, 132–133, 148- 149, 155–167, 185, 229
Graton, Cpl. Alvin S. 199, 203, 210–211
Great Eastern 18–19
Griffin, Col. Simon Goodell 113, 231

Hall, Capt. Theron 48, 99, 102, 105–106, 143, 145, 147
Halleck, Gen. Henry Wager 54
Hancock, Maj. Gen. Winfield S. 156, 165
Hardee, Lt. Gen. William J. 218
Harlow, Capt. William T. 86
Harper, Pvt. Henry M. 133
Harpers Ferry, Virginia 22–23, 28, 30, 32–34, 40, 58
Harriman, Col. Walter 33, 69
Harrington, Cpl. William 134
Harrison, Col. George P. 215
Hartranft, Brig. Gen. John Frederick 64, 68, 84, 90, 108, 110–111, 125
Hawkes, Lt. Col. George P. 34, 57–58, 60–63, 68–70, 83, 86, 88–90, 97, 99- 100, 102, 104, 119–120, 129, 139, 141, 160, 169–170, 174, 198
Hayward, Charles 35, 143–144, 153, 232–233
Haywood, Lt. Asa E. 77, 88
Head, Pvt. Truman (California Joe) 21
Hesseltine, William B. 182
Heth, Maj. Gen. Henry 168–169
Heywood, Sgt. Sidney 61
Hickman's Bridge (Camp Nelson) 98
Hildreth, Pvt. J.L. 57
Hill, Maj. Gen. Ambrose P. 23–24, 45, 197
Hill, Sgt. George C. 67, 86
Hitchcock, Dr. Alfred 234
Hitchcock, Annie Louise 6, 235
Hitchcock, Carrie Black (Walker) 233
Hitchcock, Eliza Sparhawk 7, 154, 223
Hitchcock, Pvt. George Alfred: Andersonville 178–207; Camp Lawton 208–214; captured at Cold Harbor 168–172; commentary on Union prisoners 225–231; Eastern Kentucky 81–107; Florence prison 215–218; Fredericksburg 36–54; hospital and furlough at home 148–154; Knoxville Campaign 108–136; life after the war 232-235; Maryland Campaign 22–35; return to his regiment 155–167; winter in mountains 137–147
Hitchcock, George Loring 7, 34, 97, 154, 223
Hitchcock, George Preston 233, 235
Hitchcock, Lt. Henry Sparhawk 9, 13, 25, 33, 35, 40–41, 46, 57, 60, 66–67, 69, 84, 89–91, 93–94, 96, 98, 196, 117, 121, 123, 125, 130, 132, 136, 140, 151, 154, 158, 187, 224, 232
Holmes, Oliver Wendell 8, 236
Holshoult 199
Holt, Pvt. Lyman W. 84
Hood, Maj. Gen. John B. 110, 198
Hooker, Maj. Gen. Joseph B. 36–37, 54, 56, 62–63, 66, 88, 93
hospital in Lexington, Kentucky 162–163
Howe, Capt. Edward E. 40, 87, 167, 223
Humiston, Cpl. Alvin 87
Humphrey, Brig. Gen. Benjamin 111
Hunter, Maj. Gen. David 188

Illinois Regiments: 19th 192; 60th 98, 116
Indiana Regiments: 71st 116; 117th 146
Irish, Sgt. Chauncey B. 152
Irish brigade 51
Iverson, Col. John F. 215

Jackson, Maj. Gen. Thomas J. (Stonewall) 22–23, 28, 37, 88
Jenkins, Brig. Gen. Micah 110–111, 156
Johnston, Gen Joseph E. 74, 148
Jones, Dr. Joseph 200–202

Kearny, Maj. Gen. Philip 22
Kelly, Pvt. Daniel 214
Kelt, Second Lt. John 92
Kelton, Capt. Ira J. 31
Kentucky Confederate Cavalry: 2nd 194; 8th 72
Kentucky Federal Cavalry: 10th 83, 87, 90, 92–93; 14th 81, 86, 92–94
Kentucky Federal Regiments: 47th 142; 49th 104
USS *Keokuk* 70
Kilpatrick, Brig. Gen. H. Judson 174
King, Col. William S. 94, 145–147
Kinsman, Robert 234
Knight, Pvt. Otis H. 192
Knights of the Golden Circle 152

Index

Knoxville, Tennessee, Campaign 40, 99, 108–136
Koster, Sgt. John S. 86

Lacy House 2, 58–61, 63–64
Lagara, Pvt. German 172, 197
Laird, Cpl. William Samuel 193, 201, 205–206, 210, 216, 219, 221–222
Lamb, Cpl. Walter 67, 119, 185, 195, 210
Lander, Pvt. George M. 166
Lawrence, First Lt. George F. 70, 104, 117
Leach, Pvt. Martin D. 172
Leasure, Col. Daniel 155, 168, 230–231
Leasure, Lt. S. George 231
Lee, Maj. Gen. Fitzhugh 157
Lee, Gen. Robert E. 22–24, 37–39, 54–56, 74, 88, 93–96, 108, 110, 136, 148, 155–158, 173–174
Leland, Herbert 24
Lewis, Lt. Edward R. 116
Lewis, Lt. John F. 68, 98
Lexington, Kentucky 73, 83, 88–89, 91–92, 94–95, 144–145, 148, 150, 153
Libby Prison, Richmond, Virginia 3, 172, 174
Lincoln, President Abraham 22, 24, 30–32, 36–38, 46–47, 56, 70, 72, 81, 108–109, 118, 148, 155, 192, 210–211
Longstreet, Lt. Gen. James 23, 37–38, 110–111, 123, 127–128, 137, 140, 156

Macon, Georgia 176, 178, 193–198, 200, 207
Macon Telegraph 200
Maggi, Col. Alberto C. 15, 57–58
Maine Regiment: 7th 191–192
Manigault, Louis 201
Mann, Pvt. Reuben 139, 141
March, Pvt. Isaac 222
Marshall, Col. Elisha 169
Marshall, Pvt. Thomas 172
Martin, Pvt. William H.H. 216
Marye's Heights, Virginia 5, 38–39
Maryland Heights 32
Maryland Regiments: 2nd 17, 103, 112, 121; 3rd 169, 171
Mason Dixon Line 115
Massachusetts Regiments: 1st 18; 2nd 18, 64; 8th 17; 11th 18, 193; 15th 44; 17th 18; 19th 38, 205; 20th 18, 38; 21st 2, 4, 9, 13, 15, 21–25, 37, 39, 44–45, 47–48, 57, 60, 66, 69, 81–95, 99–107, 108–136, 137–147, 151, 157, 169, 171; 22nd 17; 24th 18; 26th 222; 27th 18; 33rd 15–16, 57–58, 61, 105; 34th 188, 197, 199; 35th 16, 29, 35, 46, 57, 60, 66, 68, 83, 94, 145; 36th 30; 70, 102, 139, 146, 188, 191; 53rd 34
May, Sgt. Simon 87, 120
Mayo, Cpl. John 58, 60, 105

McCabe, Second Lt. Stephen 85
McClellan, Gen. George B. 21–23, 28, 34, 36, 53–54, 66, 210–211
McKibbin, Gen. David Bell 122
McLaws, Maj. Gen. Lafayette 23, 37, 110–111
McNulty, Cpl. Barney 92
Meade, Maj. Gen. George Gordon 38, 54, 56, 148, 166, 168
Merrimac, Confederate ship 66–67
Michigan Regiments: 2nd 46; 7th 38; 8th 93, 117, 141–142; 9th 93, 117
Middy, Pvt. George 216
military pay 91, 124
Millen, Georgia 208; *see also* Camp Lawton
Miller, Pvt. James 172, 184, 188, 191, 199, 216–217
Miller, Pvt. John M. 193
Miller, Sgt. Robert 88
USS *Minnesota* 70
Mississippi Troops *see* Barksdale
Mitchell, Lt. Col. R. Charlton 47
USS *Monitor* 66–67
Morgan, Brig. Gen. John Hunt 72, 94–97, 103
Mosby, Gen. John S. 161
Mott, Brig. Gen. Gresham 156
Mount Sterling, Kentucky 5, 72, 81–95, 108
Mulford, Lt. Col. John E. 218
Mumford, Pvt. John 192
Mun, A. 190
Muzzey, Sgt. Charles C. 90

Nagle, Brig. Gen. James 60
National Park Services 2
Nelson, Maj. Gen. William 100
New Bern, North Carolina 15, 69
New Hampshire Regiments: 6th 35, 143; 9th 31; 11th 33, 42, 46–47, 57, 60, 69, 84; 16th 144
New Jersey Regiment: 27th 70
New York Herald 31, 186
New York Regiments: 12th 192; 18th 46; 51st 29, 46, 68–69, 83, 106, 107; 76th 190; 82nd 192; 89th 38; 103rd 167
New York Times 192, 230
Newport News, Virginia 15, 65–71, 73
Newton, Brig. Gen. John 56
North Carolina Regiments: 62nd 109; 64th 109

Ohio Regiment: 129th 147
Olas (steamer) 221
Oliver, James 166
Orcutt, Pvt. Ansel 102
Orcutt, Pvt. William L. 172
Osgood, Sgt. J. Albert 68, 121, 184, 191, 222
Ould, Robert 229

Index

Paris, Kentucky 5, 73, 80–81, 97
Parke, Maj. Gen. John Grubb 65
Parker, Capt. George C. 86, 92, 96, 102, 120
Peckham, Sgt. Francis M. 102, 121
Pegram, Brig. Gen. John 72, 97
Pemberton, Gen. John 89
Pennsylvania Regiments: 48th 112, 117, 129–130, 139, 170; 51st 25, 46, 66, 69, 84; 83rd 190; 88th 190; 100th 143, 169–171
Persons, Lt. Col. Alexander W. 181
Petersburg, Virginia 53, 185, 187, 189, 197, 229
Phelps, Cpl. Buel M. 204
Phillips House 60
Piper, Pvt. Asa Franklin Van Buren 106, 121–122, 139
Pleyel's Hymn 69
Plunkett, Sgt. Thomas 50
Poe, Orlando 110–111
Pope, Maj. Gen. John 19, 22, 53–54
Port Hudson, Louisiana 96, 98
Porter, Brig. Gen. Fitz-John 53
Potter, Gen. Robert B. 106, 111, 118, 121
Potter, Pvt. Wilbur A. 68, 70, 121, 198, 222
prisons see Andersonville; Florence; Lawton; Libby
Pryor, Brig. Gen. Roger A. 65

Raiders 187–191
Ramseur, Maj. Gen. Stephen D. 171
Reno, Maj. Gen. Jesse 15, 23, 27, 31
Reynolds, Cpl. John (Jack) 68, 87, 121, 138, 167
Rhode Island Regiments: 2nd 222; 7th 123; 5th Artillery 190
Richardson, Maj. Henry H. 27, 62, 83, 97, 102, 116–117, 130, 144
Richmond, Virginia 55, 172, 173–175, 189, 222
Richmond Dispatch 174
Richmond Examiner 61, 131
Rickson, W.R. 190
Riddle's photo of Andersonville 196
Ripley, Pvt. Dwight 131
Roanoke Island, N.C. 15
Robinson, Lt. Col. Gilbert 168, 231
Rodes, Maj. Gen. Robert E. 168–169
Rosecrans, Maj. Gen. William S. 109, 117–118
Rourke, John 199
Rousseau, Maj. Gen. Lovell Harrison 192

Sampson, Capt. Orange S. 58, 104, 119, 129
Sandburg, Carl 140
Sanders, Brig. Gen. William P. 110–111
Sanderson, Capt. Fred 35
Sarfield, James 190
Saunderson, Lt. Fred 45, 47, 57, 60, 68, 86

Savannah, Georgia 186, 210–215, 218
Sawyer, Capt. William H. 161
Schouler, Adj. Gen. William 15
Seamans, B.W. 15, 58, 70
Sedgwick, Maj. Gen. John 88
Shackleford, Brig. Gen. James M. 119
Sharpsburg, Maryland *see* Antietam
Sharpshooters, Federal 21, 23
Shepard, Pvt. Levi F. 184, 191, 193, 197, 204–206, 211
Sheridan, Maj. Gen. Philip 109, 164, 209, 212, 217–218, 229–230
Sherman, Maj. Gen. William T. 73, 111, 133–136, 148, 198, 213
Sigel, Maj. Gen. Franz 64
Sigfried, Col. Joshua K. 112
slavery in Kentucky 81, 91
Smith, Maj. Gen. William F. (Baldy) 56, 65, 68, 168
Soldiers Aid Society 146
Soldier's Home 24, 102–103, 145, 153, 158–159
South Carolina Regiment: 6th 133
South Mountain, Maryland 5, 22–24, 26, 28
Sperry, Sgt. Charles H. 88
Spotsylvania Campaign 157, 160
Star of the South 221
Stearns, Adj. Frazar Augustus 62
Steele, Maj. Gen. Frederick 186
Stephens (Stevens), Sgt. Thomas 187
Stevens, Maj. Gen. Isaac Ingalls 22
Stevenson, Brig. Gen. Thomas G. 155, 157, 230
Stoneman, Maj. Gen. George 88, 194
Stuart, Maj. Gen. J.E.B. 33–34, 41, 55
Sturgis, Brig. Gen. Samuel Davis 26, 33, 37, 42, 56
Sudsburg, Col. Joseph 168, 230–231
Sullivan, John 190
Sumner, Maj. Gen. Edwin V. 23, 36–37, 56, 58–60, 63

Tarsney, John C. 226–227, 229–230
Taylor, Lt. Col. J.H. 56
Thomasville, Georgia 209
Thompson, Capt. George F. 62
Tolbert, Brig. Gen. Albert T.A. 157
Tompkins, Reverend 89, 91, 93–94, 97
train accident 200
Turner's Gap, Maryland 23
Tyler, Pvt. William H. 187

U.S. Sanitary Commission 160, 221
Upton, Col. Emory 156

Valentine, Capt. William H. 86, 89, 96, 105
Vallandigham, Clement 89

246 Index

Van Dorn, Maj. Gen. Earl 88
Vicksburg, Mississippi 73, 89–91, 95, 98, 101–102
Vowles, Capt. D.W. 208

Walcott, Capt. Charles Folsom 69, 80, 86, 141, 227–229, 232, 234
Walker's Ford 141
Wallace, Sgt. John 27, 51, 63, 88, 90, 92–94, 97, 135
Warren, Maj. Gen. G.K. 156, 168, 197
Warrenton, Virginia 42–43
Webster, Sgt. George 192–193, 201, 205
Wheeler, Capt. Asahel 61, 86
Wheeler, Gen. Joseph 110
White, Brig. Gen. Julius 110
White's Ford 22
Whitney, Pvt. Lem 15–16, 25, 29, 31–35, 51–52, 63, 67, 87, 90, 93, 102, 107, 117, 121, 138, 143–144, 150, 157, 162

Wilder, Cpl. Charles S. 89, 121, 138
Wilderness 156–157, 160
Willcox, Maj. Gen. Orlando 118, 126, 141
Wilson, Pvt. Robert 197
Winder, Gen. John Henry 181, 188, 192, 200–201, 206, 209
Winn, Sgt. Thomas 187
Wirz, Capt. Henry 6, 181–184, 188, 201–202, 204–205, 207
Wise's Field (Battle of South Mountain) 27
Wolford, Brig. Gen. William 111, 120, 127, 131, 134
Wood, Rev. Charles W. 17, 60, 158
Woodbury, Augustus 82
Wright, Maj. Gen. Horatio 72
Wright, Pvt. Samuel 76
Wyman, Charles 48, 60, 98, 101, 105

Zollicoffer, Brig. Gen. Felix 113

www.ingramcontent.com/pod-product-compliance
Ingram Content Group UK Ltd.
Pitfield, Milton Keynes, MK11 3LW, UK
UKHW041936140426
5217IPUK00014B/514